Yale French Studies

NUMBER 124

Walter Benjamin's Hypothetical French Trauerspiel

Yale French Studies

Hall Bjornstad and Katherine Ibbett, *Special editors
for this issue*

Alyson Waters, *Managing editor*

Editorial board: Alice Kaplan (Chair), R. Howard
Bloch, Edwin Duval, Thomas Kavanagh,
Christopher L. Miller, Maurice Samuels,
Christopher Semk, Edwige Tamalet-
Talbayev, T. Chapman Wing, Yue Zhuo

Editorial assistant: Elizabeth K. Hebbard

Editorial office: 82-90 Wall Street, Room 308

Mailing address: P.O. Box 208251, New Haven,
Connecticut 06520-8251

Sales and subscription office:

Yale University Press, P.O. Box 209040
Hew Haven,Connecticut 06520-0940

Designed by James J. Johnson and set in Trump
Medieval Roman by Newgen North America.
Printed in the United States of America by Sheridan
Books, Ann Arbor, Michigan.

ISSN 044-0078
ISBN for this issue 978-0-300-19420-3

HALL BJORNSTAD AND
KATHERINE IBBETT

Editors' Preface: Calling on the *Grand Siècle* with Walter Benjamin

The French seventeenth century preoccupied Walter Benjamin throughout his life. Traces of this fascination remain in the margins of his critical output, and in his correspondence and diary entries. The most surprising testimony can be found in one of the last letters Benjamin wrote, to his long-time correspondent Gretel Adorno, on 19 July 1940. The letter was written from Lourdes, in French, shortly before Benjamin's attempt to escape from France. Right before his final salutation, almost as an envoi, Benjamin writes, "I have brought with me only one book: the memoirs of the cardinal de Retz. Thus, alone in my room, I call on the 'Grand Siècle.'"[1]

This was not the first time Benjamin had called on what is still often referred to in France as the *grand siècle*, meaning the great heights of classicism under Louis XIV. Benjamin had published the *Ursprung des deutschen Trauerspiels*, his famously complex book on German early modern theater, in 1928. The English title, "The Origin of the German Tragic Drama," is a mistranslation, since Benjamin in fact takes great pains there to distinguish tragedy from *Trauerspiel* or, literally, "mourning play." In the summer of 1927, Benjamin had written to his friend, Hugo von Hofmannsthal, about a possible future project:

> I sometimes think about writing a book on French tragedy as a coun-
> terpart to my *Trauerspiel* book. My plan for the latter had originally
> been to elucidate both the German and the French *Trauerspiel* in

---

1. Walter Benjamin, *Gesammelte Briefe*, vol. 6, ed. Christophe Gödde and Henri Lonitz (Frankfurt am Main: Suhrkamp, 1995), 470. English translation ours. The Cardinal de Retz was a leader of a faction in the *Fronde* or civil wars of the mid-seventeenth century, and was imprisoned by Louis XIV before eventually coming back to favor. His voluminous *Mémoires* were first published in 1717.

YFS 124, *Walter Benjamin's Hypothetical French "Trauerspiel,"* ed. Bjornstad and Ibbett, © 2013 by Yale University.

1

terms of their contrastive nature [*das deutsche und das französische Trauerspiel in ihrer kontrastierenden Natur zu entwickeln*]. But something must be added.[2]

In another letter to von Hofmannsthal later that summer, he seemed to be more certain about the project:

> In fact, I will be spending some time on French culture from this era (the sixteenth and seventeenth centuries) in order to see whether I am getting any closer to writing a work on French tragedy.[3]

Then the project dissipated, as academic projects often do, and in later letters Benjamin dropped the topic and turned instead to talk about what would eventually become the Arcades project on nineteenth-century Paris.

In this volume, we have invited an international team of scholars of early modern Europe to take their cue from Benjamin and build the case for a hypothetical French *Trauerspiel*, imagining how Benjamin might have pursued his announced project. Our return to Benjamin's abandoned project may come as a surprise to readers of Walter Benjamin and of French seventeenth-century texts alike. In the vast scholarship on Benjamin's work, the *Trauerspiel* book he did in fact write has certainly received ample critical attention. Although perhaps more often cited than read, it has, since its translation in 1977, been a crucial text for the formulation of a number of questions within Anglophone critical and cultural studies, ranging from allegorical interpretation to the relations between early and late modern forms of sovereignty.[4]

2. Walter Benjamin to Hugo von Hoffmannsthal, June 5, 1927 in *The Correspondence of Walter Benjamin, 1910–1940*, trans. Manfred R. Jacobson and Evelyn M. Jacobson (translation modified), ed. Gershom Scholem and Theodor W. Adorno (Chicago: University of Chicago Press, 1994), 315; Walter Benjamin, *Gesammelte Briefe*, vol. 3, ed. Christophe Gödde and Henri Lonitz (Frankfurt am Main: Suhrkamp, 1995), 259.

3. Walter Benjamin to Hugo von Hoffmannsthal, August 16, 1927, in *The Correspondence of Walter Benjamin, 1910–1940*, 318.

4. Recent Anglophone scholarship includes the following three important titles: Sigrid Weigel, *Walter Benjamin's Images, the Creaturely, and the Holy*, trans. Chadwick Truscott Smith (Stanford: Stanford UP, 2013); Jane O. Newman, *Benjamin's Library: Modernity, Nation, and the Baroque* (Ithaca: Cornell UP, 2011); Samuel Weber, *Benjamin's –abilities* (Cambridge: Harvard UP: 2008), esp. chap. 10. See also Beatrice Hanssen, *Walter Benjamin's Other History: Of Stones, Animals, Human Beings, and Angels* (Berkeley: University of California Press, 1998); Lutz P. Koepnick, "The Spectacle, the *Trauerspiel*, and the Politics of Resolution: Benjamin Reading the Baroque Reading Weimar," *Critical Inquiry* 22/2 (1996): 268–91; Max Pensky, *Melancholy Dialectics: Walter Benjamin and the Play of Mourning* (Amherst: University of Massachusetts Press, 1993); Bainard Cowan, "Walter Benjamin's Theory of Allegory," *New*

At the same time, Benjamin's engagement with early modern France and its theater has received only minimal attention; a recent issue of the specialist French language journal *XVIIᵉ siècle* on German contributions to seventeenth-century French studies did not have a single mention of Benjamin, though it devoted ample space to his contemporaries Auerbach and Spitzer, and also cited Vossler and Curtius.[5]

So why should we take seriously today the book on the French *Trauerspiel* that never materialized in 1927–28? Our mode in this journal issue may be the hypothetical, but it is important to observe that our starting point is much more than the fleeting idea behind an abandoned project. As Benjamin stated in the 1927 letter to von Hofmannsthal quoted above, his intention for the book on the German *Trauerspiel* was to contrast the German and French theater. If we are to believe a diary entry from the summer of 1938, the origin of Benjamin's investigation into origins came about in an encounter with French classical drama:

> June 29. Brecht speaks of the epic theater. He mentions children's theater, in which errors in presentation, functioning as alienation effects, can impart to a performance the qualities of epic theater. The same thing could happen in the standing-room pit of provincial theater. This reminds me of the Geneva performance of *The Cid*, where the sight of the king's crooked crown first made me think of what I wrote in my book on the *Trauerspiel*, nine years later.[6]

Even Benjamin's existing *Trauerspiel* thus took its first inspiration from the founding act of French classical drama, Pierre Corneille's

---

German Critique 22 (1981): 109–22. From the immense scholarship in German, we will highlight only the following two recent titles: Bettine Menke, *Das Trauerspiel-Buch. Der Souverän—das Trauerspiel—Konstellationen—Ruinen* (Bielefeld: Transcript, 2010); Daniel Weidner, "Kreatürlichkeit: Benjamins Trauerspielbuch und das Leben des Barock," *Profanes Leben - Walter Benjamins Dialektik der Säkularisierung*, ed. Daniel Weidner (Frankfurt: Suhrkamp, 2010, 120–138). We would also like to draw attention to Antonia Birnbaum, *Bonheur Justice Walter Benjamin* (Paris: Payot, 2009).

5. *XVIIᵉ siècle* 254 (2012). Existing Anglophone scholarship on Benjamin's French early modern has focused on comedy: see Christopher Braider, "Talking like a Book: Exception and the State of Nature in Benjamin and Molière," *Comparative Literature* 64/4 (Fall 2012) and Adrienne Bontea, "A Project in its Context: Walter Benjamin on Comedy," *MLN* 121 (2006): 1041–71. See also Romain Jobez, *Le théâtre baroque allemand et français. Le droit dans la littérature* (Paris: Garnier, 2010), which pursues similar questions, but in relation to an earlier corpus of French plays.

6. Benjamin, "Diary Entries, 1938," trans. Gerhard Richter and Michael W. Jennings in *Selected Writings*, vol. 3, ed. Howard Eiland and Michael W. Jennings (Cambridge: Harvard University Press, 2002), 336.

Le Cid. Where scholars of the French tradition have understandably focused on Benjamin's interest in much later French material, as evidenced in the *Passagen-werke* or Arcades Project, we pursue instead Benjamin's early interest in what we now call the French early modern, and ask what purchase that interest allows us to have on both French drama and Benjamin's ways of thinking historically.

Benjamin's account of his glimpse of the crooked crown is not the only way in which the *Ursprung des deutschen Trauerspiels* has an estranged relation to origin: its own publication history is also evidence of the difficulties of the discontinuous. After his Francophone epiphany, the project hiccupped into life in two brief, unpublished essays on Tragedy and *Trauerspiel* (written in 1916), and appeared in different form as a thesis for his would-be habilitation in 1925. Famously, it failed to secure the desired end of an academic position but nonetheless lived on in a series of afterlives, making it into print in 1928. It has since then gained a reputation as the most arcane of Benjamin's completed books.[7] Benjamin's work took up the German-language dramas produced by a group of playwrights writing in the second half of the seventeenth century, in the run up to and in the wake of the Peace of Westphalia; separating the sacred from the terrestrial orders, Westphalia managed to bring the Thirty Years War to a close in 1648. Already, by the eighteenth century, these plays had fallen out of fashion, but Benjamin's explorations of the post-Westphalian condition led him to take an insistently "minor" and under-read literature with its "laborious efforts" seriously; he argues that "the form itself becomes evident in the lean body of the inferior work, as its skeleton so to speak."[8]

How do the German plays about which Benjamin wrote differ from tragedy? Where tragedy is concerned with myth, *Trauerspiel*

7. As Benjamin states in the dedication of the *Trauerspiel* book, it was "Conceived in 1916" and "Written in 1925" (*The Origin of German Tragic Drama*, trans. John Osborne [London: Verso, 1998, 25]). We know that the last part of the statement is inaccurate, since Benjamin's correspondence shows that it was rather written in 1923–1925. As for the earlier "conception" or "sketch" (German: *Entwurf, entworfen*), things are more uncertain, especially regarding the Geneva anecdote. We do know, however, that Benjamin was in Geneva in the spring of 1915 to visit Herbert Belmore. See George Steiner's introduction to the English translation (7–24, esp. 8–11) and the chronology for the years 1915–1916 in Benjamin, *Selected Writings*, vol. 1, by Marcus Bullock and Michael W. Jennings (Cambridge: Harvard University Press, 2002), 499–500.

8. Benjamin, *The Origin of German Tragic Drama*, hereafter cited as *OGTD*, 58.

turns its attention to history and the art of government, he writes; in the pursuit of these issues, Timothy Hampton in his essay follows the language of treaty-making in Pierre Corneille's *Rodogune*, arguing that tracing the relations between an international political order and the nascent nation state can help us think about the specificity of the French as opposed to the German *Trauerspiel*. Treaty-making takes us far from the Attic tragedy dear to the Germanic philosophical tradition, with its focus on tragedy as *agon*. In the *Trauerspiel*, the characters cannot shake off their earthly immanence, their creatureliness; these are plays about the estate of man rather than his transcendence of it. Nevertheless, these plays have an almost-relation to the comic; as Benjamin puts it "Comedy – or more precisely: the pure joke – is the essential inner side of mourning which from time to time, like the lining of a dress at the hem or lapel, makes its presence felt." They not only represent but also satisfy a newly melancholy affect that Benjamin sees as central to the post-Westphalian condition: "For these are not so much plays which cause mourning, as plays through which mournfulness finds satisfaction: plays for the mournful."[9] The plays grant no eschatology, finding consolation for the loss of transcendence in a "figurative spatial simultaneity"[10] or a "spatial continuum, which one might describe as choreographic."[11] Through this courtly labyrinth slips the all-important figure of the intriguer, making choreography out of chaos. Meanwhile, the figure of the sovereign who appears in the *Trauerspiel* is severely compromised: often, the monarch is also a martyr, but before and beyond that he is always melancholy. Denied transcendence by the rigorous structure of Lutheranism, man is stuck in creaturely life, and the ruler more than anyone else. The sovereign no longer resides with the creator nor claims a divinely transcendent relation to God, and so he bears his creatureliness especially hard: "in the ruler, the supreme creature, the beast can reemerge with unsuspected power."[12]

This last quotation is essentially a variation on Benjamin's early epiphany in Geneva: an alienating gap opening up between sovereign and creature, between crown and king, between the creature on stage and the role he plays. In Benjamin's reading, the *Trauerspiele* stage these moments where the king's crown slips and his creatureliness gets the best of him.

9. Ibid., 125–26; 119.
10. Ibid., 66.
11. Ibid., 95.
12. Ibid., 86.

But what happens when we move from what we just heard Benjamin call "the lean body of the inferior work" to the grandeur of the French *grand siècle*, which was after all where Benjamin first saw that crooked crown? Several of the contributors to this volume make the allegorical contemplation of the crooked crown a guiding image in their explorations. This is the case in Hélène Merlin-Kajman's meditation on Benjaminian allegory and the deep sense in which *Le Cid* is not a *Trauerspiel* but could have been one. Equally, to Claude Haas, what in Corneille's *Horace* might at first look like a mere "straightening" of the crown, is rather a mourning of this sovereign act itself. The crooked crown also appears at a central point of Hall Bjornstad's essay as an emblem of the creaturely melancholy of the king; an emblem whose inscription, the longest quotation in Benjamin's *Trauerspiel* book, is borrowed from Pascal. At the same time, creatureliness is inflected rather differently in these essays from the way it was for Benjamin, since we are dealing with theater produced in a Catholic rather than a Lutheran context. Katherine Ibbett takes this sectarian difference as point of departure to argue for a distinctly Gallican *Trauerspiel* that recuperates the awkward embodiment of French martyr drama in general and Corneille's *Polyeucte* in particular, from the traditional relegation of that genre as a failed tragic experiment.

Benjamin's study does not merely return to long-forgotten post-Westphalian plays; it also serves as a theoretical reflection on what it means to do literary or indeed any kind of history. Though the book purports to look at what in English is translated as "the origin," it challenges an easy understanding of linear historical time and allows for a reflection on untimeliness that winds around the term *Ursprung*: "Origin is an eddy in the stream of becoming, and in its current it swallows the material involved in the process of genesis."[13] The *Trauerspiel* project is itself an eddy in the stream of Benjamin's critique of understandings of history, particularly Marxist conceptions, that lean on progress or causality, and that pushes him to supply instead other figures to describe history: repetition, constellation, the now-time, and the ruin. Seen through a certain rudimentary historical lens, the texts that follow the 1928 publication of the *Ursprung*, such as the unfinished Arcades fragments and the autobiographical writings about his Berlin childhood, represent what Benjamin was writing

13. Ibid., 45.

when he was *not* writing his French *Trauerspiel*. Eric Méchoulan's contribution to this volume suggests, in fact, that we might read the *Trauerspiel* otherwise by reading it through Benjamin's later French interests. Méchoulan's investigation into the sounds of Racine's late plays challenges the standard literary historical narratives of origins and continuities.

Benjamin's French moderns, as opposed to his early moderns, pursued a critique of the faith in progress and chronology seen in historical materialism, and negotiated many ways to think historically *otherwise*. Such a method, Benjamin writes in the Arcades project, was intended to "liberate the enormous energies of history that are bound up in the 'once upon a time' of classical historiography."[14] Pointing to a recent "temporal turbulence" in literary studies, Rita Felski describes Benjamin as "the patron saint of all those wary of periodizing schemes, chronological containment, and progressive histories."[15] In this volume, a number of contributors pursue the "temporal turbulence" inherent to our hypothetical French *Trauerspiel*: Susan Maslan's reading of Racine's *Athalie*, for example, explores the status of the *reste* in relation to larger historical narratives, arguing that we can read the play as both tragedy and *Trauerspiel*, each of which provides a different historical lens through which to understand the play's presentation of Jewish history.

The historian Benjamin Wurgaft has astutely analyzed the repeated appeal of the contingent in scholarship about Benjamin, making along the way the larger argument that counterfactual investigation should be taken as seriously in intellectual history as it is in work on military or economic or diplomatic developments.[16] Wurgaft describes several implicitly or explicitly "counterfactual" thought experiments regarding Benjamin's "survival" and asks why the late twentieth century's attachment to Benjamin's story has prompted so much counterfactual inquiry. Even Benjamin's introduction to the American public, in the form of Hannah Arendt's *New Yorker* essay of 1968 (eventually the introduction to the essay volume *Illuminations*) laid the groundwork for an assessment of Benjamin's suicide as

14. Benjamin, *The Arcades Project*, trans. Howard Eiland and Kevin McLaughlin, ed. Rolf Tiedemann (Cambridge: Harvard University Press, 1999), 463.

15. Rita Felski, *New Literary History* 42/4 (2011): 573–91 (576).

16. Benjamin Aldes Wurgaft, "The Uses of Walter: Walter Benjamin and the Counterfactual Imagination," *History and Theory* 49 (October 2010): 361–83.

an event of unhappy circumstance that continually invites counter-factual speculation.[17] These speculatively ghoulish relations to Benjamin might counsel us to steer clear of our counterfactual *Trauerspiel*.

However, it is not just Benjamin's life that invites such hypotheses. Benjamin's own analysis of the *Trauerspiel* returns again and again to the role of chance and the contingent, a question explored here by John D. Lyons in his essay on the stage property and chance, which pursues the status of the prop as a point of encounter between the inner and outer world, a repurposed object propelling dramatic action by somehow resisting human agency. In the fragments of the baroque, Benjamin imagines a different relation to his own modernity. In the introduction to the *Ursprung*, he writes of "a dictatorship whose utopian goal will always be to replace the unpredictability of historical accident with the iron constitution of the laws of nature,"[18] and in resistance to historical or historiographical dictatorships of every sort he chooses to attend to the shifting fragments of the *Trauerspiel* that cannot be neatly organized into uniformity. In this volume, Emma Gilby addresses the historical stakes of the hypothetical mode with reference to early modern understandings of provisionality, suggesting that we take seriously the gap between ideas and their elaboration and that the provisional should be considered a serious form of intellectual inquiry.

More broadly, we suggest that paying attention to things that are not written, to the mourning drama of the unfinished project, is not merely a way of sentimentalizing the things Benjamin ought to have had a chance to do. Rather, it restores to intellectual history a way of gleaning traces of intellectual work that disappears or has been made to disappear. Our own neoliberal late modernity, as it is lived in the academy, teaches us to value only what is written down and produced, and encourages us to ignore those scholars, like Benjamin himself, known in today's academic speak as "contingent labor." In asking Benjamin's hypothetical French *Trauerspiel* to help us explore the contingent side of that seemingly so solid French *grand siècle*, we also gesture toward the unwritten history of contingent scholarship.

17. In an angrier and less sentimental counterfactual vein, see also T. J. Clark, "Should Benjamin Have Read Marx?" *Boundary 2* 30/1 (2003): 31–49, also discussed by Wurgaft.

18. Benjamin, *OGTD*, 74.

How have our contributors taken up the challenge? Many have turned not to what is sometimes—and sometimes controversially—termed the French baroque, with its bloody and hyperbolic tragedies, but rather to the canonical side of the *grand siècle*, the peak of "classicism" that supposedly defined itself against that baroque. Others, like Christopher Braider, have unpacked the categories of "baroque" and "classical" which have pushed our reading of the period in particular ways. Braider tackles the longstanding argument over the French baroque from various temporal and geographic perspectives, asking how our French *Trauerspiel* might help us undo the myth of French exceptionalism while also asserting what is specifically *French* about these cultural productions. Increasingly, scholars today claim that for all classicism's willed modernity and aesthetic clean slate, the great canon of French classical drama is stuck on the past, and not just on the perfection projected back onto Attic authorities. Indeed, classicism is still limping out of the late sixteenth century wars of religion as well as out of more recent conflicts, such as the Thirty Years War, which is so important to the German *Trauerspiel*. In keeping with these insights, the present volume argues that reading French tragedy as *Trauerspiel* allows us to see something quite other than the grandeur of the *grand siècle*.

We end the volume with a response piece from a distinguished comparatist and scholar of the baroque and of Benjamin, Jane O. Newman. If the rest of us have tackled the question of the French *Trauerspiel* from the vantage point of France, Newman brings a whole other context to bear upon the question by looking at Benjamin's German contemporaries and their urgent consideration of both the French early modern and their own political moment. We are deeply grateful to Newman for her considered response to our *Trauerspiel*, and we look forward to the conversations that her contribution will stir up in and across our respective fields. For we want to insist that this volume cannot be the final word on this necessarily fragmentary question; we can already imagine a host of other ways to conceive of the French *Trauerspiel*, and no real way of exhausting them. We invite our readers to continue the discussion.

EMMA GILBY

The Pleasures of Hypothesis: Benjamin and the Provisional French *Trauerspiel*

In 1927, Walter Benjamin makes a fleeting comment to Hugo von Hofmannsthal: "I sometimes think about writing a book on French tragedy as a counterpart to my *Trauerspiel* book."[1] Benjamin's plan for the latter work, he continues, had originally been to elucidate both the German *Trauerspiel* and the French tragic drama in terms of their contrastive nature. "But something must be added," he adds, elliptically, before going on to reflect upon his own status among the German academics and thinkers of his generation. The present volume, conceived as a way of asking about this something that had to be added (and to what, exactly, and at what point?), encourages hypothetical meditations upon the past in the context of Benjamin's own remarks about a provisional future. The interest of this approach is all the greater, I shall argue, because provisionality recurs so frequently, both as a theme and as a form of argumentative catalyst, within *The Origin of German Tragic Drama* itself. My aim here is to consider the pleasures and possibilities of the hypothetical mode with particular reference to the French texts that Benjamin mentions. There seems to me to be a crucial convergence between Benjamin's critical interest in provisionality and his critical interest in the French seventeenth century.

In the *Origin*, Benjamin offers up a remarkable analysis of the provisional. By this, I mean that he is acutely preoccupied with the relationship between beginnings and ends, with ideas and their eventual elaboration, with plans and their subsequent ruin, and with the unde-

---

1. *The Correspondence of Walter Benjamin*, ed. Gershom Scholem and Theodor W. Adorno, trans. Manfred R. Jacobsen and Evelyn M. Jacobsen (Chicago: University of Chicago Press, 1994), 315.

YFS 124, *Walter Benjamin's Hypothetical French "Trauerspiel,"* ed. Bjornstad and Ibbett, © 2013 by Yale University.

sirability of setting out with final goals already in mind. He writes in *One-Way Street* that "the work is the death mask of its conception," and this lovely phrase turns every intention into a hypothesis.[2] In the *Origin*, Benjamin sets up a situation that is provisional and experimental, in the sense of open-ended. We know that an "origin," in this critical landscape, is an "eddy in the stream of becoming": the past, the originary moment, is a moment of disturbance.[3] There can be no straightforward stream of becoming, stream of narrative, or stream of consciousness, in which the past and present are continuous with their own future. The consequences of the eddy are unpredictable and uneven. When Benjamin uses analogies, they therefore invoke unpredictability and multiplicity—they are often drawn from the vital, natural world, in "dances" and "fevers" as well as in eddies, in "entanglements" and "constellations"—and with these explanatory analogies, which never quite attain the status of explanation, Benjamin refuses outright the individual subjectivity of the single point of view or imposing methodology. The focus of the Epistemo-Critical Prologue is on the "discontinuous structure of the world of ideas,"[4] and we need to confirm the variability and context-dependency of our critical terminology: "Far from characterizing an inferior and provisional stage of knowledge, this discontinuity in scientific method could positively advance the theory of knowledge."[5] This is in fact a paean to the superiority of provisionality: Benjamin's emphasis is on what lies beyond the peripheries of present knowledge within a present system of thought.[6]

2. Walter Benjamin, *One-Way Street*, trans. Edmund Jephcott, in *Selected Writings*, vol. 1, ed. Marcus Bullock and Michael W. Jennings (Cambridge, MA: Harvard University Press, 1996), 459. As Gerhard Richter puts it, "The tropological unpredictability of presentation causes the very text that enacts an author's intention to break with that intention." See Richter, "A Matter of Distance: Benjamin's *One-Way Street* through *The Arcades*," in *Walter Benjamin and the Arcades Project*, ed. Beatrice Hanssen (London: Continuum, 2006), 132–56 (142). See also *Correspondence*, 227: "Every perfect work is the death mask of its intuition" (letter to Florens Christian Rang, January 10, 1924.)

3. Benjamin, *The Origin of German Tragic Drama*, trans. John Osborne (London: Verso, 1998), 45. Hereafter cited as *OGTD*.

4. Benjamin, *OGTD*, 33.

5. Ibid.

6. See Max Pensky, "Method and Time: Benjamin's Dialectical Images," in *The Cambridge Companion to Benjamin* (Cambridge: Cambridge University Press, 2004), 177–98. "Benjamin sought a way to actualize historical material that would *uproot* and shock what has been constructed as '*the present*,' that would disrupt the very relationship that hermeneutics assumes" (181).

Correspondingly, when Benjamin turns to the past, it is with a sense of multiple possibilities; and in this, he sees himself as a counter-example to prevailing practice: "Just as a man lying sick with fever transforms all the words which he hears into the extravagant images of delirium, so it is that the spirit of the present age sceizes on the manifestations of past or distant spiritual worlds, in order to take possession of them and unfeelingly incorporate them into its own self-absorbed fantasizing."[7] The critic according to Benjamin is not a self-absorbed maker of meanings, but an attentive observer of his or her own thought processes as they eddy around the original intention. "Tirelessly the process of thinking makes new beginnings, returning in a roundabout way to its original object."[8] This is method as digression, its primary characteristic "the absence of an uninterrupted purposeful structure;" and what this requires on the part of the critics is a "continual pausing for breath" which Benjamin states is the mode most proper to the process of contemplation.[9]

Occasional pauses for breath and moments of punctuation come in the *Origin* in the form of references to the French material that will be my focus here. We would expect to find contrasts: the contrasts to which Benjamin alludes in his letter to Hofmannsthal on French tragedy as a "counterpart" to German tragic drama. We know that, for Benjamin, the baroque *Trauerspiel* is not just unlike classical tragedy, but radically opposed to it. The site of the baroque mourning play, in contradistinction to the unified places of classical tragedy taken on by the tauter theorizing of the French seventeenth century, cannot be fixed; the tragic hero is replaced by "constellations" of figures on stage; the responses of sudden pity and terror are supplanted by a more diffuse sorrow and mourning. This emphasis on an unpredictable, unreliable "drastic externality" in the *Trauerspiel*, says Benjamin, stands in contrast to a "classicistic transparency of plot:"[10]

> If indeed surprise, even complexity, has any meaning in the structure of these dramas, and should be emphasized by contrast to a classicistic transparency of plot, then exoticism in the choice of subject-matter is also not foreign to it. The *Trauerspiel* gives more emphatic encouragement to the invention of the literary plot than tragedy.[11]

7. Benjamin, *OGTD*, 53.
8. Ibid., 28.
9. Ibid.
10. Ibid., 137.
11. Ibid., 194.

With this mention of the literary plot, Benjamin invokes a confusing sense of multiple possible outcomes. He invokes a form of textual expansion that necessarily involves redundancy, as some elements or plot-lines are rejected in favor of others. The literary plot keeps the reader reading on because of the pleasures of hypothesis and unpredictability. A classicistic transparency, he suggests, is foreign to this.

But Benjamin does not in fact cite the French dramatists who would be required for a contrastive study (had he done so, we might surmise that he would have been interested in the *intrigue*, or "plotting," of much seventeenth-century drama: the liberties taken by Corneille as he adds layers of unpredictability to his drama, or the way Racine stretches the unity of time beyond recognition, with his references to mythical pasts and anxious futures). Instead, the French authors singled out as having the most obvious critical part to play in the twists and turns of the *Trauerspiel* book are Blaise Pascal and René Descartes: Pascal "gives voice to the feeling of his age,"[12] and Descartes's work on the passions "deserves the closest consideration."[13] It is, therefore, to this engagement with Pascal and Descartes that I now turn.

Benjamin offers one very lengthy quotation from Pascal, on the status of the sovereign, taken from the section of the *Pensées* entitled "Divertissement." "Divertissement" is distraction or diversion from one's earthly state of fallenness, sinfulness, creatureliness. This quotation is designed to show how human beings are enslaved to the material, to knowledge that is conveyed through the senses. Even in the case of monarchs, Pascal's text suggests, our self-image is dependent on the external trappings of costume and artifice: the need we have, in our fallen state, for "divertissement" in the most inconsequential sense. Pascal's speaker illustrates his argument with a thought experiment: "Put it to the test . . ." ("Qu'on en fasse l'épreuve . . ."):

> Put it to the test; leave a king entirely alone, with nothing to satisfy his senses, no care to occupy his mind, with no one to keep him company and no diversion, with complete leisure to think about himself, and you will see that a king without diversion is a very wretched man. Therefore such a thing is carefully avoided, and the persons of kings are invariably attended by a great number of people concerned to see

12. Ibid., 142.
13. Ibid., 217.

that diversion comes after affairs of state, watching over their leisure hours to provide pleasures and sport so that there should never be an empty moment. In other words they are surrounded by people who are incredibly careful to see that the king should never be alone and able to think about himself, because they know that, king though he is, he will be miserable if he does think about it.[14]

"This is echoed," says Benjamin (the "this," following the very extended quotation, is unspecified, overdetermined), "on numerous occasions in the German *Trauerspiel.*"[15] Benjamin's most clearly delineated point is about sovereign fear: one of the plays he cites here and elsewhere is Andreas Gryphius's *Leo Armenius* (1650), which contains the epigrammatic statement that "where there is a scepter, there is fear."[16] In the historical period in question, suggests Benjamin, with the loss of narratives of redemption, the monarch comes to an awareness of his creaturely, rather than god-given, status: "However highly he is enthroned over subject and state, his status is confined to the world of creation; he is the lord of creatures, but he remains a creature."[17] In his anxiety, his acts become increasingly arbitrary; he suspects, as a result of his own arbitrariness, that he will himself fall victim to his opponents; through this melancholic self-destruction he becomes, in the end, a martyr as well as a tyrant. These, then, are the "two faces of the monarch:" the tyrant and the martyr.[18]

The action of the sovereign is illustrated by Benjamin with a further reference to seventeenth-century France, taken from a dissertation on the doctrine of the social contract by Frédéric Atger: "The prince develops all virtualities of the state by a kind of continuous creation. The prince is the Cartesian God transposed into the political world."[19] This quotation from Atger is also to be found in Carl Schmitt, who had proposed in his *Political Theology* that the State

14. Pascal, *Pensées*, trans. A. J. Krailsheimer (Harmondsworth: Penguin, 1966), fragment 137. This quotation, given by Benjamin in French from the Port-Royal edition of the *Pensées*, is discussed in greater length by Hall Bjornstad in his contribution to this volume. See also Bjornstad, *Créature sans créateur: Pour une anthropologie baroque dans les Pensées de Pascal* (Laval: Presses de l'Université Laval, 2010) ("l'homme perd, l'histoire naturelle gagne" [161]: "humankind loses, and natural history wins").

15. Benjamin, *OGTD*, 143.

16. Ibid., 144.

17. Ibid., 85.

18. Ibid., 69.

19. Quoted in ibid., 97. Frédéric Atger, *Essai sur l'histoire des doctrines du contrat social* (Nîmes: Imprimerie coopérative "la Laborieuse", 1906), 136.

could not be based on the rule of law.[20] Rather, sovereignty, defined as absolute will, must precede the operations of government: "Sovereign is he who decides on the exception."[21] Schmitt had summed up his notion of political theology by saying that all significant concepts of the modern theory of the state are secularized theological concepts. Accordingly, the exceptional situation is a secularized version of the miracle: it comes from outside, beyond the confines of normal time and space. Divine voluntarism is likewise mirrored in the role of the prince. It makes sense that Schmitt should at this point quote directly from Descartes, whose views on voluntarism—the notion that there is no class of entity that does not depend on God, and that God does not reckon with any criteria except those that stem from his will—are among the most trenchant to be found in his oeuvre: "As Descartes once wrote to Mersenne, 'It is God who establishes these laws in nature, just as a king establishes laws in his kingdom.'"[22]

However, as Horst Bredekamp points out, the Schmittian sovereign, established in the state of exception as the holder of dictatorial power, is evoked by Benjamin only to be spoken of in terms of his absence:

20. Carl Schmitt, *Political Theology: Four Chapters on the Concept of Sovereignty*, trans. George Schwab (Cambridge, MA: MIT Press, 1985), 46–47. "You will very quickly recognize," writes Benjamin to Schmitt in a letter of December 1930, "how much of my book [the *Origin*] is indebted to you for its presentation of the doctrine of sovereignty in the seventeenth century" (trans. Samuel Weber, in Weber, "Taking Exception to Decision: Walter Benjamin and Carl Schmitt," *Diacritics* 22 (Fall-Winter 1992): 5. Giorgio Agamben claims that *Political Theology* was itself conceived as a response to Benjamin's *Critique of Violence* (1921); on this, see Colin McQuillan, "The Real State of Emergency: Agamben on Benjamin and Schmitt," in *Studies in Social and Political Thought* 18 (2011): 96–108. On the methodological parallels between Schmitt's philosophical studies of the state and Benjamin's "art philosophical manner of research," see Jane O. Newman, *Benjamin's Library: Modernity, Nation, and the Baroque* (Ithaca: Cornell University Press, 2011), 198.

21. Schmitt, *Political Theology*, 5. On this, see Horst Bredekamp, "From Walter Benjamin to Carl Schmitt, via Thomas Hobbes" in *Critical Inquiry* 25/2 *"Angelus Novus": Perspectives on Walter Benjamin* (Winter, 1999): 247–66 (252): "The concept of the state of exception expresses Schmitt's conviction that democracy loses its foundation when different factions pursue their divergent interests to the point where a splintered political system is no longer able to guarantee the security of law. Under these circumstances, an extrasocietal force, the sovereign, must suspend the laws in order to save them."

22. Schmitt, *Political Theology*, 47. René Descartes, Letter to Mersenne, 15 April 1630, in vol. 1 (1618–1637) of *Œuvres philosophiques*, ed. Ferdinand Alquié (Paris: Garnier, 1963–73), 260. The analogy of God as all-determining legislator is a recurrent one in Descartes. For Descartes, every single law, from the most basic truths of mathematics on, is subject to the unknowable will of God.

The prince, who is responsible for making the decision to proclaim the state of exception, reveals, at the first opportunity, that he is almost incapable of making a decision. Just as compositions with restful lighting are virtually unknown in mannerist painting, so it is that the theatrical figures of this epoch always appear in the harsh light of their changing resolve.[23]

In the age of the baroque, a state of exception is impossible, given the absence of any authority to decide upon it. Instead, we find the figure of the unrestrained "plotter" or "intriguer," whose actions fill up the permanent state of exception without meaning or morality. The authority of the plotter references a chaotic, Hobbesian state of nature, as is made clearer in Benjamin's discussion of the intimate relationship between sovereign and courtier. The courtier's insight into the power of the monarch is perfect and therefore disillusioned: "The German dramatists [. . .] know the two faces of the courtier: the intriguer, as the evil genius of their despots, and the faithful servant, as the companion in suffering to innocence enthroned."[24] The two faces of the monarch, tyrant and martyr, which we have seen Benjamin discuss in relation to his extended quotation from Pascal, here necessitate the baroque duality of the courtier: intriguer and faithful servant. The Atger reference to an all-powerful, all-sovereign Cartesian God is immediately followed up in Benjamin by this acknowledgment of, and further reference to, the "other face" of that divine entity: the "evil genius" who has all the powers of deceitful transcendence. It is worth considering this reference in more detail.

We know that, in the *Meditations*, Descartes sets out on a mission to achieve absolute certainty in the sciences. In the course of this mission, he will both reject all his previous assumptions about the way the world works, and attempt to appeal to God's overarching power in order to prove the reality of his external environment. In the first Meditation, Descartes's Meditator has the direct intuition of the truth of his own existence ("I am here, sitting by the fire, wearing a winter dressing-gown, holding this piece of paper in my hands, and so on"), but goes on to subject that intuition to hyperbolic doubt.[25] Subsequently, he has to find a greater truth, of which he is just as

23. Bredekamp, "From Walter Benjamin to Carl Schmitt," 260.
24. Benjamin, *OGTD*, 98.
25. *The Philosophical Writings of Descartes*, trans. John Cottingham, Robert Stoothoff, and Dugald Murdoch (Cambridge: Cambridge University Press, 1984), vol. 2, 13.

firmly convinced, in order to answer to that doubt, prove the validity of his intuitions, and move beyond the limited confines of his intuitive self-awareness. In other words, he has to prove the existence of God.[26] This effort at proof is linked to the thought experiment that is its counterpart:

> I will suppose therefore that not God, who is supremely good and the source of truth, but rather some malicious demon of the utmost power and cunning has employed all his energies in order to deceive me. I shall think that the sky, the air, the earth, colors, shapes, sounds, and all external things are merely the delusions of dreams which he has devised to ensnare my judgment.[27]

At this point in the *Meditations*, Descartes's sense of divinity oscillates, experimentally, between a source of truth and a certain malicious demon or "evil genius." He will go on to suggest that this ultra-skeptical hypothesis in fact works to provide us with one irreducible certainty: in order to be deceived, I must exist. Both the body and the sensations assigned to the body can be doubted in the course of the deceiver hypothesis, but the Meditator can none the less say for sure that, even if he is being deceived, he knows himself currently to be a thinking thing. His knowledge of himself, he is able to conclude, comes from thinking, and not from the experiences of the senses: the deceiver hypothesis thus works to separate mind from body.

Crucially, though, this mind-body dualism is itself flexible; and this is a point referenced with striking critical confidence by Benjamin: "It is not only the dualism of Descartes that is baroque; as a consequence of the doctrine of psycho-physical determination, the theory of the passions also deserves the closest consideration."[28] Later in the *Meditations*, Descartes's Meditator will come to a sense of himself as a composite of soul and body; otherwise, he states by

---

26. When Pascal objects to Descartes's version of God as a "chiquenaude," or a flick of the fingers, he is suggesting that the supremely good entity that is the Cartesian God itself is reduced to a kind of thought experiment, or step on the path to Descartes's elevation of his own understanding. "Mémoire sur Pascal et sa famille," in *Œuvres complètes*, ed. Jean Mesnard (Paris: Desclée de Brouwer, 1964–), vol. 1, 1090–1105 (1105).

27. *The Philosophical Writings of Descartes*, vol. 2, 15. On the thought experiment of the malicious demon, see in particular Bernard Williams, *Descartes: The Project of Pure Enquiry* (Sussex: Harvester Press, 1978), 56, and Harry G. Frankfurt, *Demons, Dreamers, and Madmen: The Defense of Reason in Descartes's* Meditations (Indianapolis: Bobbs-Merrill, 1970), 87.

28. Benjamin, *OGTD*, 217.

way of example, he could not have an instructive sensation of pain in the event of danger: "I and the body form a unit."[29] An emphasis on proving the deceitfulness of the senses or the intellectual imperialism of the intellect is attenuated, and emphasis is placed instead on relationality, union. This makes way not just for the understanding that the realms of mind and body are interrelated in as much as one can make the mental decision to move one's own body, but also for wider arguments about the role of the passions in rational thought, about desires being antecedents of action.[30] The passions cross the line between body and soul, between internal and external. Via our passions, the unpredictability of the external world inserts contingency into our behavior, no matter how much we try to anticipate and regulate: "I have included among these remedies the forethought and diligence through which we can correct our natural faults [. . .] But I must admit that there are few people who have sufficiently prepared themselves in this way for all the contingencies of life."[31] As Benjamin perceives, Descartes is alert to the contradictoriness of the passions: both physical and provisional, they are subject to incessant, unpredictable renewal.

Before returning to Benjamin's vital comment on psycho-physical determination, let us examine further the intellectual *modus operandi* that Benjamin's Descartes shares with his Pascal. "Put it to the test," says Pascal; "I will suppose therefore," says Descartes. Benjamin chooses to cite these authors at the moments where their thought displays most clearly the labor it shares with irreality, with the fictive mode. The emphasis is on the pleasures and the usefulness of hypotheses. These hypotheses are not scientific, seeking confirmation. When Pascal says "put it to the test," he is not actually moving

29. *The Philosophical Writings of Descartes*, vol. 2, 56. Descartes's arguments, he writes to Elizabeth on 28 June 1643, have "distinguished three kinds of primitive ideas or notions, each of which is known in its own proper manner and not by comparison with any of the others: the notions we have of the soul, of body and of the union between the soul and the body." "The Correspondence," in *The Philosophical Writings of Descartes*, vol. 3, trans. John Cottingham, Robert Stoothoff, Dugald Murdoch, and Anthony Kenny (Cambridge: Cambridge University Press, 1991), 226. In an earlier letter written on 21 May 1643, Descartes had observed that on this union depends "our notion of the soul's power to move the body, and the body's power to act on the soul and cause its sensations and passions" (218).

30. On this, see in particular Susan James, *Passion and Action in Seventeenth-Century Philosophy* (Oxford: Clarendon Press, 1997).

31. *Philosophical Writings of Descartes*, vol. 1, 403.

toward proof via a process of experimentation (it is not as if he is really going to place a king in isolation). The process of elaborating the hypothesis itself is what is valuable; and this cognitive act—contemplating, pausing for breath rather than looking for entertainment—is what is portrayed as well as undertaken: "Man is but a reed, the most feeble thing in nature, but he is a thinking reed."[32] Pascal and Descartes are representing the process of meditation itself. As Benjamin puts the corresponding methodological point:

> Art cannot, for its part, permit what is represented, rather than the actual representation, to be the object of attention. The truth content of this totality, which is never encountered in the abstracted lesson, least of all the moral lesson, but only in the critical elaboration of the work itself, includes moral warnings only in the most indirect form.[33]

Pascal and Descartes, too, are shaping moral outcomes only in the most indirect sense, by encouraging the processes of reading on, thinking through.

So the specific moral lesson in Benjamin is subordinated to critical elaboration and indirection. There is an interesting relationship between ethics and provisionality in Benjamin's "indirect moral warnings," as the opposite of "the abstracted lesson"—the open, provisional process of experimental thought becomes a kind of ethical provision in itself—and I suggest that this is also happening in the authors he cites. We have seen the meditative provisionality to which the dualism of mind and body, attained using the "evil genius" hypothesis, is subjected in Descartes: this speculative hypothesis will in fact ramify into a discussion of relationality and the complex ethical interplay between the passions and rational thinking. These comments inevitably bring to mind the *"morale par provision"* of the 1637 *Discourse on Method*: in as much as he provides his readers with a moral lesson, Descartes is dealing explicitly with a form of provisionality. "Je me formai une morale par provision," he announces to his reader, "qui ne consistait qu'en trois ou quatre maximes, dont je veux bien vous faire part."[34] The standard translation into English is as follows: "I formed

---

32. Pascal, *Pensées*, trans. A. J. Krailsheimer (London: Penguin, 1966), fr. 200.
33. Benjamin, *OGTD*, 105.
34. Descartes, "Discours de la méthode," in vol. 1 (1618–1637) of *Œuvres philosophiques*, ed. Ferdinand Alquié (Paris: Garnier, 1963–73), 567–650 (592).

for myself a provisional moral code consisting of just three or four maxims, which I should like to tell you about."[35]

Following this standard translation, the equally standard reading of this statement paradoxically works to dismiss its importance. This reading runs as follows: we can concoct moral maxims—we can say, as Descartes does at this point in the *Discourse on Method*, that we ought to obey the laws of our country, always be firm and resolved in our decision-making, and so on—but these maxims merely serve Descartes's needs for a brief period. The maxims are a practical stopgap, because Descartes is concerned to use these hypotheses to achieve an ultimate epistemic certainty.[36] In other words, they are temporary rules that Descartes will follow while he carries out his search for certain knowledge. "Par provision" is conflated with provisional in the sense of "only temporarily useful," susceptible to replacement, and designed to be swept away when a more certain system of knowledge presents itself.

To state this, however, is to underestimate the dialectic between provisionality and moral provision that is, I suggest, of particular interest to Benjamin. Dictionary definitions of "par provision" in the seventeenth century do not take that term to mean "provisoire," but rather to be a kind of deposit or down payment: something to be added to later. As Michèle Le Dœuff points out, "par provision" in the *Dictionnaire de l'académie française* of 1694 is "ce qu'on adjuge par avance à une partie" ("that which one attributes to someone in advance").[37] To describe Descartes's *morale* as provisional can be derogatory in the sense that it designates it as inadequate, needing to be replaced. We need to understand that which is established *par provision* as being, precisely, a kind of provision: what is provided *tel quel*. The "provisional" may have negative overtones of replacement, whereas that which is "par provision" is "provisional" in the sense of "to be supplemented later," adding a general validity or positive value to what is being discussed. In talking about a "morale par provision," then, Descartes arguably makes ethics the foundational

35. *Philosophical Writings of Descartes*, vol. 1, 122.

36. See, for example, Donald Rutherford, "Descartes' Ethics," in *The Stanford Encyclopedia of Philosophy* (Winter 2008 Edition), ed. Edward N. Zalta, http://plato .stanford.edu/archives/win2008/entries/descartes-ethics/

37. Michèle Le Dœuff, "En rouge dans la marge: l'invention de l'objet 'Morale de Descartes' et les métaphores du discours cartésien," in *L'imaginaire philosophique* (Paris: Payot, 1980), 85–132.

element of philosophical certainty.[38] Ethics is given a much more important and coherent status within Descartes's thought than we might suppose if we think "par provision" simply means "temporary," and the *Discourse* can be seen to set up a relationship with his more explicitly ethical work: namely, the moral thinking of the correspondence and the *Passions*. Again, "it is not only the dualism of Descartes that is baroque; as a consequence of the doctrine of psychophysical determination, the theory of the passions also deserves the closest consideration."[39]

We have seen that, in the theory of the passions, the self is treated as the product of an interdependent mind and body, each distinct but capable of interaction. Subject to innumerable encounters with the outside world, we are necessarily integrated, in unpredictable ways, into the wider structures of society. Benjamin, too, sweeps aside any insistence on the objectification of the body-as-machine, divorced from the world of the speaking or thinking subject. He sees immediately that any view of Descartes's work as rigidly dualistic—rigidly demarcating mental and physical states, allowing no traffic between them—neglects in particular his account of the passions, of psychophysical determination.[40] A classical interiority in the process of isolated, idealized individuation is not at issue here. And this does indeed deserve "the closest consideration" in relation to the German *Trauerspiel*, where human beings, even Christ, are seen in their passionate, creaturely aspect and placed, as Benjamin says, "in the realm of the provisional, the everyday, unreliable."[41] For Benjamin, authors such as Descartes and Pascal embody this interest in a positive provi-

38. For a more detailed reading, which also does more to question Le Dœuff's emphases, see Emma Gilby, "Descartes's 'Morale par provision': A Re-evaluation," in *French Studies* 65/4 (2011): 444–58.

39. Benjamin, *OGTD*, 217.

40. Benjamin implicitly rejects here any current of Bergsonian critical idealism, immensely influential from the late nineteenth century onwards, that might equate rational thought with scientific truth, and associate Descartes with this form of antipragmatism (the claim that we need a form of knowledge beyond that available to empiricists). However, as Jane O. Newman notes in her study of the reception of Descartes in the first decades of the twentieth century, "the question of what constituted a 'traditional' approach to Descartes during these and subsequent years is crucial to pose," and certainly more complex than is often allowed in standard critical narratives about a "rationalist" Descartes. "The Present and Our Past: Simone de Beauvoir, Descartes, and Presentism in the Historiography of Feminism," in *Women's Studies on its Own: A Next Wave Reader in Institutional Change*, ed. Robyn Wiegman (Durham: Duke University Press, 2002), 141–76 (161).

41. Benjamin, *OGTD*, 183.

sionality: in experimentation, flexibility, and the myriad roles played by the passions in everyday life.

*   *   *

I have argued that Benjamin focuses on Descartes and Pascal at the intensely hypothetical moments cited because of the central place of provisionality within his own methodology. This is also why he is perceptive about the doctrine of psycho-physical determination, which takes the mediations of the passions as an essential part of human experience. We know that the *Origin of German Tragic Drama* met with academic contempt, launching Benjamin into a precarious, freelance life of essays, translations, and fragments. In his later work, and notably in *The Work of Art in the Age of Its Technical Reproducibility*, we see art lose any form of finality. Its reproducibility means that it becomes part of a process of experimentation and provisional application. Here, too, for Benjamin, as for the seventeenth-century authors cited, thinking about provisionality can itself offer a kind of ethical provision: a refusal of predetermined systems or notions of completion.

HALL BJORNSTAD

"Giving voice to the feeling of his age": Benjamin, Pascal, and the *Trauerspiel* of the King without Diversion

If, as Benjamin writes to von Hofmannsthal in the summer of 1927, the original plan for his book on the German *Trauerspiel* had been to draw out a contrast between it and French tragic drama,[1] the relative absence of French material in the finished book becomes striking. In this context, then, the one French seventeenth-century text that Benjamin actually does quote takes on increased significance. This text is Pascal's reflection on "the king without diversion" (*"le roi sans divertissement"*) and Benjamin's page-long quotation from the *Pensées* early in his chapter on melancholy constitutes, in fact, the longest quotation of the whole volume. There are, of course, other references to French works in the book, including to those of Menestrier, abbé Bossu, Alphonse Delbène, Nicolas Caussin, and, most importantly, Descartes and Claude Saumaise. Yet none of these comes close to having the same argumentative role as the mobilization of Pascal. As we shall see, Pascal is invoked as a central witness "giv[ing] voice to the feeling of his age" in a reflection that brings together many issues

---

1. "I sometimes think about writing a book on French tragedy as a counterpart to my *Trauerspiel* book. My plan for the latter had originally been to elucidate both the German and French *Trauerspiel* in terms of their contrastive nature [*das deutsche und das französische Trauerspiel in ihrer kontrastierenden Natur zu entwickeln*]." (*The Correspondence of Walter Benjamin*, ed. Gershom Scholem and Theodor W. Adorno, trans. Manfred R. Jacobsen and Evelyn M. Jacobsen [London and Chicago: The University of Chicago Press, 1994], 315.) Interestingly, Benjamin first says "French tragedy" and then "French *Trauerspiel*," referring not only to the project for a second *Trauerspiel* book, but also to the origin of the project for the book on the German *Trauerspiel*.

Throughout this essay, I will follow Benjamin's example in the quotation above and refer to *Ursprung des deutschen Trauerspiels* as the *Trauerspiel* book, as a way of avoiding the title of the English translation, "The Origin of the German Tragic Drama," which introduces a confusion pertaining to a central distinction in my argument.

YFS 124, *Walter Benjamin's Hypothetical French "Trauerspiel,"* ed. Bjornstad and Ibbett, © 2013 by Yale University.

central to Benjamin's wider project, including melancholy, creatureliness, and the conception of history as *Trauerspiel*.[2]

In this essay, I will explore the function of the reference to Pascal in Benjamin's argument and its repercussions for our understanding of the seventeenth-century thinker. More precisely, I will argue that the Benjaminian frame helps us see the fundamental stakes of Pascal's project more clearly, and that this, in turn, may help us to anchor Benjamin's argument historically. In so doing, I hope to help advance our understanding of the darker side of secularization, as analyzed by Pascal and Benjamin.

In order to prepare the ground for my close reading of the inclusion of Pascal's "king without diversion" in Benjamin's book, I will start by stressing two important distinctions regarding Pascal: first, the distinction between what he set out to do and what he really accomplished in the project that arrives to us under the name of *Pensées*; and second, between what Benjamin read as Pascal's *Pensées* back in the early twentieth century, and what we read under the same name today.

Pascal's ambition was, of course, to write an apology for the Christian faith. This text was to be as efficient in persuading the free-thinking target audience as his *Provincial Letters* had been in discrediting Jesuit casuistry. The force and modernity of the text is due not only to Pascal's rhetorical skills and his lucidity as an observer of human nature, but also to an important generic invention. Where apologetic writers before him had approached the task by proving the existence of God and evoking the felicity of man with God, Pascal famously formulated his task as one of showing *la misère de l'homme sans Dieu*—"the wretchedness of man without God"—through an analysis of the human condition.[3] Basically, Pascal was looking in

---

2. Walter Benjamin, *The Origin of German Tragic Drama*, trans. John Osborne (London: Verso, 1996), 142. In what follows, a few of the quotations from Osborne's translation have been modified to bring them closer to the German original, especially in cases where Benjamin's emphasis is on creatureliness, cf. Walter Benjamin, *Ursprung des Deutschen Trauerspiels*, ed. Rolf Tiedemann (Frankfurt am Main: Suhrkamp, 1978).

3. Blaise Pascal, *Pensées*, trans. Roger Ariew (Indianapolis: Hackett, 2005), fragment 40. Ariew follows Philippe Sellier's ordering of the fragments. In what follows, I will on a few occasions modify Ariew's translation to bring it closer to the original. I am quoting the French original from Blaise Pascal, *Les Provinciales, Pensées et opuscules*, ed. Gérard Ferreyrolles and Philippe Sellier, La Pochothèque (Paris: Librairie générale française, 2004).

a direction in which nobody else was looking at the time, neither Christian apologists or moralists, nor libertine free-thinkers. As I have argued elsewhere, Pascal, by bracketing his own perspective and adopting that of the free-thinker, writes what could be called a work of fiction whose main character is "a creature without creator," a wretched creature who inhabits an anthropological space that is neither that of his Augustinian author nor that of the free-thinker.[4]

Now, Pascal of course never finished his project. The collection of fragments that arrives to us under the name *Pensées* has its material basis in the papers Pascal left behind when he died in 1662: most of the fragments are sketches toward—if not the ruins of—a projected apology for the Christian faith. In fact, even the name under which we know the text was originally an expression of this failure. As Pascal's brother-in-law Florin Périer wrote the year after Pascal's death, expressing the general disappointment of the intellectual community gravitating toward Port-Royal: "all we found in his papers consisted only in a heap of detached thoughts [*un amas de pensées détachées*]."[5]

For a long while, it was believed that Pascal had left his papers behind without any order whatsoever. This led editors, from the Port-Royal edition in 1670 to Brunschvicg's in 1905, to organize the fragments as they found best, resulting in a fascinating variety of editions reflective of different periods and ideologies. For example, the once widely used Brunschvicg edition gives the reader a Pascal perfectly suited for the needs of a French state that had just enacted an official separation from the church. However, we now know that Pascal left the fragments in a certain order, although its exact meaning is not easy to tease out. This has lead to what optimistic editors sometimes call "objective editions" of the *Pensées* (by Lafuma, Sellier, and Le Guern) based on two slightly different copies made of Pascal's *Nachlaß* just after his death.

My reason for insisting on this distinction is that Benjamin, as well as many other twentieth-century readers of the *Pensées*, did not use a fully adequate version of the text. In fact, the Brunschvicg edition, which is fairly reliable when it comes to establishing the text, but not for the ordering of the fragments, remained influential well

    4. Hall Bjornstad, *Créature sans créateur: Pour une anthropologie baroque dans les "Pensees" de Pascal* (Laval: Presses de l'Université Laval, 2010).

    5. Florin Périer, Préface, *Traités de l'équilibre des liqueurs (. . .)* [1663], quoted here from Pascal, *Œuvres complètes*, ed. Jean Mesnard (Paris: Desclée de Brouwer, 1964–), 4 volumes to date, vol. I, 689. My translation.

beyond the appearance of the "objective" editions. Today it seems somewhat peculiar to propose a global understanding of a collection of fragments based on the classification made by a scholar in 1905 instead of the author's own classification from 1660, as did Lucien Goldmann in the 1950s and Pierre Bourdieu as late as the 1990s.[6] This is less of a problem when it comes to Benjamin, however, since he is commenting on individual fragments and not the totality they enter into. And yet, as it will soon become clear, Benjamin's philological choices were less than sound for other reasons.

Let us now turn to Benjamin's text. The passage drawing on Pascal occurs at the center of the *Trauerspiel* book, near the end of its first half that carries the title *"Trauerspiel* and Tragedy," in an untitled section often referred to as "the melancholy chapter." This chapter was in fact the first part of *Ursprung des deutschen Trauerspiels* to be published. The book itself wasn't published until 1928, after the manuscript had first been submitted as a "Habilitationsschrift" in 1925, but then had to be withdrawn to avoid the "unpleasantness of public refusal."[7] In the meantime, however, the melancholy chapter had been published in Hugo von Hofmannsthal's journal *Neue Deutsche Beiträge* in 1927, and was thus contemporary with the exchange of letters referred to in the opening of my essay. This is therefore a chapter that can be read on its own, isolated from its context.

Indeed, to Benjamin, melancholy is the point where the different characteristic features of the baroque age converge. At the same time, however, one can wonder about the relative scarcity of references to baroque sources in this chapter on *baroque* melancholy, which is instead focused on Renaissance and medieval sources and scholarly interpretations of these. As Jane Newman has shown, not only Benjamin's argument, but his use of primary sources as well are here heavily (and more heavily than Benjamin's own annotation suggests) indebted to his scholarly contemporaries, such as Warburg, Giehlow, Panofsky, and Saxl, although this is done ultimately only to refute the optimism undergirding their work.[8] Although Benjamin

6. See, for example, Lucien Goldmann, *Le dieu caché: étude sur la vision tragique dans les "Pensées" de Pascal et dans le théâtre de Racine* (Paris: Gallimard, 1955); Pierre Bourdieu, *Méditations pascaliennes* (Paris: Seuil, 1997).

7. George Steiner, Introduction to Benjamin, *Origin of German Tragic Drama* (London: Verso, 1996), 11. Hereafter cited as *OGTD*.

8. See Jane O. Newman, *Benjamin's Library: Modernity, Nation, and the Baroque* (Ithaca: Cornell University Press, 2011), 168–69.

interweaves what Newman calls "his own citations on melancholic astral-humoral issues from additional seventeenth-century texts," it is worth noting that the two primary baroque references of the chapter are of a different order and that neither of them are German, namely Shakespeare's *Hamlet* and Pascal's *Pensées*.[9] Both of these sources resonate in the title of the section in which the Pascal quotation appears, in the second of seven subsections in the chapter: "Melancholy of the Prince" (*"Trübsinn des Fürsten"*).

I would like to dwell a moment on the way Pascal is brought into the argument. The passage in question opens the "Melancholy of the Prince" section. In the multilingual original, the following five sentences by Benjamin in German are followed by two quotations from the *Pensées* in French, to which I will return shortly.

> In this imposing heritage [the theory of the melancholy disposition] which the baroque received from the renaissance, and which was the result of almost two thousand years of work, posterity possesses a more direct commentary on the *Trauerspiel* than the poetics could provide. There is a harmonious relationship between this and the philosophical ideas and political convictions which underlie the representation of history as a *Trauerspiel*. The prince is the paradigm of the melancholy man. Nothing demonstrates the frailty of the creature so drastically as the fact that even he is subject to it. In one of the most powerful passages of the *Pensées* Pascal gives voice to the feeling of his age with this very reflection.[10]

It is not immediately clear from the context exactly to which feeling Pascal gives voice, according to Benjamin. A first reading may suggest that the answer is that Pascal voices the feeling that "[t]he prince is the paradigm of the melancholy man." However, the content of the actual quotation from Pascal will show that neither "the melancholy disposition" nor "the frailty of the creature" are far away. In fact, I will argue that the passage above contains four different possible antecedents for the last line reference to the "feeling of his age," and that they all resonate in the Pascalian words to which we will soon turn:

9. Newman, *Benjamin's Library*, 169. Newman discusses Benjamin's mobilization of Shakespeare extensively, including his identification as German (esp. 115–37, 143), and the interpretation of *Hamlet* in the melancholy chapter (143–154, 169), but does not comment on the quotation from Pascal.
10. Benjamin, *OGTD*, 142.

1. . . . the theory of the melancholy disposition
2. . . . the representation of history as a *Trauerspiel*
3. . . . that the prince is the paradigm of the melancholy man
4. . . . the frailty of the creature [*Gebrechlichkeit der Kreatur*]

Before proceeding to the Pascalian quotation, two of these points require further comment. I will not dwell on the first point (the theory of the melancholy disposition, famously analyzed by Pascal as "*ennui*") nor the third (the creaturely exemplarity of the prince), since they should need no further comment than the one Benjamin provides above, and Pascal in what follows.

The importance of "the representation of history as a *Trauerspiel*" in a Pascalian context can most easily be grasped by revisiting Benjamin's distinction between tragedy and *Trauerspiel*. In short—maybe too short—we may say that the *Trauerspiel* is a non-heroic tragedy.[11] Its main characters remain royal as in the tragedy, but they are never "deified," nor do they at any point "shake off their immanence."[12] It is as if their supreme position among men, instead of making them less human, makes them more human, more fragile, more "creaturely." This is, of course, conspicuous in *Hamlet*. The greatness of the melancholy prince is not good for anything; on the contrary, his greatness only underscores his misery—if it is not the misery that constitutes his greatness. And the prince's death is accidental, unheroic, untragic, without any obvious higher meaning. As Benjamin points out, in the *Trauerspiel*, the reason for the catastrophe is no longer "moral transgression but the very estate of man as a creature."[13]

And what is true on stage also holds for the *Trauerspiel* of life. According to Benjamin, "[l]ike the term 'tragic' in present-day usage . . . the word *Trauerspiel* was applied in the seventeenth century to dramas and historical events alike."[14] In this way, *Trauerspiel* is more than a dramatic genre; it becomes a particular perception of history, a baroque way of perceiving history.

In order to suggest that this mode of thinking is not alien to Pascal, it is enough to quote the following short fragment from the *Pensées*,

---

11. See the introduction to this volume for a more thorough discussion of this distinction. My concern here is less Benjamin's reference to the actual German *Trauerspiele* than the way he mobilizes considerations of creatureliness in making the distinction.
12. Benjamin, *OGTD*, 67.
13. Ibid., 89.
14. Ibid., 63.

where we notice the same use of a theatrical language to describe life off stage: "The final act is bloody, however fine the rest of the play. In the end they throw some earth over our head, and that is it forever."[15] Pascal's most recent translator, Roger Ariew, whose translation I follow here, translates the famous opening line, "*Le dernier acte est sanglant*," quite literally with "the final act is bloody," but what about the somewhat freer and more dramatic earlier translation by W. F. Trotter, who offers: "the last act is *tragic*"?[16] This is a tricky question because in the early modern sense, the words "tragic" and "bloody" are close to synonyms in this context, as illustrated by a passage from Claude Saumaise on regicide that Benjamin cites earlier in the book when he evokes "[t]he fifth and final act" in which the drama is brought to a close "with such a tragic and bloody catastrophe [*par une si tragique et sanglante catastrophe*]."[17] And yet, to a modern ear, with the post-romantic metaphysical weight of the adjective "tragic," Trotter's choice is unfortunate. If history and the human life are perceived as a *Trauerspiel*, as here, then the last act is precisely *not* tragic, *not even* tragic—sadder than tragic, so to speak. The end portrayed here is not heroic; no victory is won in the hour of defeat, no meaning is created through an ultimate sacrifice. What Benjamin offers us is a critical idiom for thinking about the darkest aspects of Pascal's analysis of what he calls the "the wretchedness of man without God,"[18] liberated from post-romantic notions of a tragic *Weltanschauung*.

This observation brings me to the fourth possible answer to the question about what precise feeling Pascal is voicing, as quoted by Benjamin, namely "the frailty of the creature," or, in German, the even more frail "*Gebrechlichkeit der Kreatur*." At this point, a philological observation is in order. First of all, it is worth pointing out that in daily parlance the German *Kreatur* is much less commonly used than the English *creature*, or the French *créature* (the primary translation of the Latin *creatura* being rather the Germanic *Geschöpf*). With the words derived from *Kreatur*, *creature*, and *créature* (*kreatürlich* and *Kreatürlichkeit*; *creaturely* and *creatureliness*) the French terms are somewhat more in flux, but *créaturel* and *être-créature* are good

15. Pascal, *Pensées*, fr. 197.
16. Pascal, *Thoughts*, trans. W. F. Trotter (New York, F. Collier & Son, 1910), 79.
17. Benjamin, *OGTD*, 78. The passage is quoted in the original French by Benjamin. I follow the translation provided by Osborne in his annotation of the text.
18. Pascal, *Pensées*, fr. 40.

options), we enter into technical theological terminology in all three languages. Traditionally, these terms have been used to designate man in his relation to his Creator. As used by Benjamin, however, they seem to have gone through a secularization (and everything hinges here on the exact meaning of the word "secularization"); after the Creator's withdrawal from the Creation, it is as if the words based on *Kreatur* resonate with the suffering to which man is subject as a mortal creature. The notion points, so to speak, simultaneously in two directions: upward to a prelapsarian origin, where the human creature once resided with his Creator, and downward to the realm of animals and things, where he now dwells, longing or mourning for his lost state.

This tension between an upward and a downward pull is present through the whole melancholy chapter. We encounter it in the opening page, in the first quotation from Hamlet, where man is portrayed both as beast-like and god-like; later, among other places, in the discussion of the dualism inherent in the astrological idea of Saturn; and even in the melancholic dog as torn between prophetic dreams and rabies, intellectual greatness and madness.[19] And the same is of course true for Hamlet, torn between greatness and madness—and for melancholy itself. In all its loftiness, "melancholy emerges from the depth of the creaturely realm."[20]

Before finally reading the Pascal passage quoted by Benjamin, a curious philological observation is in order, as hinted at above. Benjamin read Pascal's *Pensées* in an outdated edition: not Brunschvicg's

---

19. Cf. Benjamin, *OGTD*, 138, 150, 146.

20. Benjamin, *OGTD*, 146. The reading I propose here would not have been possible without the increased attentiveness to creaturely concerns in Benjamin's writing in the last two decades by such scholars as Beatrice Hanssen, Julia Lupton, Françoise Proust, Eric Santner, Daniel Weidner, and Sigrid Weigel. See Beatrice Hanssen, *Walter Benjamin's Other History. Of Stones, Animals, Human Beings, and Angels* (Berkeley: University of California Press, 1998); Julia Reinhard Lupton, "Creature Caliban," *Shakespeare Quarterly* 51/1 (2000), 1–23; Françoise Proust, *L'histoire à contretemps. Le temps historique chez Walter Benjamin* (Paris: Cerf, 1994); Eric Santner, *On Creaturely Life. Rilke, Benjamin, Sebald* (Chicago: University of Chicago Press, 2006); Daniel Weidner, "Kreatürlichkeit: Benjamins Trauerspielbuch und das Leben des Barock" in *Profanes Leben - Walter Benjamins Dialektik der Säkularisierung*, ed. Daniel Weidner (Frankfurt: Suhrkamp, 2010, 120–138); Sigrid Weigel, *Walter Benjamin. Die Kreatur, das Heilige, die Bilder* (Frankfurt am Main: Fischer Taschenbuch, 2008). I would like to thank Jane Newman for having brought my attention to this emerging reorientation of Benjamin scholarship already in the late 1990s.

fairly reliable (although "subjective") edition from 1905, but a 1905 Flammarion edition in the series "Les meilleurs auteurs classiques," based on the 1670 Port-Royal edition of the *Pensées*, where the editors took great liberties in rewriting the text and even adding new passages in order to make the fragmented text seem a little less fragmented. Unfortunately for Benjamin, the first part of his quotation from the *Pensées* was not written by Pascal; it is a pastiche written by the editors, most likely by Pierre Nicole.[21] In this way, the passage is still a "voice of the age of Pascal," and it sounds like Pascal; it is Pascalian in its content, but it is still definitely not authentically Pascalian.

How should one proceed in such a situation? How is the status of Benjamin's text altered by his mistake? Luckily, in this instance, the first passage does not say much that is not present in the longer second passage on "the king without diversion." Therefore, I will skip the pastiche (easily available in any edition of Benjamin's *Trauerspiel* book, and in older editions of the *Pensées*) and move directly to the longer quotation, replacing Benjamin's text with the more accurate version from the Sellier edition of the *Pensées*, as rendered into English by Roger Ariew. Before doing so, I would like to stress that this last substitution is not entirely unproblematic, due to the alterations in the text Benjamin read. The most important of these concerns the proverbial "king without diversion," which is in fact missing from the Port-Royal edition of the text: where Pascal wrote "*un roi sans divertissement*," Nicole changed it to "*un roi qui se voit*," "a king that sees himself." This is quite a fascinating dislocation to have taken place in the 1660s, in the early years of Louis XIV's personal reign, a period that saw an unprecedented level of royal mirroring and which would ultimately lead to the construction of the Hall of Mirrors at Versailles, where the most important mirrors are not the ones on the walls, but the paintings of the exploits of Louis XIV's reign by Charles Le Brun in the vault. Ironically, therefore, it could seem that where Pascal's original wording is more explicit in its anthropological analysis, Nicole's rewrite gives an even more forceful voice to the obsessions (and anxiety) of the age.

Now, finally Pascal's text. The title of the fragment, not quoted by Benjamin, is "Diversion":

21. For this attribution, see Marie Pérouse, *L'invention des "Pensées" de Pascal. Les éditions de Port-Royal (1670–1678)* (Paris: Champion, 2009).

"Is not royal dignity sufficiently great in itself to make its possessor happy by the mere contemplation of what he is? Must he be diverted from this thought like ordinary people? I quite see that it makes a man happy to be diverted from thinking about his domestic woes by filling his thoughts with the concern to dance well. But will it be the same with a king, and will he be happier in the pursuit of these idle amusements than in considering his greatness? And what more satisfactory object could be presented to his mind? Would it not spoil his delight to occupy his soul with the thought of how to adjust his steps to the rhythm of a tune, or of how to place a bar skillfully, instead of leaving him to enjoy quietly the contemplation of the majestic glory surrounding him? Let us test this. Let us leave a king all alone to reflect on himself at his leisure, without anything to satisfy his senses, without any care in his mind, without company, and we will see that a king without diversion is a man full of misery. So this is carefully avoided; there never fail to be a great number near the retinues of kings, people who see to it that diversion follows the kings' affairs of state, watching over their leisure to supply them with pleasure and games, so that they have no empty moments. In other words, they are surrounded by people who take wonderful care to insure that the king be not alone and able to think about himself, knowing well that he will be miserable, king though he is, if he does think about it."[22]

We recognize the tension between the upward and downward pull structuring the passage: the tension between the royal office, on the one hand, and the royal person on the other; between the king's immortal body politic and his fragile body natural. Which of the two royal bodies prevails in the king, *is* in reality the king? Is he more *king* (that is royal office: "royal dignity," "greatness," "the majestic glory surrounding him") than *man*? Is the glory of his office in itself enough to repress his creatureliness? The importance granted to the king's vision is here significant: Should not "the mere *view* of what he is," "the *view* of his greatness," "the *contemplation* of the majestic glory surrounding him" be enough to make him happy?[23] Or in other words: Should not the peaceful contemplation of the royal portrait, of his immortal body politic, be the most satisfying way possible for the king to fill his time?

Pascal's answer is, of course, "no." Without his "affairs of state," his "diversions," "pleasures," and "games" the king will inevitably

22. Pascal, *Pensées*, fr. 169.
23. My emphasis in all three expressions.

be miserable, since he will end up "think[ing] about himself." And this miserable "think[ing] about himself" contains implicitly the answer to the first series of questions raised above. The "self" of the king resides not in his portrayed royal glory, but in frail, mortal man. The king is less king than man—"king though he is [*tout roi qu'il est*]." Or, as Benjamin puts it: "However highly he is enthroned over subject and state, his status is confined to the world of creation; he is the lord of creatures, but he remains a creature [*er ist der Herr der Kreaturen, aber er bleibt Kreatur*]."[24] His royalty and humanity are here opposed as *Herr* and *Kreatur*, as lord and creature, and his "self" ultimately resides less in his *Herr-lichkeit* (which, interestingly, is the German theological counterpart to the French *gloire* and the English *glory*) than in his Kreatür-lichkeit. Consequently, to avoid melancholy, the king needs to be diverted from the recognition of what Benjamin calls "the misery of mankind in its creaturely estate [*das Elend des Menchentums in seinem kreatürlichen Stande*]."[25] The king—"king though he is"—is just a mortal creature, inexorably approaching the end of his reign. He may be playing a decisive role in History through his body politic, but at the same time his body natural is "subject[ed] to nature."[26] Faced with death, he is no different from his subjects. In the theatrical language of Pascal's fragment 197, the king's last act will also be bloody, however happy all the rest of the play has been; in the end a little earth will be thrown upon *his* head, too, and that will be it forever.

This is the drama of the modern, secularized creature, whose constitution is infused with theological residue limiting its agency (passivity, opacity, abjectness, dependence), but for whom, in Benjamin's famous formulation, there is "no eschatology."[27] As Pascal puts it, in lapidary fashion, in an important but under-studied fragment: "Description of man. / Dependence, desire for independence, needs."[28] The king may conceive of himself as a tragic hero within a lofty script of glorious transcendence toward autonomy, but he will in the end have to realize that his life is not a tragedy but rather a *Trauerspiel* in which the natural history of man inevitably trumps the epic-heroic history of the king. This recognition presents itself through what

24. Benjamin, *OGTD*, 85; Benjamin, *Ursprung des Deutschen Trauerspiels*, 66.
25. Benjamin, *OGTD*, 146.
26. Ibid., 166.
27. Ibid., 66.
28. Pascal, *Pensées*, fr. 113.

Benjamin analyzes as melancholy and Pascal as *ennui*. Its most exact description can be found in the following remarkable fragment, where three puzzling accumulations of nouns, in a language of languishing, already point to the depth of the fall of what might have looked like an autonomous modern subject:

> Nothing is so intolerable for man as to be in complete tranquility, without passions, without dealings, without diversion, without effort. He then feels his nothingness, isolation, insufficiency, dependence, weakness, emptiness. Immediately there arises from the depth of his soul boredom, gloom, sadness, chagrin, resentment, despair.[29]

And yet, both in Benjamin and Pascal there seems to take place a reversal through which the melancholy prince becomes a figure of hope. In Benjamin's section on melancholy, the prince plays the role of both the archetypal melancholic and the one who transcends melancholy. As we have seen, the prince is introduced in the first role early in the section, in a way that anticipates the lesson from Pascal's "king without diversion," which is quoted immediately afterwards: "The prince is the paradigm of the melancholy man. Nothing demonstrates the frailty of creatures so drastically as the fact that he is subject to it."[30] Hamlet is obviously present already in the melancholic sovereign who despises his royal office and portrait, who prefers to be "sans divertissement," who enacts—and stages—his own *Trauerspiel*. At the very last page of the section his example is explicitly evoked, since "[o]nly in a princely life such as this is melancholy redeemed": Hamlet's "life, the exemplary object of his mourning, points [. . .] to the Christian providence in whose bosom his mournful images are transformed into a blessed existence."[31] Hence, more than any other, the prince demonstrates the transitoriness of man, and only in the prince can this transitoriness itself become transitory.

In Pascal, too, royalty is used both to depict the melancholic misery of man and to signal a way out of this misery. As we have seen above, the melancholy of the "king without diversion" has its source in the creaturely misery of his body natural; in fact, in the last analysis, the purpose of the diversion is nothing more than to make the king forget the inevitable "last bloody act" of the *Trauerspiel* he is

---

29. Pascal, *Pensées*, fr. 169. For an elaboration of this perspective, see chapter 5 of Bjornstad, *Créature sans créateur*, esp. 147–63 and 178–79.
30. Benjamin, *OGTD*, 142.
31. Ibid., 158.

living. The counterpart to the Pascalian melancholic "king without diversion" is to be found in the following passage: "All these forms of wretchedness prove his greatness. / They are the wretchedness of a great lord, the wretchedness of a deposed king."[32]

To bring out the close yet complex relation of symmetry and inversion that exists between the two Pascalian kings (the "king without diversion" and the "deposed king"), Louis Marin juxtaposes the relevant passages in the following way: "a king without diversion is a man full of misery (. . .) but all these forms of misery are the misery of a great lord, the misery of a deposed king."[33] This is still Hamlet's territory: A "king without diversion"—even he is a man, even he is subject to melancholic misery; a "deposed king"—but only in a "princely life such as this"[34] can melancholy be redeemed. In Pascal, there is, of course, an underlying apologetic agenda here: if you sustain melancholy creaturely misery, you too can attain a "princely life such as this." Even the king is a (miserable) man, and even you are a (deposed) king. Pascal can obviously not promise immediate redemption—the way back to the lost throne may be long and hard for the deposed and exiled king—but he shows a possible way out of what Benjamin, at the end of the *Trauerspiel* book, calls "the supposed infinity of a world without hope."[35]

In this way, both Benjamin and Pascal seem to insert hope into a baroque world that, according to their common comprehension of the misery of its creaturely estate, should be without hope. In fact, in the way these images of redemption are linked to the recognition of human misery, not only a baroque melancholy will emerge, as Benjamin says, "from the depth of the creaturely realm,"[36] but so may also a baroque hope.

32. Pascal, *Pensées*, fr. 148.
33. Cf. Louis Marin, *Le portrait du roi* (Paris: Seuil, 1981), 267; and *The Portrait of the King*, trans. Martha Houle (Minneapolis: University of Minnesota Press), 218–19; translation modified.
34. Benjamin, *OGTD*, 158.
35. Ibid., 232.
36. Ibid., 146.

JOHN D. LYONS

Material Fatality: Props and the Baroque Drama of Chance

"Chance, in the sense of the breaking down of the action into fragmented elements or things, corresponds entirely to the meaning of the
stage-property."[1]

Benjamin says of the principal figures of *Trauerspiel* that

What is conspicuous about them is not so much the sovereignty evident in the stoic turns of phrase, as the sheer arbitrariness of a constantly shifting emotional storm in which the figures of Lohenstein
especially sway about like torn and flapping banners. And they also
bear a certain resemblance to the figures of El Greco in the smallness of their heads, if we understand this in a metaphorical sense. For
their actions are not determined by thought, but by changing physical
impulses.[2]

This contrast between thought and action, or rather between thought
and feeling, on one hand, and the physical, material world, on the
other, is typical of Benjamin's description of the baroque drama. In
mentioning the stoic expressions of these heroes, he gives us a clue
to the tradition in which the spiritual (or mental) and the physical are
divorced. The latter is the world of fortune, which is specifically com-
prised of physical things, of all that can be stolen, or lost, or burned,
or that simply disintegrates. The former is the world of will and idea,
which consists of things that are not subject to fortune and that only
change when we decide to change them. This representation of the
world is familiar to us because we recognize it as the legacy of sto-
icism or even more specifically of Boethius's *Consolation of Philosophy*. Benjamin notes the continuity of the baroque with the middle

1. Walter Benjamin, *The Origins of German Tragic Drama*, trans. John Osborne
(London: NLB, 1977), 133. Hereafter cited as *OGTD*.
2. Ibid., 71.

YFS 124, *Walter Benjamin's Hypothetical French "Trauerspiel,"* ed. Bjornstad and Ibbett, © 2013 by Yale University.

ages, which, as he says, were not even recognized as a distinct historical period under that name until the seventeenth century, and Boethius's image of *Fortuna* is most powerfully persistent throughout that period.[3] For Boethius, the inner world of thought is only subject to fortune if we allow it to be. In other words, our thoughts do not change by chance, unless we have decided to let them be subject to the invasive power of the material world. Random thoughts happen, not by chance, but by a decision to abdicate the properly decisive role of thought and to allow thought to ape the world of matter. Outside, it is quite another thing, and all of that outside world is in a state of unpredictable flux precisely because that is what matter does. It is because the inner world is not governed by chance that Boethius can hold people morally accountable for what they think.[4] In referring to the metaphorically small-headed heroes who flap about, Benjamin is simply pointing to the underdeveloped state of these princes who stud their speeches with stoic expressions but who do not have actually stoic mastery (big heads). Fortune is so much located within and upon the material world that it is sometimes tempting to think of fortune as a synonym for matter—something like this happens when we say that someone "has a fortune" or has "lost a fortune," meaning lots of money and property—and to say that fortune is a way of describing how matter moves. And matter that moves is easy to mistake for something that is alive. This is precisely the error or the illusion that Aristotle encounters in trying to point out what we call chance (*tyché* or *automaton*).

It is within this background in the baroque-medieval worldview that Benjamin says "Once human life has sunk into the merely creaturely, even the life of apparently dead objects secures power over it. The effectiveness of the object where guilt has been incurred is a sign of the approach of death."[5] Metaphorically there is an exchange or draining of life into matter where the sign of the deadness of an individual is the increased dominance of things. The latter seem almost to come alive in proportion to the death of the individual over whom they have power, as in fungus growing on a corpse. In this context Benjamin writes of the way the prop or stage-property (*das Requisit*)

3. Ibid., 77.

4. John D. Lyons, *The Phantom of Chance: From Fortune to Randomness in Seventeenth-Century French Literature*, Edinburgh Critical Studies in Renaissance Culture (Edinburgh: Edinburgh University Press, 2011), 12–15.

5. Benjamin, *OGTD*, 132.

corresponds to chance (*Zufall*) as the disintegration into pieces of what happens.

Here I take the liberty of considering the prop in an enlarged sense, not simply as the real or fake item that is actually handled on stage, but also as a thing, mentioned by the speakers, that in its material being takes on particular significance and even seems to alter the course of events. But to be a "prop" offstage, as I take it, the thing would have to be mentioned with particular attention to its material qualities and, in order to fully justify the appeal to chance, it would have to show a certain resistance to human control. In other words, if the characteristic of the material world that makes it notably different from the inner world is that it is not subject to our decisions, then the prop as point of encounter of the inner world and the outer world must be neither simply *there* as part of the background nor simply an extension of the human agent. Rather, it must be too much like a part of a human agent, yet in a certain sense not enough a part, not obedient enough to human intention. Benjamin gives the example of the dagger in one of Calderón's tragedies of jealousy, and this seems entirely right because when we speak of props we usually mean things that human beings can handle and use: a dagger, a sword, a bowl, a book, a pin, a portrait, a skull.

For Benjamin, the prop is a mark of modernity. The exclusion of the stage-property "is a sign of the genuine influence of antiquity, or a genuine Renaissance trait. For there is hardly any more pronounced distinction between modern and ancient drama than the absence from the latter of the profane world of things. And the same is true of the classical period of the baroque in Germany."[6] If ancient tragedy dispenses altogether with props and *Schicksalstragödie* is dominated by props, *Trauerspiel* occupies an intermediate position, since these two modern genres, in Benjamin's view, are situated on a scale of increasing materiality.[7] Shakespeare makes use of props in *Hamlet*, which has a "drastic externality characteristic of the *Trauerspiel*." Concurrently with the emphasis on the external, Benjamin notes the dominant role of chance in *Hamlet*, where the hero "wants to die from some accident, and as the fateful stage-properties gather around

6. Ibid., 133–34.
7. Benjamin, though surely correct in general on this point, may have exaggerated the absence of stage properties in ancient drama. See David Raeburn, "The Significance of Stage Properties in Euripides' 'Electra,'" *Greece & Rome* 47/2, Second Series (October 1, 2000): 149–68.

him, as around their lord and master, the drama of fate flares up in the conclusion of the *Trauerspiel*, as something that is contained, but of course overcome, in it. Whereas tragedy ends with a decision."[8]

Given Benjamin's clustering of stage prop, fate, and chance as indicators of the new drama that broke with the ancient genre of tragedy, we can recognize much of seventeenth-century French drama as resembling his *Trauerspiel*. This kinship between French and German baroque drama is somewhat obscured for modern readers, including no doubt Benjamin himself, by the triumph of Corneille and Racine as quasi-exclusive representatives of seventeenth-century French dramaturgy. Even in their works, the prop has a significant and now under-appreciated role, as we will see. Yet if we take a broader view of the drama of early modern France and consider some of the repertory that no longer claims a place in the classroom and on the stage, we see that the prop has an overwhelming importance. Moreover, many, if not most, French tragicomedies and tragedies of the first third of the seventeenth century confirm Benjamin's intuition about the relation between the material world and chance or fortune. Repeated and vivid displays of props are the hallmark of the French tragicomedy. Hélène Baby has written of the way the prop is used to display the inner life of characters: "it seems as if there was an absolute need for sentiment to pass from the interiority of the character to the exteriority of the object, and thus from abstraction to materialization."[9] Benjamin gives us another way of looking at the prop, not simply as a way of externalizing feelings but as a manifestation of humanity's subjugation to a material world in which virtue, merit, and intention are swept away in the vortex of what Benjamin calls "the unpredictability of historical accident" (*schwankenden historischen Geschehns*).[10]

Consider the 1643 tragicomedy (or tragedy) *Bélisaire*, by Jean Rotrou (1609–1650).[11] The hesitation about the generic classification of Rotrou's play—on the title page of the first edition it is called a "tragedy," but a few pages later, between the list of *dramatis personae* and

---

8. Benjamin, *OGTD*, 136–37.

9. Hélène Baby, *La tragi-comédie de Corneille à Quinault* (Paris: Klincksieck, 2001), 662. In the notes to her edition of Rotrou's plays, Marianne Béthery describes his work as "a dramaturgy of the stage-prop" (*une dramaturgie de l'accessoire*) in Jean Rotrou, *Théâtre complet*, ed. Georges Forestier and Marianne Béthery (Paris: Société des textes français modernes, 1998), 1:27.

10. Benjamin, *OGTD*, 74.

11. Rotrou, *Théâtre complet*, 1:69–199. The play was first published in 1644.

the first scene, it is called a "tragicomedy"—is paralleled in Benjamin's later hesitations about the exact contours of the drama he attempts to describe, for he finds some of the essence of the German baroque *Trauerspiel* in the work of Calderón.[12] In *Bélisaire*, the hero, a Roman general in the service of the emperor Justinian, is hated by the empress Théodore. He survives four attacks by dagger and an attempt to trap him in a staged sexual seduction, but finally succumbs when Théodore accuses him of making a sexual advance to her, and he is executed by Justinian's orders, just before the truth comes to light. The whole play could be described as a series of exchanges (or attempted exchanges) of a variety of props: daggers, a gold chain, rings, a scarf, a glove, and four written documents. These props are mentioned in the copious stage directions (e.g. "he draws a dagger," II, 8, after verse 594) as well as in dialogue ("I dropped one of my gloves, / Yet you do not even oblige me by picking it up," IV, 2, 1393–94) and their functions assume a fascinatingly systematic quality. For instance, saving a life or giving up an assassination attempt earns a gold chain or ring in return (I, 2; II, 18), and the sight of a ring—mark of an earlier intervention to prevent a murder—subsequently prevents an assassination (III, 2).

With striking frequency the characters link these physical objects to the effect of chance. To choose a lieutenant, Bélisaire takes three written nominations (three *mémoires*) and shuffles them before picking one at random (II, 7). He then announces his choice to the emperor, saying "I placed my faith in chance and made it the judge" ("J'en ai cru le hasard, et l'en ai fait l'arbitre" II, 10, 664). As it was for Benjamin, in Rotrou's dramatic world chance (*hasard* and *fortune*) is equivalent to fate (*sort*, *destin*, and one's *astre*). The point the play seems to make is that while the hero tries repeatedly to reward and encourage merit, what finally decides the outcome of his own life is simply chance. A material object (a love letter) that has no explicit mark of its addressee falls into the hands of the wrong person (the empress), and despite the evidence of the hero's life-long virtue and loyalty, he is stripped of all honor and killed. As Marianne Béthery writes in the introduction to her edition of Rotrou's theatrical works, "the adventures of Bélisaire and other characters . . . are lived under the sign of injustice and absurdity. A good man can achieve nothing

---

12. Benjamin, *OGTD*, 81;125. Benjamin mentions the way intrigue in the *Trauerspiel* is related to comedy as well as to mourning.

and evil ultimately triumphs."[13] In the case of the tragicomedy *La force du sang* by Alexandre Hardy (1570–1632), the outcome of this drama of rape and reconciliation depends on chance as mediated by an object found in the dark.[14]

Today's readers and theater audiences know seventeenth-century French tragic drama only through the work of Corneille and Racine. In their plays, props generally do not have the importance that Benjamin attributes to them in *Trauerspiel*. We should remember, however, that Pierre Corneille started writing for the stage when tragicomedy was the dominant genre of serious (i.e. not explicitly comic) plays, and in tragicomedies chance and its actualization in material objects play a decisive role. In the year of *Le Cid* (1637) there were 21 tragicomedies performed or printed, alongside 17 tragedies.[15] One of the best examples of Corneille's early use of props in a plot driven by chance is *Clitandre, ou l'Innocence délivrée* (1631).[16] The first act of *Clitandre* is a masterpiece in the dramaturgy of chance. Caliste has come into the forest to catch her lover Rosidor at a tryst with another woman. Caliste's information about her lover's infidelity comes from Dorise, who has planned this visit to the woods and accompanies Caliste. However, the audience learns shortly before Caliste does, that this supposed assignation and Rosidor's infidelity are entirely inventions of Dorise herself who loves Rosidor and plans to kill Caliste while they are in a secluded place where there will be no witnesses and no one to protect Caliste. Unbeknownst to Caliste and to Dorise, Rosidor is indeed in the same forest, but to fight a duel against Clitandre, who is also in love with Caliste. But unbeknownst to Rosidor, the message sent to him challenging him to a duel did not come from Clitandre, but was a forgery. The supposed duel was the invention of Pymante, who is in love with Dorise and who plans to ambush

13. Rotrou, *Théâtre complet*, 1:57.

14. Alexandre Hardy, *La force du sang*, ed. James Herbert Davis (Athens: University of Georgia Press, 1972). The date of performance of *La force du sang* is unknown, but Lancaster estimates that it was staged sometime between 1615 and 1625. It was printed in 1625. Henry Carrington Lancaster, *A History of French Dramatic Literature in the Seventeenth Century* (Baltimore, MD: Johns Hopkins University Press, 1929), Part I, vol. 1, 45.

15. Lancaster, *History*, Part II, vol. 2, 777–78. Roger Guichemerre, in *La tragicomédie* (Paris: Presses Universitaires de France, 1981), notes that the years 1631–1642 were the apogee of tragicomedy in France. (38).

16. For a fuller treatment of *Clitandre* and chance, see Lyons, *The Phantom of Chance*, 37–44.

Rosidor with a number of henchmen and kill him to eliminate the object of Dorise's affections. Thus, there are two simultaneous murder plots located in the same part of the forest for the same time: Dorise against Caliste and Pymante against Rosidor.

The two plots are perfectly but unwittingly coordinated in time and space by the two separate conspirators, and their convergence illustrates the paradoxical permeability with opacity that often characterizes tragicomic space. Rosidor, without seeing Dorise poised to strike Caliste, seizes Dorise's sword—a sword that from his point of view comes out of nowhere—to defend himself against his attackers. This crossing of the two murder attempts in the first act, in the concrete form of the transfer of a prop from one performer to another, is the major incident from which the rest of the tragicomic plot derives: Dorise's escape and subsequent disguise, Pymante's escape and subsequent encounter with Dorise, the accusation against Clitandre that he organized the attempt on Rosidor's life, and finally the king's permission for Rosidor and Caliste to marry. But this incident is the pure result of chance. If Rosidor's sword had not broken at that precise moment, he would not have needed another sword and would not have seized the one that Dorise held suspended over Caliste.

The dozen different chance events in *Clitandre* are quite varied in nature, in magnitude, and in sheer improbability. The exchange of the swords is the most remarkable and has the largest number of consequences, but it depends on the earlier discovery of the sword by Dorise, which is itself entirely unremarkable, and rather random. The bolt of lightning that kills the Prince's horse is the most conventional and the most spectacular kind of chance, that is, an incident that is so widely identified as being unpredictable, unavoidable, and yet hugely important that it is a "classic" case of chance, often studied as such (e.g. in the *Logique* de Port-Royal, chapters 13–16).[17] But the lightning bolt can belong to another related category, also ruled out of tragedy by Aristotle: the *deus ex machina*.[18]

As exemplified strikingly in *Clitandre*, the tragicomedies of this period intensify contrasting extremes. The dramatic characters pro-

---

17. Antoine Arnauld and Pierre Nicole, *La logique; ou, L'art de penser; contenant, outre les règles communes, plusieurs observations nouvelles, propres à former le jugement* (Paris: Flammarion, 1970), 413–31.

18. Aristotle, *The Poetics of Aristotle: Translation and Commentary*, trans. and ed. Stephen Halliwell (Chapel Hill: University of North Carolina Press, 1987), chapter 15, 47–48.

duce extraordinarily intricate schemes that advance the pretention to subject the world to total human control (in the early decades of the twenty-first century we may be tempted to compare this to complex and expensive procedures of "risk management"), while on the other hand the plot of the play includes the most improbable and far-fetched incidents of randomness. In the case of the two crossed murder plots, we can see actual human intentions that are strangely, uncannily parallel yet opposite, so that while the bolt of lightning is impressive because of something entirely *unintended* that happens, the crossed plots are impressive because of an *excess of intention* that is, moreover, exquisitely symmetrical. The two forms of chance meet at this point, in this extra or excess intention. Apparently we cannot help thinking that "this is too good to be true," precisely because there seems to be an intention that we, at the same time, deny. The term used by the characters in Corneille's play is *dessein*, which expresses the intention of the human plotters. And this intention meets the unintended, in the form of material reality: the tree branch on which the sword breaks, the bolt of lightning, and the body of the horse.

To draw still more attention to the role of chance in the form of the material world, there is the very first incident of the story that is mentioned last, in the fourth scene of the fifth act (v. 1789), so that the play ends by returning to its beginning and reminds the audience of the mysteries of causality: Dorise finds a sword in the forest. Human intention, the *dessein*, turns out to depend on material reality. At the end of the play Dorise is suddenly and weirdly rehabilitated and married to the Prince's favorite Clitandre, and one effect of the flashback to the discovery of the sword is an attempt to transfer the guilt to the material world itself. That is, in order to displace guilt from the murderous Dorise at the moment when she is betrothed to the prince whose name gives the play its title, Corneille makes it seem that Dorise would have been innocent all along had she not chanced upon this corrupting object. When we consider how thoroughly seventeenth-century literature is (for modern, that is, post-nineteenth-century readers) lacking in material detail, the few objects that are named, though not described, take on proportionately more intensity. In *Clitandre* this is true of the sword and also the hairpin that Dorise inadvertently left in place and that allowed Pymante to recognize her. The sword and the hairpin—easily seen as "phallic" objects—converge insofar as they are both used by Dorise as weapons.

She tries to kill Caliste with the sword, and she succeeds in putting out one of Pymante's eyes with the hairpin.[19]

In the tragedies of the later seventeenth century, props play a smaller role, or at least there are fewer of them. It may be, however, that the smaller number of props only intensifies the focus on the one or two that remain. As in *Clitandre*, swords are among the survivors. Rodrigue's bloodied sword in Corneille's *Le Cid* and Don Sanche's sword in that same play are good examples. The rarefaction of the prop culminates in Racine's tragedies, which most closely align with Benjamin's view of "tragedy" (as opposed to *Trauerspiel*) as a dematerialized genre. However, even here a prop can have a crucial function, as we see in the case of the sword in *Phèdre*.[20] It really is a prop in the most narrow, practical sense, a *Requisit*, since without it the conclusion of the scene in which Phèdre confesses to Hippolyte that she loves him would make no sense.

PHÈDRE:

This frightful monster must not now escape.
Here is my heart. Here must your blow strike home.
Impatient to atone for its offence,
I feel it strain to meet your mighty arm.
Strike. Or if it's unworthy of your blows,
Or such a death too mild for my deserts,
Or if you deem my blood too vile to stain
Your hand, lend me, if not your arm, your sword.
Give me it!

OENONE:
    Ah! What are you doing? God!
Someone is coming. You must not be seen. (II, 6, 701–12)

The sword is mentioned; it is clear from the dialogue that Phèdre has grabbed it, and yet the actual taking of the sword is never made

19. Perhaps Corneille has further coded these objects in terms of gender types. Dorise fails in her aim when she uses the masculine sword as weapon but succeeds when she uses the feminine hairpin, an object that has specifically been designated as laden with gender significance because it has betrayed her when she tried to pass as a man.

20. Jean Racine, *Œuvres complètes: Théâtre-poésie*, ed. Georges Forestier, La Pléiade (Paris: Gallimard, 1999), 815–76. *Iphigenia; Phaedra; Athaliah*, trans. John Cairncross (Harmondsworth: Penguin, 1970), 127–214.

entirely explicit in words. Between Phèdre's "Donne" and Oenone's "Que faites-vous . . . ?" the gesture takes place as if in a kind of hole in the text, something that is so unmentionable that it can only be designated by an interrogative pronoun. If a prop is a thing that can be handled, here we have one that is handled more than it should be. It is a metonymic, as well as metaphorical prop, since when Phèdre reaches for the sword, its proximity to Hippolyte's crotch may very well leave both the hero and the audience wondering for a second exactly what she is grabbing—and this signification through proximity is, of course, echoed by the conventional phallic virtue of the instrument. The sword again figures in the text, but does not appear on stage, three acts later. It disappears from the stage and, temporarily, from the text, by chance—that is, there is apparently no intention to take it for later use; the seizing of the sword is an end in itself. But the sword returns repurposed, so to speak, as evidence against Hippolyte, and the gap between the absence of intention at the moment of the sword's disappearance and this repurposing marks the sword with the classic characteristics of chance, in which a material thing is repurposed.

Thésée's words are particularly precise in this regard in the first scene of act IV:

> To gain his lustful and nefarious ends,
> The shameless villain had to resort to force.
> I recognized the sword he drew on her,
> That sword I gave him for a nobler use. (IV, 1, 1008)

Thésée recognizes that the sword has changed purpose, though for us he draws attention to the fact that he actually does not recognize the purpose to which the sword is being put. It seems notable here that what had been called an *épée* in act II is now twice called a *fer*, an "iron" ("J'ai reconnu le fer, instrument de sa rage, / Ce fer dont je l'armai pour un plus noble usage"), as if to stress its gross materiality, as if the sword itself has fallen from its noble father-intended aim. The weird property of the prop is that it speaks very loudly for something that is mute and dumb, iron, and this specious capacity of the prop to speak is amplified by the silence of the principals involved who actually know what happened: "Rather did Phaedra spare a father's tears. / Ashamed of a distracted lover's suit" (1012–13). But what happens with the prop here is typical of the role of objects in dramatic accounts of chance: a mute inanimate thing is open to "interpretation" that consists of allowing the user of the prop to pour his or her meaning—that is, fear or desire—into the thing.

It has often been noted that Thésée's way of reading this prop and the situation that surrounds it is a characteristic projection of Thésée's habits and desires onto the blank space that is his knowledge of his very different son. And his interpretation is facilitated by Phèdre's silence and by Hippolyte's relative silence. Benjamin quotes with approval Franz Rosenzweig's statement, "The tragic hero has only one language that is completely proper to him: silence" (108). This silence, or rather speechlessness, appears here when Hippolyte argues in his own defense in a form of preterition, by saying that things should speak for themselves, beginning,

> Rightly indignant at so black a lie,
> I ought, my lord, to let the truth speak out,
> But I shall not resolve this mystery
> Out of the deep respect that seals my lips.
> And, if you will not deepen your distress,
> Look at my life; remember who I am.
> Like virtue, crime advances by degrees . . . (IV, 2, 1087–1093)

Hippolyte builds his case entirely in terms of verisimilitude, showing that there is nothing in his past that would lend credence to this accusation—this supposed crime would have to *come out of nowhere*, it would be a truly freak occurrence. And we know that in neo-Aristotelian poetics such causeless occurrences are proscribed. Yet the *Poetics* leave the chance event in a particular limbo, because such events should not occur, yet they have a certain appropriateness when they do occur—they serve someone's intention or correspond to someone's desire.[21] Hippolyte's attempt to defend himself by arguing along the lines of plausibility is doomed to failure because it supposes, but in the wrong sense, that *things speak for themselves*. He makes the major mistake of confusing inside and out, moral purpose and the purposeless material world of *fortuna*, saying "The daylight is not purer than my heart" (1112), when he might more accurately have said that "daylight is much less pure." He stumbles precisely because he cannot account for something that happened by chance and for which there is a material proof.

---

21. Lyons, *The Phantom of Chance*, 4–5.

Benjamin offers us a particularly apt way of understanding Hippolyte's predicament with reference to the reappearance of the *fer*, when he writes, "Fate is the entelechy of events within the field of guilt."[22] The relation between fate and chance, between *Schicksal* and *Zufall*, is not obvious, yet we can see that the two are frequently mentioned together in a myriad of texts, including Benjamin's, and that examples of the one are often interchangeable with examples of the other, almost like Thésée's and Hippolyte's different ways of trying to get a mute thing to speak.

In the *Poetics*, Aristotle gives the example of Mitys's statue, which falls on the very man who killed Mitys, as a chance event that produces the desired dramatic effect of wonder, because on one hand the audience (in Aristotle's view) knows that this was just an accident and on the other hand it seems like something that happens with a purpose.[23] This story of the falling statue shows how events can be repurposed when they suit the stories that we would like to tell, which are in many cases stories of the ineluctable character of justice. People throughout the ages have done such "repurposing," despite the evidence that there is nothing at all ineluctable about justice. Bossuet, in his *Sermon on Providence*, cites *Ecclesiastes*:

> I saw that under the sun the race is not to the swift, nor the battle to the strong, nor bread to the wise, nor riches to the intelligent, nor favor to the men of skill; but time and chance happen to them all.[24]

The sense that there is no justice is somehow converted into the depiction of a world in which there is justice, even though it may be an unjust justice. This is the situation of Hippolyte and this is where his sword plays a role that can be compared to the falling statue. In the case of *Phèdre*, the "field of guilt" is an apt way to describe the situation of all the major characters. All are in some way guilty. Thésée's adulteries, seductions, and betrayals of women provoke his son's shame in the first scene of the play. Phèdre's desire for her step-son has plunged her into what appears to be a terminal illness. Aricie, the object of Hippolyte's affection, lives as hostage to her family's previous attempt to dethrone Thésée. Her inherited guilt—and we should not forget that inherited guilt was for the Catholic Church of Racine's

22. Benjamin, *OGTD*, 129.
23. Aristotle, chap. 9 in *The Poetics*, 42.
24. Herbert G. May and Bruce Manning Metzger, *The New Oxford Annotated Bible with the Apocrypha* (New York: Oxford University Press, 1973), 812.

time just as much a central doctrine as it was for the Lutheran authors of *Trauerspiel*—made her a sexual pariah, for Thésée had forbidden her to marry. Finally, and most importantly, Hippolyte is guilty of having violated his father's command by proposing marriage to Aricie. Therefore, while he is not guilty of the crime of which Thésée accuses him, he appears, by chance, to be guilty of another crime against his father. Hippolyte fears the return of his father because he knows himself to be guilty of one thing and then is struck speechless by the weird accusation that befalls him. This is precisely the kind of situation that Benjamin intends when he writes of the "entelechy of events within the field of guilt" because the crushing sense of guilt and the mournful result do not come from any act of the individuals. They are already guilty, in advance:

> The core of the notion of fate is [. . .] the conviction that guilt (which in this context always means creaturely guilt—in Christian terms, original sin—not moral transgression on the part of the agent), however fleeting its appearance, unleashes causality as the instrument of the irresistibly unfolding fatalities.[25]

The radiating effect of guilt as a fantasy of our own importance in the world and as a way of countering the random functioning of the world as depicted by the Ecclesiast, brings together chance and fate in a way that makes Benjamin's frequent pairing and blurring of these concepts understandable. As an *entelechy* fate is self-sufficient. It thus can function separately from the cause-effect chains that govern ordinary events. And guilt is the field within which events detach themselves from the chain and foreground themselves as radiant with meaning, a meaning that, in the case of fate, we pre-understand or, in the case of chance, that we construct, so to speak, in the subjunctive as something that remains suspended in terms of a cause in which we renounce belief (too good to be true, too dreadful to be true), but which figures in our way of detaching the event from a multitude of others that do not correspond so precisely to our fears and desires.

Chance is measurable in terms of the human belief that material things, things not in any way in our control, are somehow to be measured and described in terms of their importance for human beings, an importance that tragedy in particular projects and that we com-

---

25. Benjamin, *OGTD*, 129.

monly describe by the casual term "dramatic" when we say something had a *dramatic* effect.

Hippolyte's sword can, in a certain sense, be considered an idol of guilt. It returns to convict him of a crime that he did not commit. It is available because of no human plan or forethought and there is, between the sword and the "crime" that Hippolyte committed (the crime of loving Aricie) no direct causal relationship. But if fate is the entelechy of events in the field of guilt and if a chance event is one that no one planned but that has a marvelous appropriateness, we can see that this material object, this prop or *Requisit* is precisely the kind of repurposed thing that makes dramatic sense.

HÉLÈNE MERLIN-KAJMAN

The Crooked Crown: Reading
Le Cid after *La Mariane*

Presenting the allegorical dimension of the *Trauerspiel*, Benjamin makes it clear that the spectator is somehow a reader:

> [. . .] the *Trauerspiel* [. . .] which grew up in the sphere of the allegorical, is, in its form, a drama for the reader [. . .]. It does make it clear that the chosen spectators of such examples of the *Trauerspiel* concentrated on them with at least the same thought and attentiveness as the reader [. . .].[1]

But this is a strange kind of reader because he is also a melancholic. If he has to concentrate, it is because in the presence of allegory, meaning is not clearly given, or, more precisely, its integrity is lost. Being able to read an allegory, or to *attempt* to read it, means being able to measure the paradoxical presence of signification as ruin or specter; and this knowledge engenders sadness.

But it was by chance that Benjamin seems to have had his first ideas about the importance of the allegorical loss of meaning. As he observes in a diary entry in 1938, it was during the performance of *Le Cid* in Geneva that "the sight of the king's crooked crown first made me think of what I wrote in my book on the *Trauerspiel*, nine years later."[2] It is easy to understand the logic that leads from this unessential incident to the deep analysis of the *Trauerspiel* book. The detail—and of course, it is important that it was a detail—liberates the emblematic value of the crown precisely when it appears out of

---

1. Walter Benjamin, *The Origin of German Tragic Drama*, trans. John Osborne (London: New Left Books, 1977), 185. Hereafter cited as *OGTD*.
2. Benjamin, "Diary Entries, 1938," trans. Gerhard Richter and Michael W. Jennings in *Selected Writings*, vol. 3, ed. Howard Eiland and Michael W. Jennings (Cambridge: Harvard University Press, 2002), 336.

YFS 124, *Walter Benjamin's Hypothetical French "Trauerspiel,"* ed. Bjornstad and Ibbett, © 2013 by Yale University.

harmony with the whole. When it stops being natural, or realistic, it suddenly discloses its allegorical function and captivates Benjamin's attention, awakening the dormant allegorist who had been deceived by the apparently natural kingly dress: no longer merely looking, he begins to read. This is exactly the process Benjamin explains in the passage from which the first quotation was taken:

> "From somewhere else," the allegorist then takes it up, by no means avoiding that arbitrariness which is the most drastic manifestation of the power of knowledge [. . .]. It may not accord with the authority of nature; but the voluptuousness with which significance rules, like a stern sultan in the harem of objects, is without equal in giving expression to nature. It is indeed characteristic of the sadist that he humiliates his object and then—or thereby—satisfies it. And that is what the allegorist does in this age drunk with acts of cruelty both lived and imagined.[3]

Here we have one of the few passages in which Benjamin evokes the context of the Thirty Years War.[4]

And now, another, more laconic statement:

> Considered in allegorical terms, then, the profane world is both elevated and devalued.[5]

Yet *Le Cid* is not a German *Trauerspiel*, nor even a "Herodian drama," which to Benjamin constituted the quintessence of the genre. In 1636, the very same year it was first performed, there was, however, a Herodian drama staged in Paris with the same actors: *La Mariane*, a tragedy written by Tristan L'Hermite. It was a huge hit and near the end of the century, in 1674, the poetic theorist Rapin recalled the strange effect it had had on its spectators: "When Mondory played La Mariane of Tristan, people always left contemplative and pensive,

---

3. Benjamin, *OGTD*, 184–85.

4. Benjamin never speaks about the stories or arguments of the *Trauerspiele* he evokes: even in the details he gives, he works against the linearity of plot and breaks any illusion of continuity, of causal or chronological links. He refutes any kind of representation: the plays do not *represent* anything natural or historical in the ordinary meaning of these words, and they are often defined as self-sufficient works—or if they are not self-sufficient, it is because of the *presence* of physicality itself, because of the allegorical meaning that results from "a strange combination of nature and history," as Benjamin frequently asserts (*OGTD*, 167).

5. Benjamin, *OGTD*, 175.

reflecting on what they had seen, and filled at the same time with a great joy."[6]

This effect may be compared to the melancholic's sadness. The relation posited between the incident of the crown and the sadness of allegorical attentiveness allows us to measure a paradox: the crown should not be crooked on the king's head in *Le Cid* (even if we will see that things are a little bit more complex), but in the last act of *La Mariane*, on the contrary, it should be, allegorically speaking, because of Hérode's ultimate madness. *La Mariane* is, as Benjamin tells us about the *Trauerspiel*, "haunted by the idea of catastrophe."[7] In contrast, we may recall Corneille's famous comment on the audience's reaction when seeing Rodrigue in Chimène's house after he has killed her father:

> I noticed at the first performances that when this wretched lover appeared before her, the audience shuddered, betraying an extraordinary curiosity and an intensified attention to what they wanted to share with each other in such a pitiful condition.[8]

The audience's reaction, as described by Corneille, is in no way one of sadness. Perhaps this is partly because, in this case, there is nothing to read, nothing to look at contemplatively and pensively.

La Mariane, as I have said, is a Herodian drama in the Benjaminian sense: a general configuration of the dramatic relationship between the tyrant and the martyr, and a third character, the intriguer.[9] In Tristan's play, Hérode is the tyrant, his wife Mariane is the martyr, and Salomé, Hérode's sister, is the intriguer whose perfect familiarity with "the life of the soul"[10] affords her the capacity of manipulating

6. René Rapin, *Les réflexions sur la poétique de ce temps et sur les ouvrages des poètes anciens et modernes*, ed. Elfrieda T. Dubois, facsimile of the first edition (Paris, 1675; repr., Genève-Paris: Droz-Minard, 1970), 102.

7. Benjamin, *OGTD*, 66.

8. Pierre Corneille, "Examen," *Le Cid*, in *Œuvres complètes*, ed. Georges Couton, vol. 1 (Paris: Gallimard, "Bibliothèque de la Pléiade," 1980), 702. My translation.

9. See Benjamin, "Calderon's *El Mayor Monstruo, Los Celos* and Hebbel's *Herodes und Mariamne*," trans. Rodney Livingstone in *Selected writings*, vol. 1, ed. Marcus Bullock and Michael Jennings (Cambridge: Harvard University Press, 1996), 363–86. The basic plot of the Herodian drama could be summed up as follows: Deceived by an intriguer, Hérode comes to believe that his wife, Mariane, cheats on him and is going to kill him, while Mariane, remembering that Hérode killed her brother Aristobule, is filled with hatred toward her husband and refuses to justify herself. Hérode's jealousy makes him have her killed, after which he sinks into madness.

10. Benjamin, *OGTD*, 99–100.

a person (and predicting his movements) as if he were a clock or a machine.[11]

But the sources for Tristan's plot were not only other tragedies like Thomas Hardy's; he also certainly read Caussin's allegorical narrative *Le politique malheureux*, the first edition of which was published at the end of his *La cour sainte* in 1624.[12] Caussin, who inspired Gryphius, appears in Benjamin's book because he wrote the *Polyhistor symbolicus*:

> Nor could any kind of writing seem better designed to safeguard the high political maxims of true worldly wisdom than an esoteric script such as this, which was comprehensible only to scholars. In his essay on Johann Valentin Andreä, Herder even speculated that it provided a refuge for many ideas which people were reluctant to voice openly before princes.[13]

This final remark confirms one of the points I tried to make in my book *L'absolutisme dans les lettres et la théorie des deux corps*.[14] Besides the evident or explicit allegorical meaning of Caussin's narrative (whose full title, *Le politique malheureux ou l'innocence opprimée* is, as Benjamin emphasized, a double one customary of the baroque),[15] a secret meaning is intended to condemn the politics of tolerance of Protestantism. Just as Mariane is persecuted as a wife by her historical royal husband, so the Church cannot be married to the State once the State is no longer subject to considerations of salvation. Hérode stands for the modern sovereign exactly as Benjamin describes him (a description that is inspired, as is well known, by his reading of Carl Schmitt), but in Caussin's view, his fate must show that to know "no eschatology" (I am paraphrasing this famous sentence: "The baroque knows no eschatology"[16]) is a serious mistake and a reason for him to be deemed guilty. And just as Mariane very clearly announces the coming of Christ, and as Hérode announces his death, she also may announce the last judgment and the end of history. The secret

---

11. As Iago does in *Othello*. For the comparison between Herodian drama and *Othello*, see Benjamin, "Calderon's *El Mayor Monstruo, Los Celos* and Hebbel's *Herodes und Mariamne*," 367–68.

12. R.P. Nicolas Caussin, *La cour sainte* (Paris: Sébastien Chappelet, 1624).

13. Benjamin, *OGTD*, 172.

14. Hélène Merlin-Kajman, *L'absolutisme dans les lettres et la théorie des deux corps: Passions et politique* (Paris: Champion, 2000).

15. Benjamin, *OGTD*, 195.

16. Ibid., 66.

message could thus be that the actual, present king should fear the last judgment when "den[ying] direct access to a beyond"[17] and acting as an absolute king whose only preoccupation is a political one.

I just stated that Mariane announces Christ's coming. Benjamin does not mention the special link an allegorical figure establishes between two moments in ancient Christian allegory, one in the Old Testament that prophesizes the second one in the New Testament, which prophesizes yet another one in the future of the Church, or on an eschatological level. In general, Benjamin distinguishes between medieval and baroque forms of allegory; he claims that baroque allegory "is descended from antiquity."[18] I don't know if he had read Auerbach's work on Dante (1929).[19] But for my understanding of Benjamin's analysis itself, the ancient mechanisms of allegorical figures are of great importance. When he says that the baroque knows no eschatology, and then that "in the field of allegorical intuition the image is a fragment, a rune,"[20] I understand this to mean that, once the eschatological signification is lost, the allegorical figure remains bare, without any certainty of what it announces, all while conserving a memory of having announced something. As in the example of the torso, the past is lost, but known to have been, and therefore it still remains. On the contrary, in Christian allegory, the figure is not exactly complete, but, in a way, entire: entirely turned toward another future event to which it gives its meaning, so that the whole meaning is present in every figure. History is a figure of providential will that links events even when they seem to happen without any meaning. With the baroque, however, Benjamin says, even if eschatology has disappeared, allegory remains, but only as a ruin: as a figure of a dead, vanishing, purely creaturely estate. And this is how I interpret the following sentence: "all the wisdom of the melancholic is subject to the nether world: it is secured by immersion in the life of creaturely things, and it hears nothing of the voice of revelation."[21]

Such is the universe of *La Mariane*. The relationship between past and future becomes obscure. One only knows that there is such a re-

17. Ibid., 79.
18. Ibid., 171.
19. Erich Auerbach, *Dante als Dicther der irdischen Welt* (Berlin: Walter De Gruyter, 1929).
20. Benjamin, *OGTD*, 176.
21. Ibid., 152.

lationship, and that time is condemned to repeat itself, as Benjamin explains:

> These dramas should not have had an odd number of acts, as was the case in imitation of the drama of the Greeks; an even number is much more appropriate to the repeatable actions which they describe. In *Leo Armenius*, at least, the action is complete by the end of the fourth act.[22]

In *La Mariane*, everything is as Benjamin has stated. Hérode himself is so immersed in physicality that he cannot understand the figures of his nightmare at the beginning of the play, nor the meaning of Aristobule's specter when it appears in the nightmare and announces the repetition of death.[23] Hérode illustrates perfectly what Benjamin writes about the prince who is condemned by the baroque concept of sovereignty to be a tyrant: "The prince, who is responsible for making the decision to proclaim the state of emergency, reveals, at the first opportunity, that he is almost incapable of making a decision."[24] And Benjamin gives this detail, which applies perfectly to Hérode: "The conflict between sensibility and will in the human norm [. . .] is particularly striking in the person of the tyrant. In the course of the action his will is increasingly undermined by his sensibility: and he ends in madness."[25]

But above all, Mariane herself becomes ambiguous. Though she is supposed to be the allegorical figure of virtue as in Caussin's example, she is in fact also immersed in corporality because of her desire to avenge her dead parents: her chastity, mentioned by Benjamin as a sort of private state of emergency[26] because it functions as "the stoic technique" that "aims to establish a corresponding fortification against a state of emergency in the soul, the rule of emotions,"[27] is caused by her melancholic love for her dead brother, Aristobule. She is turned to the historical past more than to a promised or announced future, of which she remains a figure. Yet in the final act devoted to revealing this eschatological level, it is Hérode who announces the future between two bouts of madness. And the only thing he announces very

22. Ibid., 137.
23. Ibid., 152.
24. Ibid., 71.
25. Ibid., 99.
26. Ibid., 74.
27. Ibid., 74.

clearly is the malediction of his people, the Jewish people, while the allegorical meaning of this malediction remains unclear: his people are accused of not being able to kill the tyrant, that is to say Hérode himself, who does in fact present himself as an allegorical figure of the tyrant. But killing the tyrant was, as Benjamin recalls, forbidden. And here the indecision typical of the tyrant becomes that of the people itself, lacking any clear lesson. It is easy to understand why "people always left contemplative and pensive . . . ," as Rapin noted.

But even if it gives new depth to this allegorical interpretation, Benjamin's analysis is less interesting as a way of reading *La Mariane* than as a way of reading *Le Cid* after *La Mariane*. Corneille's tragedy attracted wide commentary immediately after it was first performed, starting with the famous quarrel. These comments oriented later interpretations toward Aristotelian concepts, toward problems of truth and verisimilitude, as is very well known. But if we compare *Le Cid* to *La Mariane* while remembering the allegorical dimension of the latter, we can measure the nature of the difference in the effects of the two tragedies, a difference we can sum up by saying that *Le Cid* is *not* a melancholic play. And by "is *not*," we must understand *it could have been*. In fact, *Le Cid* liberates the spectator from melancholy, precisely because its plot *could* be a melancholic one, as its many similarities to *La Mariane* demonstrate.

These resemblances start with the names themselves: Hérode-Rodrigue. If we remember Benjamin's analysis of baroque language, "the anagrams, the onomatopoeic phrases and other examples of linguistic virtuosity," where "language is broken up to acquire a changed and intensified meaning in its fragments,"[28] we must conclude that there is something fateful written in Rodrigue's name. Or maybe Hérode is something of a specter haunting Rodrigue's character: almost just like a tyrant, he kills Chimène's father because of honor, whose role, Benjamin notes, derives "from the creaturely estate of the dramatic character."[29] *Le Cid* gets its very allegorical meaning when it is confronted with the Herodian drama. Let us look at some of the main differences between the two tragedies.

The state of emergency is central to *Le Cid*, but comes from "real" history; it is not provoked by the schemer as it is in *La Mariane*.

28. Ibid., 207–08.
29. Ibid., 86.

But it is not exactly the king who averts it (nor is it the king who makes the decision); it is Rodrigue, without much hesitation, in two or perhaps three moments that run through all possible figures of emergency. The first one is a personal emergency, when he decides to provoke Chimène's father in order to avenge his own father: even if it is not a stoic decision, one can say that it "establishes a corresponding fortification against a state of emergency in the soul, the rule of emotions."[30] But in reality, he obeys both his honor and his love for Chimène. The second one is a political emergency, when the Moors menace Seville; the third and final one comes when Rodrigue is faced with an exception while fighting against Don Sanche. Each time, the solution is not given in advance and does not consign "earthly things" "to their end."[31]

Le Cid is as ostentatious as a *Trauerspiel* is, but because of honor and love, not because of the melancholic consideration of allegorical ruins. On the contrary: think, for instance, of the moment when Rodrigue arrives with the sword he used to kill the Count. It is his first melancholic moment because he wants Chimène to kill him. Chimène recognizes her father in the sword, and the sword could thus have the meaning that Benjamin saw in the object of baroque drama: "The effectiveness of the object where guilt has been incurred is a sign of the approach of death."[32] But the sword will not be an allegorical object, and the Count will not be a specter, though he is the only corpse in the play, and even a corpse that speaks to Chimène allegorically. The sword will not be a fatal sign: refusing to kill Rodrigue, refusing to look at it any longer, Chimène obliges Rodrigue to hide it, because she loves him in spite of his murder.

Le Cid stages "the midnight hour" ("The midnight hour of the *Trauerspiel* stands in contrast to the daytime setting required by every tragic action"[33]), which is the time of Rodrigue's second melancholic moment, exactly as it was his father's. But when they meet to confer, Don Diègue recognizes the right to love and advises Rodrigue to fight against the Moors: he is the good counselor, not an intriguer, only because he accepts hearing what Rodrigue tells him about his love (and because what he hears sounds new to him).

---

30. Ibid., 74.
31. Ibid., 66.
32. Ibid., 132.
33. Ibid., 135.

There is in a way a schemer in *Le Cid*: the king himself, because he has the knowledge of the life of the soul that Benjamin attributes to the intriguer, and because he makes a kind of joke when he announces to Chimène that Rodrigue is dead. He wants to know if she loves him or not. During the quarrel, Scudéry accused Corneille of having given a burlesque role to the king. Benjamin says that "with the intriguer comedy is introduced into the *Trauerspiel*."[34] This is exactly Scudéry's point: he observes that, by making his joke, the king no longer appears in his dignity, that his crown falls from his head[35] —and we recognize here the detail that struck Benjamin and provided the beginning of his reflection on the *Trauerspiel*.

In *Le Cid*, love has the structural place that mourning has in the baroque drama. This is in fact a possibility of which Benjamin seems aware: Corneille is confronted as much as anyone with what Benjamin says ("since therefore neither rebellion nor submission was practicable in religious terms, all the energy of the age was concentrated on a complete evolution of the content of life"[36]), but thanks to love, he invented a solution other than death.

In *Le Cid*, something similar to what Benjamin elsewhere calls an experience is made possible, but a new one—not a story told by tradition, by a storyteller. Rodrigue incarnates the sentence that is his answer to the Count: "Valor has no need of years."[37] He is the allegorical figure of Newness. As in *La Mariane*, there is no eschatology—but this time, this means that there is newness; there is something to be invented. And as the king helps the heroes give room to the "creaturely estate" in order to liberate them from their fathers' fate (the fate of the past), history can begin—not as stage-property,[38] but rather as an open, creaturely sphere that is not oriented toward salvation even if it is not contrary to it; it has no specific orientation, because history is not yet viewed as the telos it would be later.

34. Ibid., 125.
35. See Georges de Scudéry, "Observations sur le Cid," in [Armand Gasté], *La Querelle du Cid, pièces et pamphlets publiés d'après les originaux avec une introduction*, facsimile of the first edition (Paris, 1898; repr., Geneva: Slatkine Reprints, 1970), 93.
36. Benjamin, *OGTD*, 79.
37. Corneille, *Le Cid*, act II, scene 2, v. 406. My translation.
38. Benjamin, *OGTD*, 170–71: "The transfixed face of signifying nature is victorious, and history must, once and for all, remain contained in the subordinate role of stage-property."

Now, one could object: is the difference I described between *La Mariane* and *Le Cid* something other than the difference between baroque and classicism? Do I need Benjamin's analyses to arrive at such a conclusion?

Here is where I am perplexed. In *L'absolutisme dans les lettres*, my analysis did not mobilize the concepts of the baroque and classicism, except to conclude that Corneille (and of course, he is emblematic here) was *classico-baroque*. And I could come to this conclusion because of the allegorical meaning I found in his plays.

Reading French "classical" tragedies as allegorical plays is not a usual way of interpreting classicism: as I suggested earlier, we are used to reading them in relation to Aristotelian rules, poeticians' debates, and the general problems of representation, in other words the relation the plots are supposed to have, or not to have, with external, historical reality; or with the expectations of the public, its pleasure, and so on. The reason for this is the meaning we attribute to "classical": a certain universal quality of clarity and rationality. Or, on the contrary, a refusal to give "classicism" anything more than a historical meaning, which leads us to examine these works by placing them in a general way in the seventeenth century, in their context, and then we leave it at that. I will return to this idea.

What does it mean, then, to say that Corneille is classico-baroque?

Baroque *vs* Classicism: there would be no point in rehearsing the history of this pair of concepts here. They are anachronistic applied both to France and Germany, and all the more so since they function as an echo chamber. No German classicism without reference to French classicism; no French baroque without reference to a European baroque or Nietzsche's Dionysian. When it comes to the German *Trauerspiel*, the reference to (German) classicism serves to highlight, by contrast, the singularity of the baroque. When it appears ("the baroque, that contrasting prelude to classicism"[39]), it does not gain any new meaning. Benjamin inherits the opposition from literary historians, and does not contest the corpus it designates. But as he wrote in 1923 to his friend Florens Christian Rang, he wanted to save a previous literature[40] and give it back to the Germans, because

---

39. Benjamin, *OGTD*, 160.

40. Quoted by Pierre Bouretz, *Témoins du futur: Philosophie et messianisme* (Paris: Gallimard, 2003), 255.

the baroque drama was scorned by German scholars. Benjamin added this strange remark: he wanted to recover secret relations between Germans and Jews. This is odd if you realize that for Benjamin, the baroque drama is illustrated by Herodian drama, the impossible marriage between Hérode and Mariane. The allegory as ruin could mean that there is still a link, and also that there is no longer a link. In the Christian interpretation, it is the link between Old Testament —Ancient Jewish Law—and New Testament that is established. But for Benjamin, this structural place of the Old Testament is attributed to Antiquity.

Benjamin wanted to exhume a forgotten past, a forgotten work. Nietzsche could be the model, but the "origin" in Benjamin's philosophy is not a "genealogy" because allegory for him is rotten. Instead, it looks like Derrida's *différance*.

In *Les mots et les choses*, Foucault describes the "Renaissance episteme" in words very similar to Benjamin's, as scholars have long noted. But for Foucault, literature, in its modern meaning, has saved the lost alliance between objects and signification—between things and words—that characterized the "Renaissance episteme" (or the baroque moment). On the other hand, Foucault shares with Benjamin the idea that history as telos has been accomplished and written by the victorious. Just as Benjamin refuses Ranke's will to restore the past as it happened, so Foucault refuses to write the story of what he calls "historical work." He wants to write the story of the lack of work: like Benjamin, he wants to exhume hidden voices and knowledge from the past.

In Foucault's view, the rupture between silence and history reveals the structure of power. And resistance is the preservation of a relationship with that which has been reduced to silence.

This is very different from what Benjamin does. Everyone knows this statement, for instance:

> Then our coming was expected on earth. Then, like every generation that preceded us, we have been endowed with a *weak* messianic power, a power on which the past has a claim.[41]

The present has been anticipated by the past of which it conserves an imprint, even if it has been forgotten. And this is precisely the struc-

41. Benjamin, "On the Concept of History," trans. Harry Zohn in *Selected Writings*, vol. 4, ed. Howard Eiland and Michael W. Jennings (Cambridge: Harvard University Press, 2003), 390.

ture of allegory: past is both lost and kept, and the allegorical figure signifies this tension. There is something in human time itself that is denied by the chronological, causal conception of history, something that the allegorist (or the literary critic) must recover: this is what Benjamin calls a "weak messianic force." It is the structure of the melancholy as well—or of the symbolic. And when I say "or," I don't in any way mean that these are identical. I only mean that there are different kinds of proof that time is not always linear, that it is also as if it were folded.

Let us return to the question of the baroque and classicism: in recent years, these categories have been abandoned. They were deemed anachronistic and seen as having been canonized by the institution. Here, Ranke's prescription to write history as it really happened meets the idea that it must not be written from the victor's point of view, and one could think this represents progress in the discipline of history. However, it still implies that human time can be fully described by chronological discourse, with its linear causality and nominalism. I prefer to agree with two of Benjamin's propositions. The first one comes from the *Trauerspiel* book, "Beauty, which endures, is an object of knowledge. Philosophy must not attempt to deny that it reawakens the beauty of works."[42] The second one appears in an essay, "Literary History and the Study of Literature":

> Only a discipline that abandons its museum characteristics can replace illusion with reality. [. . .] For the crisis in education stands in precise correlation to the fact that literary history has now completely lost sight of its most important challenge [. . .] its pedagogical task.[43]

Even if I am not sure that Beauty is, or is only, an object of knowledge, I almost agree with these pieces of advice. And this is why I practiced the allegorist's method with *La Mariane* as well as with *Le Cid*. To liberate allegorical meaning is to put the work of literature back into motion—to *quote* the work; and Benjamin did not devalue the revolutionary quotation of ancient Rome as Marx did.

It seems clear that allegory implies a difference between two moments. To be an allegorist does not mean one has to search for a key:

---

42. Benjamin, *OGTD*, 182.
43. Benjamin, "Literary History and the Study of Literature," trans. Rodney Livingstone in *Selected Writings*, vol. 2, ed. Michael W. Jennings, Howard Eiland, and Gary Smith (Cambridge: Harvard University Press, 1999), 462.

it means setting up a game, a device capable of making two moments play together, without one functioning as a key for the other (unlike exegetical endeavors where the New Testament provides the key to the Old). Because the past is past but not completely lost, there can be a future. Our comment "was expected by the text"—it is a structural consequence of a text.

But even if the allegorical meaning of *Le Cid*—which confers to it what I call its classico-baroque dimension—is enlightened by its relation to the allegorical meaning of *La Mariane*, I choose to *quote* the former work, in Benjamin's meaning, rather than *La Mariane*— rather, we could say, than a *Trauerspiel*.

"The historian [. . .] grasps the constellation into which his own era has entered, along with a very specific earlier one."[44] And I wonder why Benjamin chose the Herodian drama as the main type for the *Trauerspiel*. Or was it rather the existence of Herodian drama that led him toward the *Trauerspiel*? Is the Herodian drama the drama that troubles the rupture between the Old and the New Testament, and thereby the allegorical value of Judaism for Christianity? It would be very interesting to compare Benjamin and Auerbach, who wrote on Christian allegory and creatureliness but chose French classicism and its "public" (split into two elements—like Jews and Christians are, but brought together by literature[45]). I wonder what echo Benjamin wanted to produce when he chose to restore these old, baroque works to Germany. What was the messianic force, the hope?

I am no less haunted by catastrophe than Benjamin or the melancholic person. Who could avoid feeling melancholy after World War II? But I think that the allegorical meaning of Corneille provides us with the opportunity to detach ourselves from mourning, without denying it. Allegory always preserves the opportunity to turn back to another past—here, the past of baroque catastrophe, which may also be the past of the civil massacres; but in *Le Cid*, allegory turns us away from the melancholic fascination with catastrophe and its claim to renounce any desire for the whole.

It does not announce the future or any kind of eschatological interpretation, and it has no obvious key to the present. But death is no longer its main stage-property. As everyone knows, the melan-

44. Benjamin, "On the Concept of History," 397.
45. See Merlin-Kajman, "Le public au XVIIe siècle et au-delà selon Auerbach," in *Erich Auerbach, la littérature en perspective*, ed. Paolo Tortonese (Paris: Presses Sorbonne nouvelle, 2009), 91–115.

cholic person does not want to recognize the separation between the dead and the living: he has to shelter the dead in his own person, to keep them alive by means of his own body, his own soul. The past is not past, but present: entirely present, so present that no future—no subject—is possible. And, in this case, the sadistic solution may be the only one. I prefer to choose what Benjamin in the quotation above called a "pedagogical task," a task where pedagogy may have something to do with a therapeutic duty.

Teaching literature with this type of allegorical view allows us to play with texts in a ludic and transitional space, where literature is a sort of transitional object in the way that Winnicott described it; it has an allegorical function but is not a key to the past; rather, it is entirely turned toward the future. We must do this to avoid the risk of "museumification" that is otherwise inherent in the transmission of literary history.

SUSAN MASLAN

Melancholy Racine: Benjamin's
Trauerspiel and Literary Jews

Is it plausible, or even possible, to read French classical tragedy with Walter Benjamin's *Origin of German Tragic Drama*? After all, Benjamin himself noted the "contrastive natures" of the two traditions.[1] Indeed, Benjamin's reading of the baroque German *Trauerspiel* incessantly marks its difference from tragedy. Tragedy is bound by its adherence to Aristotelian laws; *Trauerspiel* is supremely uninterested in Aristotelianism. Tragedy's subject is myth; *Trauerspiel*'s is history. Tragedy's aesthetics and ethics are those of transcendence; *Trauerspiel* "is taken up entirely with the hopelessness of the earthly condition."[2] Those who articulated and promoted the cause of French classical theater underscored its strict observance of Aristotelian "rules"; its superiority to the detail and muck of history; its essentially transcendent aim and meaning.

In this essay I want to suggest that Jean Racine's *Athalie* (1691) is really two plays at once: a neo-classical tragedy and a Benjaminian *Trauerspiel*. Critics have often assumed that Racine's sacred tragedies—*Esther* and *Athalie*—are not concerned with Jewishness or Judaism despite their source in the Hebrew bible.[3] In this view, *Es-*

1. "My plan for the latter [the *Trauerspiel* book] had originally been to elucidate both the German and the French *Trauerspiel* in terms of their contrastive nature." Walter Benjamin, letter to Hugo von Hoffmannsthal, June 5, 1927 in *The Correspondence of Walter Benjamin, 1910–1940*, trans. Manfred R. Jacobson and Evelyn M. Jacobson (translation modified), ed. Gershom Scholem and Theodor W. Adorno (Chicago: University of Chicago Press, 1994), 315.

2. Benjamin, *The Origin of German Tragic Drama*, trans. John Osborne (London: Verso, 2009), 81. Hereafter cited as *OGTD*.

3. Two important yet very different exceptions are Lucien-Gilles Benguigui, *Racine et les sources juives d'"Esther" et d'"Athalie"* (Paris: Harmattan, 1995), which argues that Racine was a philo-Semite and that *Esther* and *Athalie* both demonstrate

YFS 124, *Walter Benjamin's Hypothetical French "Trauerspiel,"* ed. Bjornstad and Ibbett, © 2013 by Yale University.

ther and *Athalie* transcend their Jewishness with the simplest, quickest sort of allegory: the Jews in *Esther* are figures for Jansenists; the Temple in *Athalie* is a figure for Port-Royal.[4] But such a reduction of allegory to a key does justice neither to the depths of Racine's erudition and intellectual curiosity, nor to the complexity of his theater. *Athalie*, I will argue, develops two kinds of allegory: a Christian allegory through which the preservation and coronation of the child-king Joas portends the arrival and glory of the Messiah; and a Benjaminian allegory in which the play's Jews stand for Jews who remain Jews and who are thus bypassed or discarded by the movement of (divine) history. The trace of Jews who fail to read or live allegorically is what makes them the subject of a Benjaminian allegory—an allegory in which they stand for their own "dead materiality."[5] In other words, *Athalie* bears within it irreducibilities that stubbornly resist and remain despite the eschatological framework that ostensibly consumes the drama and transforms it into sublime, sacred tragedy. Despite Benjamin's distinction between tragedy, with its ethos and aesthetics of transcendence, and what George Steiner called the heaviness of the "earthbound" mourning play, I am suggesting that we can find a *Trauerspiel* within Racine's tragedy and that the subject of that *Trauerspiel* is the Jews.[6]

Athalie abounds with elements and figures Benjamin identifies with the mourning play. Athalie herself, the proud, awful, impious, and merciless usurper corresponds to the figure of the tyrant/martyr Benjamin identifies as so central to *Trauerspiel*. Like Herod, who, Benjamin notes, was depicted—to the delight of audiences—battering out the brains of infants, Athalie is described as relishing the murder of her own infant grandchildren.[7] Moreover, Athalie's downfall stems from her indecisiveness, which Benjamin calls "a feature peculiar to

the playwright's deep knowledge of Judaism and, on the other hand, John Trethewey, "Antijudaism in Racine's *Athalie*," *Seventeenth Century French Studies* 18 (1996): 167–75, which argues that Racine was an unconscious anti-Semite and that *Athalie* paints a negative portrait of Judaism.

4. Jean Orcibal, *La genèse d'Esther et d'Athalie* (Paris: Vrin, 1950) argues for *Athalie* as an allegory for the Glorious Revolution of 1688. René Jasinski argues that *Esther* should be read as an allegory for religious and political conflicts of late seventeenth-century France in *Autour de l'Esther racinienne* (Paris: Nizet, 1985).

5. Gordon Tesky, *Allegory and Violence* (Ithaca: Cornell University Press, 1996), 12. In Tesky's gloss of Benjamin, baroque allegory produces "signs that emphasize their dead materiality."

6. George Steiner, "Introduction," to Benjamin, *OGTD*, 16.

7. Benjamin, *OGTD*, 70.

Trauerspiel."[8] Mathan, the apostate priest of Baal and close advisor to Athalie, seems the very essence of the political "intriguer" Benjamin associates with *Trauerspiel*. This piecemeal matching of structures and types may illuminate Racine's thinking about politics and its relation to the theater, but my goal in reading *Athalie* with Benjamin is different: the reading I seek brings into focus the melancholic aspect of Racine's play, it helps us extricate Racine from the breathless confines of classicism, and it allow us to see Racine's Jews as the subject of *Trauerspiel*.

By Racine's Jews I do not mean the Jews just waiting to be Christians that the conventional allegorical mode assumes all literary Jews to be, but rather, for example, the modern Jews celebrating Purim to whom Racine refers in the last sentence of his preface to *Esther*: "They say that even today the Jews still celebrate the day when Esther delivered their ancestors from the cruelty of Haman with sacred ceremonies of Thanksgiving."[9] Here, for one moment, the Jews of *Esther* and the Jews of *Athalie* are the ancestors of the Jews of Racine's seventeenth-century world, rather than figures for future Christians. The Jews who recall and celebrate Esther's heroism demonstrate their continuity and identity with ancient Jewry. Racine suggests this continuity with the word "still [*encore*]," while "today [*aujourd'hui*]" underscores the real presence of real Jews. When Racine reminds his readers of the continued presence of Jews, he casts the temporality of *Esther* and *Athalie* not in eschatological time but in historical time. Moreover, even this historical time is something other than linear chronological movement, for while the descendants of Racine's ancient Romans and ancient Greeks walk Racine's earth as modern Italians and modern Greeks, no longer subject to the law of the terrible pagan Gods who defined action and law in *Iphigenie* and *Bérénice*, by contrast, the Jewish descendants of Esther and Joas live on as Jews and thus as ruins. "Allegories are, in the realm of thought, what ruins are in the realm of things," Benjamin writes luminously.[10] And as Hélène Merlin-Kajman explains in an essay in this volume, allegory without eschatology—which is essentially Benjamin's definition of the Baroque—produces and discloses a remainder. It harkens us to

8. Ibid., 71.

9. Jean Racine, *Œuvres complètes*, ed. Raymond Picard (Paris: Gallimard [Bibliothèque de la Pléaide]), 1:814. My translation.

10. Benjamin, *OGTD*, 178.

an "other" that has disappeared but not transcended. For this reason, as she puts it, we can conceive of allegory as a ruin.[11] The Jews of *Esther's* preface are those who have refused to be *aufgehoben*, to be sublated at the moment of the arrival of Jesus, the descendant of David and Joas so often invoked in *Athalie*. Those same Jews, I argue, are present as future hypotheticals within *Athalie*. They are the Jews who crowd the temple with offerings for God at the outset of the play, they are the Jews who sing of their love for Jerusalem, and perhaps above all, they are those who have remained faithful to the law despite Athalie's introduction of the worship of Baal. The law is the object of their affection and their veneration. It is the law of which the chorus in *Athalie* sings, "But His pure law, His sacred ways/ Are far His richest gift to men . . . O Divine, O enthralling law!"[12] Indeed, from the Christian point of view, those Jews remain—like Corneille's Pauline—excessively dutiful to the law, so much so that they will not recognize Christ as "His richest gift to men." And that Christ comes to free the Jews from their law, as Paul so vehemently insists in the letters to the Galatians, only discloses that the love of the Jews for the law in *Athalie* might have a melancholic and ruinous aspect.

Paul chastises the Galatians: "Before this faith came, we were close prisoners in the custody of the law, pending the Revelation of faith. Thus the law was a kind of tutor in charge of us until Christ should come, when we should be justified through faith; and now the faith has come and the tutor's charge is at an end."[13] Paul writes here to remonstrate with those new Christians who sought to maintain the laws of Judaism—notably circumcision. "If righteousness come by law, then Christ died for nothing," Paul expostulates.[14] The new Christians Paul aims to correct are too attached to the law. Like the Jews of Racine's France, they do not easily (or do not at all) relinquish their relation to the law and to the earthly, material practices it prescribes. Perhaps the transcendence that faith offers in the place of the law seems too insubstantial: all that is solid melts into air. So the Jews, as ruins, remain stubbornly creaturely, pure material, pure

11. See Merlin-Kajman in this volume, 54.
12. Racine, *Iphigenia/Phaedra/Athaliah*, trans. John Cairncross (Harmondsworth, UK: Penguin, 1986), 250–251. For the French see Racine, *Athalie* in *Œuvres complètes*, 1:886.
13. *The New English Bible* (New York: Oxford University Press), 232.
14. Ibid.

resistance to transcendence. "Such a ruin," Benjamin quotes Borinski as explaining, "appears as the last heritage of an antiquity which in the modern world is only to be seen in its material form."[15] The material practices that seemed to promise continuity, solidity, and self-presence, become traces, vestiges, emblems of loss. Allegory in the *Trauerspiel*, Gordon Tesky explains, "encourages the production of signs that emphasize their dead materiality."[16]

The Jews who remain Jews in the future that *Athalie* projects and that is present within the play are those signs. With their props and their practices, with their devotion to blood sacrifice and to the book, *Athalie's* Jews continually point to their own afterlives as ruins. *Athalie* represents the Jewish commitment to Jewish law and Jewish practices; it suggests that this commitment defines Jewish identity. Yet the play's entire plot and tension revolve round the securing of King David's lineage, not in order to protect the Jewish people or to defend the land, but in order to preserve the line from which Jesus will spring. The plot recounts and celebrates the achievement that will lead—from the Christian point of view—to the loss of the Jews' status as God's people, to the criminalization and marginalization of the Jews, and from the point of view of Racine's seventeenth century, to the loss of Jewish territory, dignity, and autonomy. Thus, Racine's Jews—that is the good Jews rather than those who seem ready to worship idols at the drop of a hat—are always already melancholic, always defined by their commitment to their loss.

Athalie is Racine's second sacred tragedy and the last of his plays. Like *Esther* (1689), Racine wrote *Athalie* for the demoiselles de Saint-Cyr but, unlike *Esther*, *Athalie* is a full-length tragedy for which Racine imagined strikingly elaborate staging. *Athalie* represents the story of a wicked queen of Judah, daughter of Jezebel and Ahab, who has usurped the throne after her son's death and who eventually loses power and her life when the existence of the rightful king, Joas, is revealed. Racine stages the revelation that Joas, a child of eight and Athalie's grandson, lives despite Athalie's belief, shared by nearly all those in the kingdom, that Joas died a victim in Athalie's massacre of her grandchildren. Joas is crowned and Athalie is killed. But this is sacred history, not mere political history. For the throne at stake is the throne of David.

15. Benjamin, *OGTD*, 178.
16. Tesky, *Allegory and Violence*, 12.

1. THREE TEMPORAL SCHEMES

There are three temporal schemes or orientations in *Athalie*. Athalie's own temporal orientation is essentially regressive and her bias toward the past is what unleashes the play's action. The crisis whose consequences unfold and reach their climax in *Athalie* begins when Jehu, who has been chosen by God, punishes the house of Ahab by killing his son (and Athalie's brother) Joram, King of Israel, along with Athalie's mother Jezebel, and by exterminating every descendant of Ahab's house. Athalie's own son Ochosias, King of Judah, happens to be visiting Joram at the time and he too falls victim to Jehu's divinely legitimated rampage. Athalie's reaction is immediate and unhesitating: she slaughters Ochosias's children, her own grandchildren. Racine underscores Athalie's personal participation in these murders; Josabeth, Joas's savior and aunt recalls, in a typically Racinian hallucinatory account, a primal scene of violence:

> Alas! his plight when heaven showed me him
> Returns incessantly to harrow me
> With princes slain the palace floor was strewn.
> A dagger in her hand, implacable,
> Athalie urged her soldiers on to kill,
> And then herself pursued her murderous way.[17]

Racine's description of Athalie—dagger in hand, urging on the soldiers who, barbarous as they may be, perhaps falter before the massacre of infants and children—makes clear that her concern is not only—or even primarily—political. Certainly, Athalie will profit from the occasion to declare herself ruler of Juda, but the moment Josabeth recounts is one of mad vengeance rather than political calculation. To have "avenged my parents on my progeny," as Athalie herself explains she has done, is to have a sense of lineage oriented solely to the past.[18] Obligation to the forces of the past trumps any relation to futurity. Athalie sees only a battle between the House of David and the House of Ahab and she sees in her grandchildren only their origin in the house of David:

> And thus, in short, your God, implacable,
> Between our houses broke all amity.

17. Racine, *Iphigenia/Phaedra/Athaliah*, 247. I am retaining the use of the French character names.
18. Ibid., 269.

Yes, I loathe David's line; and that king's sons,
Though of my blood, are yet no kin of mine.[19]

Athalie will not recognize her grandchildren as her kin because she cannot envision their movement forward in time—she cannot see that since they are "of [her] blood" they would carry her "blood" into the future. Such a thought is, however, thinkable; when Josabeth worries whether Joas will be a good king she explicitly entertains two possible futures: one in which Athalie's "odious line" might determine Joas's character, another in which God would incline Joas toward David's "line."[20] But Athalie's ethics can grasp only the stakes of origin, of ancestors rather than descendants.

The Christian temporal framework, on the other hand, is that of tragedy and transcendence: it is oriented toward the future, toward the necessary unfolding of things to come. This point of view is not embodied by one character in the play: rather it is the justification for the play itself. From this position, the entire crisis of the play is whether the last remaining embodiment of the lineage from which the Messiah is to be born will be preserved long enough to have children of his own. Athalie, Joas, the kingdom of Juda, are not important in themselves but only insofar as they endanger or safeguard the future for Jesus. Racine explains in his preface, "[t]he aim of the action was not just to keep the scepter in the house of David but to preserve intact for that great king the chain of descendants from whom the Messiah was to spring. For the Messiah, so often promised as the son of Abraham, was also to be the son of David and of all the kings of Judah."[21]

Thus, even the fact that the high priest Joad, in his moment of visionary prophecy, foresees and foretells that Joas will become impious—that he will murder his cousin and Joad's own son the prophet Zachariah; that from "fine gold" Joas will degenerate into "basest lead,"—does not impede the play's triumphalist, transcendent movement toward the future.[22] Indeed, Joad, in his prophecy, contemplates Joas's future corruption, his son's murder, the destruction of the Temple and of Jerusalem, and the Babylonian captivity as so many necessary steps toward the arrival of the Messiah:

19. Ibid., 270.
20. Ibid., 247.
21. Ibid., 235.
22. Ibid., 288.

Weep, weep Jerusalem, deceitful town,
O you! Who kill the prophets of the Lord,

. . . .

The Lord has laid the queen of cities low,
Its kings rejected, and its priests enchained.

. . . .

What new Jerusalem ascends
From out of the desert in a blaze of light,
With, on its forehead, an immortal mark?
Sing, peoples of the earth!
Jerusalem is born again.[23]

Joad predicts the coming of Jesus and the establishment of the Church (the new Jerusalem). His ultimate aim is not political—the reestablishment of the rightful king—but religious and eschatological.

Athalie's compulsions push her toward the past; the Christian plot is concerned with the future. But there is one more point of view present in the play: the Jewish point of view. The time of the Jews is the present; they are in the here and now of the play. The Jewish characters express their desire to see a descendant of David on the throne of Juda; but throughout much of the play they believe that Joas is dead and that the House of David is extinct. When the chorus praises Joas after his encounter with Athalie, they do not praise him as the "precious remains" of David that will secure the birth of the Messiah; they liken him instead to "pleasing Samuel."[24] The Jews' belief that the House of David has been destroyed does not foreclose or interfere with their religious observances, their rituals, or their beliefs. If the peril to the future Christians evoked by Racine is that the lineage from which the Messiah is to be born might be extinguished, the danger to the Jews in the play is the immediate threat Athalie poses to them as she surrounds the Temple with her soldiers. Read from the transcendent Christian view, the child Joas is a pre-figuration of the child Jesus; but from the Jewish perspective in the play, Joas is the charming child-king whose establishment on the throne will rid them of the threatening Athalie.

The Jews in the play—Abner, Josabeth, the chorus, the crowds of Levites and priests—consider Athalie a usurper and a blasphemer, but their own religious practice and their own relation to God do not depend on replacing her with a descendant of David. In fact, when

23. Ibid., 288–89.
24. Ibid., 272.

the play opens, the Jews are observing Shavuot—the celebration of the giving of the Torah. Racine notes in his preface that "[h]istory does not specify the day on which Joas was proclaimed."[25] Racine sets the action precisely on a major festival day in order to pack the play with descriptions, representations, and evocations of Jewish religious practice. References to offerings, sacrifices, and purification by blood abound; characters speak of incense and holy oils; the stage is populated by Levites and priests; and of course the entire play takes place within the Temple. Raymond Picard notes "All these details and explanations show the degree to which Racine was preoccupied with historical precision. Ordinarily, Racine was concerned with psychological color; in this case he is concerned with local, material color."[26] The "local color" is of course Jewish color—or at least what Racine imagined it to have been. Likewise, Picard observes "in *Athalie*, unlike in his other tragedies, Racine did not hesitate to put actions themselves on stage."[27] Racine, I am suggesting, underscored the materiality and the "presentness" of Judaism.

David Hume, otherwise a warm admirer of Racine's theater, grasped that the depiction of the Temple and of Jewish religious practice in *Athalie* conflicted with the ethos and aesthetics of tragic transcendence. In "Of the Standard of Taste," Hume laments that in *Athalie* an "intemperate zeal for particular modes of worship"— what is, in the play, marked out as Jewish worship—"is set off with all the pomp imaginable and forms the predominant character of the heroes."[28] The worship that is depicted, Hume writes, is a "particular mode"—that is, it does not attain a universal. It cannot transcend its particularity and its materiality, its pomp, it props, its things. This helps explain why zeal in its commission is necessarily "intemperate." For Hume, the pomp of which he writes so disapprovingly clearly points to the absence of an immediate and transparent correspondence between sign and signifier, between rite and divinity. Thus, the pomp is all that is imaginable to the dramatist, not all that is demanded for the recognition of God. This pomp is theatrical excess—the literary or theatrical remainder that is not transcended. It is not a vehicle for sublimity and thus it cannot exercise a transcen-

25. Ibid., 236.

26. Racine, *Œuvres complètes*, 1162, note 1. My translation.

27. Ibid., 1166, note 1. My translation.

28. David Hume, "Of the Standard of Taste," in *Essays Moral, Political, and Literary*, ed. Eugene F. Miller (Indianapolis: Liberty Classic, 1985), 248.

dent function. This material excess is akin to Benjamin's props, the intrusion of the world of things—inanimate things that rule events—into the stage world of the *Trauerspiel*.

The zeal Hume condemns is the playwright's, not that of the Jews. *Athalie* is marred, Hume implies, by Racine's Catholic bigotry. Racine, Hume suggests, cannot detach himself from his own particularity, cannot transcend his own finite position and thus the play cannot achieve the transcendence required of great art: it will be cheered in Paris but greeted with dismay in London. Hume presumes that *Athalie's* pomp, the "modes of worship" it stages, are Catholic; I am arguing that they are Jewish. But Hume's fundamental insight into *Athalie's* "pomp"—his understanding that it collides against the play's subject and aesthetics of transcendence—remains compelling.

Because the play's Jewish plot is in the present, the Jews are also already melancholic remnants. *Athalie's* triple temporal register—at once present tense (Jews), proleptic (Joad's prophetic anticipation of Christ), and retrospective (Racine and his spectators' certain knowledge that Christ did come)—means that the Jews' Judaism is always already bypassed by history. As readers and spectators of the play, we know that Christianity has rejected and abandoned the very practices that Racine presents as so dear to his Jewish characters. The spectacle and exoticism of Racine's Judaism calls attention to its materiality rather than its spirituality, and makes of Jewish ritual a stage prop in Benjamin's sense. But in so doing, it also underscores Judaism's anachronism. For Racine's world, Jewish belief and Jewish practice can have theological legitimacy and religious meaning only prior to the arrival of Christ: thus, those Jews who persist in their Jewishness after Christ are, like their rites, "signs of their own dead materiality." Their continued existence makes them vestiges of a bypassed world.

Racine evokes the future persistence of these "Jewish" Jews in the figure of Abner with his frequent references to Abner's faithfulness to the Jewish God and to his laws. Even as he recognizes that so many of his fellows have left behind their Jewish faith and adopted the worship of Baal encouraged by Athalie, Abner's commitment is unshakeable. Indeed, Racine represents a small, besieged, faithfully Jewish band, surrounded by hostile practitioners of an alien but politically and militarily powerful religion.

Some of *Athalie's* characters, for example Joad in his prophetic moment, clearly point toward their future Christianity. But at other moments the steadfast love they express for the Jewish God, the

Jewish law, and Jewish rite suggest that their stubborn attachment will persist in the future. The chorus, with its different voices, seems to embody the possibility of future divisions. Some may become Christians; others may remain Jews. Their exchange following Joad's prophecy portends the two different perspectives:

> A VOICE: Zion will be no more. A cruel flame
>   Will raze its temples to the ground.
> SECOND VOICE: God watches over Zion. And it rests
>   Upon his everlasting word.
> FIRST VOICE: I see its brilliance met before my eyes.
> SECOND VOICE: I see its light shining throughout the world.
> FIRST VOICE: Zion is swallowed in a deep abyss.
> SECOND VOICE: Zion's head towers to the heavens.
> FIRST VOICE: What sad abasement!
> SECOND VOICE: What immortal glory![29]

The first voice hears in the prophecy only the destruction and loss of the Israelite world she knows; the second places her faith in a transcendent, immortal second Christian "Zion." The first voice laments, the second praises. Racine does not resolve the opposition; instead he introduces a third voice that advises the chorus: "Be no more troubled."[30] Rather than transcending the opposition or subsuming the first voice in the second, Racine leaves both the voice of ruin and the voice of immortality in place.

Perhaps the first voice also heard Joad's implication that the new figural "Zion"—the Church—that will replace the real, material Zion is not necessarily destined for the Jews. Joad's vision conjures the joy and amazement not of the Israelites but of non-Jews:

> Sing, peoples of the earth!
> Jerusalem is born again.
> Whence come from every side
> These children that it did not bear?
> Lift up, Jerusalem, lift up your head.
> See all these kings astounded by your fame.
> Kings of the nations shall bow down to you
> And kiss the dust from off your feet.
> The nations vie in marching to the light.[31]

29. Ibid., 291.
30. Ibid., 292.
31. Ibid., 289.

Kings and peoples from all over the world recognize the arrival of the Messiah and join in the new Jerusalem, but Jews are not mentioned. Jews are the necessary source for the birth of the Savior but, like Joas, after their contribution to divine eschatology they may become "basest lead."

2. THE LAW AND JEWISH LITERALISM

Athalie moves between two opposing representations of the Jews' relation to the law: on the one hand, all the calamities that befall the Jews are a direct result of "forgetting the law." Indeed Racine represents such forgetting as so easy as to be almost inevitable. In his preface, Racine tells us that at the time of the narrative in *Athalie* nearly everyone in Juda and Israel was either an "idolater" or "schismatic." In the play's opening speech, Abner laments the ease and speed with which Jewish religious practice has been replaced:

> The merest handful of the faithful dares
> Bring back for us, how faintly, former times
> The others are forgetful of their God
> Or even, hastening to the shrine of Baal
> Initiates of his shameful mysteries.[32]

Indeed, forgetting the Jewish God and the Jewish law seems seductively easy. Athalie's husband and son, both late kings of Judah, both descendants of David, fall away from Jewish law and become followers of Baal. The only character who seems to have actively turned away from Jewish law rather than having simply "forgotten it" is Mathan—the apostate priest of Baal. He knows and announces that the Jewish God is the only real God and that his decision, his conversion, was a political calculation. We know, too, that the adult Joas will turn away from Jewish religious practice and will have his cousin Zachariah executed for having reminded him of his obligations to the Jewish God. Leaving Judaism behind is so common in the world of *Athalie* that it is the majoritarian position. The ease with which the characters who populate *Athalie* stray from Judaism, on the one hand prefigures the shift from Judaism to Christianity and, on the other, underscores the stubbornness of those who remain practicing Jews.

But if forgetting the law seems almost to be a natural state in the play, the law also appears as a fetish: not only in the repetitive

---

32. Ibid., 239.

canticles like the one I cited above, and in the way the laws that regulate the space of the temple are invoked with such solemnity, but also in the way that the law forms nearly the unique occupation of Joas in the temple:

> ATHALIE: What is your daily task ?
> JOAS: I worship God; His laws are taught to me
> And in His sacred book I learn to read.
> Already I've begun to write it out.[33]

This is a far cry from the "rex" as "lex." Here, writing the law means literally re-copying the law. In his preface, Racine underscores the mechanical, material relation of Judaism to the law when he mistakenly asserts:

> They were taught the Holy Scriptures not only as soon as they had attained the age of reason but, to quote Saint Paul, at their mother's breast. Every Jew was obliged, once in his lifetime, to write with his own hand the whole volume of the Law. Kings were even compelled to write it twice.[34]

Jewish religious life in Racine's vision is defined by its material, rather than spiritual, its literal, rather than its allegorical, character. Such a vision of Judaism was an important part of the Christian tradition. As Daniel Boyarin explains "Origen also attributed the failure of the Jews to a literalist hermeneutic, one which is unwilling to go beyond or behind the material language and discover its immaterial spirit."[35]

We can see now why Racine chose to place the action of his play on Shavuot, the holiday that recalls God's giving of the law. Making the Jewish liturgical celebration of the law the framework for the play highlights Jewish material practices and beliefs. The chorus sings praises of the gift of the law:

> Mount Sinai, keep the memory of that day,
> August and solemn to the end of time,
> When on the summit ringed with fire,
> Wrapped in a cloud, the Lord appeared
> And let His radiance shine on mortal gaze.
> Wherefore this lightening, why these flames,

---

33. Ibid., 266.
34. Ibid., 235.
35. Daniel Boyarin, *A Radical Jew: Paul and the Politics of Identity* (Berkeley: University of California Press, 1985), 13.

Torrents of smoke and stirrings in the air,
The thunder and the trumpets' blare?
Mount Sinai, keep the memory of that day.

And a voice answers:

He came to tell the children of the Jews
Of the immortal splendour of His laws.[36]

The law is the object of glory, this member of the chorus explains. Moreover, the "splendour [*lumière*]" of those laws is not finite—not destined, according to the singer, to be replaced by the redeemer; it is immortal—unending. Racine emphasizes the spectacular in this account: the flames, the fire, the flashes of light. These spectacular effects are once again literal; the lights and flames of which the chorus sings are neither inner lights nor spiritual flames. They are the flames and lights and flashes that accompany God's presence and God's gift of the law. And in that moment, on the mountain, Daniel Boyarin explains, "For the rabbis, what is found are the words themselves, as radiant, joyful, and sweet—no interpretations and no knowledge of truth—as when given on Mount Sinai."[37]

The law, then, is fixed, objectified in the book as book. As Josabeth instructs Joas, the book as object has a magical, ritual, and also sovereign quality. But it is also a prop:

My son, place on the table reverently
The dreaded volume of our holy law.
And you too, dear Eliacin, lay down
This diadem beside the book divine.
Levite, Joad orders you to place
Beside the crown the sword that David bore.[38]

The book seems to be consubstantial with its own force; it does not serve as a medium to something higher, something outside, beyond itself.

And what of the materiality—so heavily underscored in the play—of the ritual offerings to God? Even the high priest Joad, his hands stained with the blood of the sacrificial victims, announces that these

36. Racine, *Iphigenia/Phaedra/Athaliah*, 251.

37. Boyarin, "Origen as Theorist of Allegory," in *The Cambridge Companion to Allegory* ed. Rita Copeland and Peter T. Struck (Cambridge: Cambridge University Press, 2010), 53.

38. Racine, *Iphigenia/Phaedra/Athaliah*, 293.

sacrifices are meaningless to God. Joad presumptuously ventrilo-
quizes God and questions Abner: "Think you I need the blood of goat
or ox?"[39] The gifts and the blood seem not so much to please God as
to mark out the Jews who persist in the ritual and to distinguish them
from the Jews who have, as Abner laments, abandoned the Jewish
God and the Jewish practices in favor of a new religion: that of Baal.

The choice to place the action of his play on Shavuot allowed
Racine to stage the material ostentation of Jewish religious practice,
but more importantly it throws into relief the melancholy nature of
Racine's Jews. Shavuot is a day that looks back, rather than forward.
It is a celebration of that which makes the Jews into relics. The Jews
in *Athalie* venerate the law, but from the Christian point of view that
very adherence to the law forecloses the Jews from a future in which
the law is transcended by faith. When he centers his play around
the observance of Shavuot, Racine makes the Jews the subject of a
Trauerspiel.

---

39. Ibid., 241.

ERIC MÉCHOULAN

Noise, Meaning, and Music in the Racinian *Trauerspiel*

Quoi?... Quoi?... Enfin... Oui... Il est vrai, Cléobule... Crispe, il
n'est que trop vrai... Quoi! Monsieur... Quoi perfide!... Quoi!...
Quoi!... Dieux... Enfin... Quoi?... Oui... Quoi?... Oui... Oui...

The troubled thresholds of French tragedies are often crossed thanks
to little words such as these, often without any immediate significance beyond punctuating a beginning, initiating an action, or tear-
ing surprised or saddened voices from silence. These ritual exposi-
tory scenes expose the noises of language before the appearance of
any conflict or danger. They immediately testify to the gap between
sound and signification that, according to Walter Benjamin, is the
mark of the *Trauerspiel*, which

> does not describe the motion through the spheres that carries feel-
> ing from the pure world of speech out to music and then back to the
> liberated sorrow of blissful feeling [. . .] [M]idway through its journey,
> nature finds itself betrayed by language, and that powerful blocking of
> feeling turns to sorrow [*Trauer*]. [. . .] The interplay between sound and
> meaning remains a terrifying phantom for the mourning play.[1]

The world of meanings is a "purgatory" where sounds dwell and make
the complaint of their petrified echoes heard. This is a paradoxical
complaint because it starts in silence and is rooted in the petrification
of sounds. The multiplying discourses resonate all the more given
that the noises composing them are forgotten in them. In this movement through three terms—sound, complaint, meaning—where one
feels the beginnings of a dialectics, music is what overcomes noises
and meanings.

1. Walter Benjamin, "Language in *Trauerspiel* and Tragedy," trans. Rodney Livingstone, *Selected Writings*, vol. 1, ed. Marcus Bullock and Michael W. Jennings (Cambridge: Harvard University Press, 1996), 60.

YFS 124, *Walter Benjamin's Hypothetical French "Trauerspiel,"* ed. Bjornstad and Ibbett, © 2013 by Yale University.

Walter Benjamin writes this first reflection in two brief essays in 1916,[2] at a time when sound and fury are deafening Europe. When he finalizes his project almost ten years later, he returns to this opposition between sound and meaning, seeing in the written word the weight of signification and in the "inspired song"[3] the music that never escapes it. Yet he does find felicitous forms of resistance to communication in the onomatopoeic nature of originary language and in the "phonetic violence" of the alexandrine.[4] This is why

> the language of the baroque is constantly convulsed by rebellion on the part of the elements which make it up . . . In its individual parts, language in ruins has ceased merely to serve the process of communication, and as a new-born object acquires a dignity equal to that of gods.[5]

Might we not understand the recurring use of these little words at the threshold of French tragedies as fragments more than half sunk into their sonorous accents, sound effects of feelings rather than meaningful words? French tragedies would thus begin their disturbing cycle with the phatic ruins of language: *quoi, oui, enfin!* We need to understand, along with the apparent paradox of beginning with the word "finally," how temporal stakes are thus redefined. It's what comes after that must serve as a beginning, just as "language in ruins" becomes "a new-born object."

In order to hear and understand this strange temporal rhyme (a rhyme that of course only appears with its second occurrence), one needs to grasp the fact that an

> origin [*Ursprung*], although an entirely historical category, has, nevertheless, nothing to do with genesis [*Entstehung*]. The term origin is not intended to describe the process by which the existent came into being, but rather to describe that which emerges from the process of becoming and disappearance . . . There takes place in every original phenomenon a determination of the form in which an idea will constantly confront the historical world.[6]

2. In addition to "Language in *Trauerspiel* and Tragedy," there is a second essay entitled "*Trauerspiel* and Tragedy," quoted below.

3. Benjamin, *The Origin of the German Tragic Drama*, trans. by John Osborne (New York: Verso, 1998), 200. Hereafter cited as *OGTD*.

4. Benjamin, *OGTD*, 206.

5. Ibid., 207–08, translation slightly modified.

6. Ibid., *OGTD*, 45.

It is thus a matter of abandoning any kind of genealogy (in the familial sense of the term): the origin is not constituted by a chronological point whose laborious movements we could follow; it is composed anachronistically, by time's turning back on itself in which the Now and the Past touch one other as two extremes. The origin arises in the force-field opened in the actuality of a becoming and a disappearance. It seeks both to recompose its form and to reopen its fate. A past stabilized by a placid science of history thus does not exist. One cannot contemplate an origin that has appeared once and for all on the pediment of the temple of the past.

The origin is certainly related to what *has taken place*. Yet if it were not also what *takes place*, it would not be an origin. "In history, it is a methodological mistake to use the future perfect," Paul Ricoeur reminds us, condemning the supreme sin of anachronism.[7] Yet to say this implies ignoring another concept of history that adopts an analytics of reading, what we might call an *anachronics* written in the future perfect. In this frame of mind, the writing of history is less the product of time than a reading of contretemps. Because the points that measured time in relation to a before and an after appear henceforth as vectors of divergent forces, there can materialize in an image not a process of mediation, but a *dialectical immediacy*: "To thinking belongs the movement as well as the arrest [*Stillstellen*] of thoughts. Where thinking comes to a standstill in a constellation saturated with tensions—there the dialectical image appears. It is the caesura [*Zäsur*] in the movement of thought."[8] In these words one can hear a speculative echo of the Hölderlinian caesura, the "counter-rhythmic interruption" that brings to light tragic transport and the rhythm of signs and that is both a suffering in which "there exists nothing but the conditions of time and space" and a way to give balance to or, even better, to protect rhythm.[9] The caesura is both the improbable sign that tears through meaning and the untimely trace that protects time.

Far from classical figures of discontinuity in which the past, cut off from the present, needs an expert historian in order to become

7. Paul Ricoeur, "Histoire et mémoire," in *De l'histoire au cinéma* (Paris: Complexe, 1998), 280, translation mine.

8. Benjamin, *The Arcades Project*, trans. by Howard Eiland and Kevin McLaughlin (Cambridge: Harvard University Press, 1999), 475.

9. Friedrich Hölderlin, "Remarks on Oedipus," in *Friedrich Hölderlin: Essays and Letters on Theory*, trans. Thomas Pfau (Albany: SUNY Press, 1988), 108.

understandable, so foreign does this past seem to us, the idea of the origin implies another relation to time and another conception of the discontinuous. This is also true in terms of geography: thinking a French *Trauerspiel* perhaps demands that we seek baroque drama at the end of what tradition conceived of as classical tragedy. In this sense, an instructive equivalent to the *Trauerspiel* would be not so much what is qualified in France as the "baroque period," the bloody tragedies of the late Renaissance, but rather the height of perfection of Racinian tragedy, *Esther* and *Athalie*. Let us then explore both these relations to time and these stagings of noise and music in order to better hear tragic *lamento* in the French style.

THE INTRIGUER, AN OBSTACLE TO ONOMATOPOEIA

"Quoi? Enfin! Oui . . ." bring us across the threshold of the tragic dream. Participating in the register of signification, these noises first of all provide points of contact between the expression of emotions and an audience's attention. Preceeding the existence of any intrigue, before the intriguer sets traps by playing with meaning, they uncover the insistence of sounds: "The intriguer is the master of meanings. In the harmless effusion of an onomatopoeic natural language [meanings] are the obstacle, and so the origin of a mourning for which the intriguer is responsible along with them."[10] Phonetic madness and the apparent autonomy of sound replay the score of onomatopoeia, the origins of language, thus renewing ties with something that is beneath signification.

Long before Freud grasped the value of signifiers in the dream process, tragic dreams enlightened us as to the originary ruins of language. In *Esther*, the sovereign's nightmare testifies to discourse's fragmentation into enigmatic words:

> His Majesty seems plunged in deepest gloom;
> Last night some dreadful nightmare haunted him.
> While all the world lay silent sleeping,
> His voice cried out in terrifying tones.
> I rushed to him. His words were all distraught:
> He murmured of some threat, aimed at his life;

10. Benjamin, *OGTD*, 210.

He mentioned enemies, wild ravishers;
Even the name of Esther passed his lips.[11]

Devoured by melancholy, the sovereign is nothing more than a voice, and that voice is a cry. When it is a matter of explaining himself or of telling a story, there is nothing but the disorder of detached words. At most, a few elements of signification emerge like an inhabited archipelago torn from the night: enemy, ravisher, Esther—and "the very fact that they still have a meaning in their isolation lends a threatening quality to this remnant of meaning they have kept. In this way, language is broken up so as to acquire a changed and intensified meaning in its fragments."[12] The defining characteristic of this language game consists in effacing the sonorous elements and even the production of meaning in communication in order to give the impression of immediate availability. Yet these words, the *remnants* of whose signification we see at play underneath the sounds heard, take on an unexpected intensity.

What does the sovereign then command? That the registry of his reign be read. The fragmented word must be followed by the glorious continuity of history, which can provide an antidote: "There lie inscribed each golden deed and bad, / Eternal moments of love and vengeance."[13] Yet what does he discover in this past that catches up with him? One of his subjects who, having uncovered a plot against his life, had never been rewarded. The dream seemed to be describing a disquieting future; history provides a reminder of a stolen past.

> Too damnable neglect of such a service!
> Most certain consequence of royal cares!
> A prince, surrounded by tumultuous tasks,
> Is ceaselessly enticed to fresh horizons.[14]

Just as the dream wrapped around the king and only allowed a few fragmented phrases through, the tumultuous world of objects surrounds the king and hides deserving subjects. The problem is that this man who is finally to be rewarded is one of those Jews whose

11. Jean Racine, *Complete Plays*, vol. 2, trans. by Samuel Solomon (New York: Random House, 1967), 330 (II, 1).

12. Benjamin, *OGTD*, 208.

13. Racine trans. Solomon, 331 (III, 1).

14. Ibid., 337 (II, 2).

death has been decreed according to the instructions of the king's most prized adviser, Aman. This is an exemplary contretemps where recognition of what came before energizes the fate of the now. History does not therefore allow us to leave the temporal fragmentation of the dream. On the contrary, it reveals secret corners that bring extremes together: to reward and to order execution.

This effect of discontinuity is superposed with the caesura that punctuates the first scene of the second act. Once Hydaspe has spoken of how the registry was able to calm the king, he folds the royal unrest onto the king's favorite and asks him what is worrying him. Aman confesses that it is the obsessive presence of Mardochée, this Jew who refuses to acknowledge his greatness. Yet this leap from the king to his favorite, from the dream to reality, provides only an appearance of discontinuity. In fact, an ironic and secret thread unites the two: the man forgotten by the king is none other than the individual with whom Aman's memory is obsessed. Through an unexpected echo, the person the king wants to remember is also the one his favorite is counting on forgetting.

The intriguer is indeed the master of meaning, for he carries out his work in the field of knowledge and regulates power by controlling meanings. But the tragedy shows his ignorance of sonorous echoes and secret continuities—which go on to provoke the following ironic reversal. The king consults his favorite; he asks him how to "honor a worthy subject."[15] Aman thinks the sovereign is intending to reward him, Aman. He thus recommends that he offer this subject a glorious parade to be led by an eminent lord. Yet the king intends to recognize the services of Mardochée the Jew. This is how Aman has to glorify in the streets of Suse the very man he had dreamed of seeing disappear; all of a sudden he falls into *clowning*:

> Not only over me he won the day,
> I, sad wretch, had to herald his proud way!
> The traitor! At my groveling how he gloated;
> And all the people with derision noted
> My blushing face, that told my shame and gall,
> And drew the presage of my certain fall.[16]

In a rather unusual way for French tragedies, the intriguer is here not merely foiled, he is above all ridiculed. He works at a loss to himself

15. Ibid., 339 (II, 5).
16. Ibid., 351 (III, 1).

and offers the pathetic parade of this fact to the public. "With the intriguer, comedy is introduced into the *Trauerspiel*. But not as an episode. Comedy—or more precisely: the pure joke—is the essential inner side of mourning."[17]

One can now understand the effect of inversion between the king and his favorite adviser: it is not only forgetting and memory, recognition and revenge, friendship and hatred, discourse's sound fragments and meaning's mastery that switch places for them, but more fundamentally, melancholy and clowning. Contrary to what one might expect, it is not in tragicomedy that one finds the most comical intriguers, but rather in the kind of religious tragedy to which *Esther*, at the end of the seventeenth century, restores such strange glory. For "if the mourning of a prince and the mirth of his adviser are so close to each other this is, in the last analysis, only because the two provinces of the satanic realm were represented in them."[18]

THE ENIGMA OF THE PAST: GHOSTS, REMNANTS, SECRETS

One must take literally the announcement Elise makes at the start of the play, saying Esther is on stage even though she is dead: "Grief-stricken by the rumor [*bruit*] of your death, / I lived, secluded from the haunts [*reste*] of men."[19] The barely significant little noises that stay at the threshold of tragedies can also take on the scale of the noises of crowds, like organs without particular bodies or meanings detached from a unique referent. The rumble's noise is dispersed as were the stones of the Holy Temple, engendering separation and unraveling. Likewise, in *Athalie*, rumor has it that Joas is dead, even if he is hidden in the Temple under the name of Eliacin. Athalie does not fail to recognize his nature: "Soldiers, deliver me from hateful ghosts."[20] These two very young people are on stage like specters. Esther and Joas only promise the future because they are already no longer of this world. The *Trauerspiel*'s spell works through this ghostly nature of characters that occupy a key position precisely because of their absence: under pressure from opposing forces, without really

---

17. Benjamin, *OGTD*, 125.
18. Ibid., 127.
19. Racine trans. Solomon, 316 (I, 1).
20. Ibid., 455 (V, 5).

acting on their own, they allow for the play's architecture to hold as if it were suspended in tragic air.

They present *remnants*: "He is the most *precious remnant (reste)* of the faithful David,"[21] repeated by Abner as a hypothetical reading based on the reactions he observes: "What more would you do, if this boy was a *precious remnant [reste]* of your royal ancestors?" (my italics).[22] Joad recognizes this in turn through a gesture of defiance against Athalie: "Of David's treasures only he remains" (voilà ce qui me *reste*).[23] Yet this is also a way to qualify those people who have not fled and who in the end give their support to the heir: "The rest (*reste*) have loudly pledged their loyalty," Ismaël announces to Joad.[24] Just as the ghost becomes king or queen, the treasure that is only a remnant allows the Jewish people to be recomposed as a whole. The remnant is what resists passing time: both a piece of the past's debris and the presence of what was. This is the *Trauerspiel*'s historical shading.

Mathan, the apostate priest who is jealous of Joad, commits a fundamental error because he does not understand this logic of the remnant: "Happy if I, by ravaging His Temple, / Could thus show up his hate as impotent, / And plunging in the ruin [*parmi le débris*], sack and corpses, / with crime on crime, drown all my vain remorse!"[25] He thinks that the piece of debris bears witness to his personal strength, while actually the remnant forms the very heart of the Temple, its hidden treasure, the secret place where immortality is housed: the very idea of transmission.

This would no doubt be a way to bring together something Benjamin places in opposition. In the *Trauerspiel*, says Benjamin, objects and stage props or accessories reign, but not in tragedy:

> But alongside [accessories] there are dreams, ghostly apparitions . . .
> All of these more or less closely orientated around the theme of death,
> and in the baroque they are fully developed, being transcendental phenomena whose dimension is temporal, in contrast to the immanent, predominantly spatial phenomena of the world of things.[26]

21. Racine, *Athalie*, I, 2, translation mine.
22. Racine, *Athalie*, V, 2, translation mine.
23. Racine trans. Solomon, 455 (V, 5).
24. Ibid., 457 (V, 6).
25. Ibid., 421 (III, 3).
26. Benjamin, *OGTD*, 134.

Like in *Esther*, dreams and ghosts in *Athalie* occupy a preeminent place in the torments reserved for sovereigns. The logic of the remnant certainly presupposes a tension that is above all temporal. Spatiality is nonetheless also very important, starting with the setting for the action: "The scene is in the Temple of Jerusalem, in a vestibule of the High Priest's apartments."[27]

In his preface, Racine slips in a justification for the chosen setting: priests and Levites had their

> lodging in the porches or galleries around the Temple, which formed a part of the Temple itself. The whole edifice was generally known as the holy Place. But more particularly this was the name given to that part of the inner Temple where were the golden Candlestick, the Altar of the incense, and the Tables of the showbread. And this part was further distinct from the Holy of Holies, where lay the Ark . . .[28]

The temple is thus composed of a series of interiors that are themselves given rhythm by series of objects: consecrated accessories whose sacredness is marked by capital letters, yet accessories nonetheless that refer to the history of the Jewish people. The vestibule of the Great Priest is thus both a space in which the different characters can move around and a reserved and sacred place, a blurry boundary between the profane and the sacred that pushes the dynamic of the objects of the *Trauerspiel* to an extreme: their accessory (and thus profane) nature has, precisely, been consecrated as an accessory.

Profanation puts ordinary objects back into the order from which they had been separated (one separates something as a better way to make it sacred). This is the major point of contention between the adversaries concerning the limit-space of the temple, including that object of power *par excellence*, the sword: "And you, come, I will arm you in that place / Where hidden lies, remote from prying eyes, / That mighty stock of lances and swords, / Dipped formerly in Philistine blood."[29] With these words, Joad gives the Levites arms that have been consecrated by Biblical history and God's grace and conserved in the secret of the Temple.

In this play between interior and exterior, the figure of the secret is what mobilizes all energies, since the secret is what has been set

27. Racine trans. Solomon, 380.
28. Ibid., 374, translation modified.
29. Ibid., 430 (III, 7), trans. modified.

aside, separated from the rest of the messages, removed from daylight's ordinary communication. The vestibule unveils the enigma of the past for the audience and nonetheless keeps it hidden:

> SALOMITH: Has word of this, our secret, spread abroad?
> ZACHARIE: The secret is still kept within the Temple.[30]

This secret is thus suspended in time as much as it is in space, waiting to be sowed and then reaped during the people's harvest. The secret of the dream that must be interpreted, the hidden treasure that is not the treasure one thinks, even the secret of the uprising and of the king found again: these are all public stagings of interiority. For the secret has no doubt more to do with the publicity of its operations than with the content of what is hidden. It serves more as a way of affirming power than of veiling knowledge. It is less a matter of being aware than it is of being able.

The unity of place chosen by Racine thus testifies to an extremely deep play on the closing and opening of the world of objects and of the theatrical stage. Just as "the remnant" (*le reste*) testifies to the closing of a world that is maintained in history, even to its opening to time, the Great Priest's vestibule is the interior threshold of the sacred and the intimate border of the profane. Here again, we find a common point and a profound difference between Racine's tragedies and the *Trauerspiel*:

> In the European *Trauerspiel* as a whole the stage is also not strictly fixable, not an actual place, but it too is dialectically split. Bound to the court, it yet remains a travelling theater . . . In Greek eyes, however, the stage is a cosmic topos . . . the *Trauerspiel*, in contrast, has to be understood from the point of view of the onlooker. He learns how, on the stage, a space which belongs to an inner world of feeling and bears no relation to the cosmos, situations are compellingly presented to him.[31]

The court is in fact shifted to the temple's threshold, renewing with one sense of the cosmos, and, with the young women at Saint Cyr who interpret the roles for Louis XIV's scaled-down court, giving new life to a Christian community. Yet this cosmos is entirely interior. Like the temple closed off to the profane, like the closed theater of Saint-Cyr or even of the court, like affects closed up into bodies: "The

30. Ibid., 448 (V, 1).
31. Benjamin, *OGTD*, 119.

evaporation of the tragic under the scrutiny of psychology goes hand in hand with the equation of tragedy and *Trauerspiel*."[32] In *Esther* or *Athalie*, this clearly psychological scrutiny nonetheless rejoins the order of the sacred cosmos more than individual desire. This is why the lamentation and sadness of the *Trauerspiel* is, after the necessary deaths of the tyrants and intriguers, ultimately absorbed in communitarian joy and the chorus's singing.

DIALECTICS OF MUSIC:
THE ORGANIC WITHOUT BODY

The sound-meaning-music trio Benjamin speaks of in his 1916 text is differently arranged in the final work. He has changed his point: "The phonetic tension in the language of the seventeenth century leads directly to music, the opposition of meaning-laden speech. Like all the other roots of the *Trauerspiel* . . . such words [the "passion for the organic"] refer not so much to the external form as to the mysterious interiors of the organic. The voice emerges from out of these interiors."[33] What are these interior, organic spaces that are said to preside over the destinies of language? One can find a trace of them in the opposition between two ways of articulating the voice with meaning. When Aristotle speaks of what characterizes man, the political animal, he makes a clear distinction between the voice (*phone*), which is "an indication of pleasure or pain, and is therefore found in other animals" and "the power of speech" (*logos*), proper to naturally political man, which "is intended to set forth the expedient and inexpedient, and therefore likewise the just and the unjust."[34] One need only turn to one of Racine's contemporaries, John Locke, someone who will be widely heeded on this point, to find that, on the contrary, there is a fundamental continuity between the two: "Things then are good and evil only in reference to pleasure or pain."[35] This is where the organic allows for a dialectics of voice and meaning through the music of pain and pleasure. This is not the body without organs that Deleuze and Guattari sought to describe; rather, these are organs

32. Ibid., 118.
33. Ibid., 211.
34. Aristotle, *Politics*, I, 1253 a 9–18, in *The Politics and the Constitution of Athens*, ed. by Stephen Everson, trans. by Benjamin Jowett (Cambridge: Cambridge University Press, 1996), 13.
35. John Locke, *An Essay concerning Human Understanding*, ed. A. D. Woozley (London, Fontana, 1964 [1689]), II, XX, 159–60.

without bodies, organs situated at the limit of the modern field of consistency of the organism, of community. For Benjamin, they offer resources for dialectics and not for desire.

In effect, music no longer sounds like the overcoming or synthesis of the opposites constituted by phonemes and meanings; it constitutes instead their point of passage:

> it would have to bring oral and written language together, by whatever means possible, which can only mean identifying them dialectically as thesis and antithesis; to secure for music, the antithetical mediating link, and the last remaining universal language since the tower of Babel, its rightful position as antithesis; and it would have to investigate how written language grows out of music and not directly from the sounds of the spoken word.[36]

In other words, music does not come to subsume opposites, to tear them away from constant contradiction; it is rather a capacity for opposition and linking.

This leads us away from the mythology of musical harmony intervening to absorb social conflict. Just as the noises of language in onomatopoeia open onto social regimes of inequality,[37] music gives rhythm to dispersed noises, a fact that provides an unexpected resource for the written world of signification. This can be seen in an exemplary way in the moment of prophecy that animates Joad in the middle of the tragedy (Act III, scene 7) since the biblical scripture is conveyed through a chorus that sings it. Thus, "just as tragedy marks the transition from historical to dramatic time, the mourning play represents the transition from dramatic time to musical time," as Benjamin affirmed at the end of his second 1916 essay.[38] In *Athalie*, music is articulated with the historical time of biblical scripture and opens onto the dramatic time of prophecy. Racine's last play is both a tragedy and a *Trauerspiel*.

This is why the dispersal of sounds, things, and beings in passing time is actually what we need to attempt to absorb into music. "Sion, repaire affreux de reptiles impurs / Voit de son temple saint les pierres dispersées" ("Zion, the dreadful den of unclean dragons, / beholds her

---

36. Benjamin, *OGTD*, 214.

37. On this point, see my forthcoming article in *Du bruit à l'œuvre. Actes de la 2ᵉ Rencontre internationale Paul Zumthor*, Geneva.

38. Benjamin, "*Trauerspiel* and Tragedy," trans. Rodney Livingstone, *Selected Writings*, vol. 1, 57.

holy Temple's stones still scattered!") Esther laments,[39] before calling to her side the young women of the chorus who we hear "behind
the theater" as so many ties—announced by the repeated phonetic
reversal of "rep" (*repaire, reptiles*) into "per-" (*p(i)erres, dispersées*)—
between the past and the present, between the off-stage of the past
and the welcoming stage of the now:

ESTHER:
They must be called. Come now, my maidens, come,
Companions once of my captivity,
And ancient Israel's green posterity.

ONE OF THE ISRAELITE MAIDENS (SINGS OFFSTAGE):
Sister, whose voice is calling us?

ANOTHER:
I know those accents sweet [*les agréables sons*].
It is the Queen.[40]

The queen's identity is sonorous above all else. She is a voice that
emerges into the world of noises with pleasant sounds that ensure
her recognition before the meaning of her words is perceived. The alliance between the past and the now relies on the spoken music of a
queen and the singing of her maidens.

The moment that Racine seems closest to ancient tragedy—
through the chorus and music, through the sacred heights of conflicts that no longer concern merely the personal emotions or court
intrigues of his earlier plays—he is in fact most radically distanced
from it. Or rather, as with the *Trauerspiel*, "an interpretation won
through, on the strength of which the new, in a gesture of submission,
secured for itself the most convincing authority, that of antiquity."[41]
In this play between past and present, the anachronistic is not merely
something blindly pasting the new over the old, or tradition openly
recycling the past into the present. Rather, the anachronistic, in sub-
mitting itself to the authority of the past, masters the past, replaying
the habitual gesture of Racinian heroines who, as captives, in fact
captivate the sovereign. The canonization of classical works must appear as natural as a scream and becomes as social as the noise of collective clamor.

39. Racine trans. Solomon, 318 (I, 1).
40. Ibid., 319–320 (I, 1–2).
41. Benjamin, *OGTD*, 100.

THE IDEA OF THE FRENCH *TRAUERSPIEL*

For Benjamin, the *Trauerspiel* is less a poetic form than it is an "idea."
If one intends to work with the hypothesis of a French *Trauerspiel*,
one must understand what an "idea" can be and what its link to the
empiricity of historical and geographical phenomena is. Above all,
one must dissociate the "idea" and the "concept." The contingent
historical event may be taken up, in its singularity, by the concept.
It is a question of content. The idea, on the other hand, changes its
information: it conserves the event by giving it a structure or, even
better, a "configuration." The idea is a monad that stems from the
configuration of a truth, of a discerning, and not from the production of knowledge: "If representation is to stake its claim as the real
methodology of the philosophical treatise, then it must be the representation of ideas . . . Knowledge is possession. Its very object is determined by . . . this quality of possession . . . For the thing possessed,
representation is secondary."[42] With ideas, one must thus leave behind the possession concepts allow (*Begriff* comes from *greifen*: to
grasp): a concept captures, an idea discerns.[43] And in this case, the
very form of the representation of ideas becomes vitally important.

Allegory provides such a representation, one that escapes the logic
of the general and the particular the better to seize their temporal
configuration: "Allegory established itself most permanently when
transitoriness and eternity confronted each other most closely."[44]
This is not a matter of denying the weight of history's contingency or
of sinking into the banal disappearance of passing time: we are touch-
ing on the superposition of different times and readings. Far from cov-
ering up the empirical realities of history, one saves their manifestation: "As the salvation of phenomena by means of ideas takes place,
so too does the representation of ideas through the medium of empirical reality. For ideas are not represented in themselves, but solely and
exclusively in an arrangement of concrete elements in the concept: as
the configuration of these elements."[45]

---

42. Ibid., 29.
43. One might compare this "dialectics at a standstill" to the "static genesis"
Gilles Deleuze speaks of in *Difference and Repetition*, trans. by Paul Paxton (New
York: Columbia University Press, 1995), 183.
44. Benjamin, *OGTD*, 224.
45. Ibid., 34.

An idea is both an artifice and a reality, not a generality that gathers phenomena in their possible repetition, but a way of intensifying phenomena: "Ideas are to objects as constellations are to stars . . . Just as a mother is seen to begin to live in the fullness of her power only when the circle of her children, inspired by the feeling of her proximity, closes around her, so do ideas come to life only when extremes are assembled around them."[46] The constellation remains dependent on the empirical reality of the sky. Yet it is not in the same register: it proposes both an arrangement and a reading of it. To a certain extent, one can wonder whether Benjamin, with allegory, is not trying to read the majestic page of the theater of the seventeenth century with a Baudelairean watermark, as if he were arranging ancient works in the melancholic mirror of the "Andromache, I think of you!" where "Paris changes! but nothing of my melancholy has lifted. New palaces, scaffoldings, blocks, old outer districts, for me everything becomes allegory."[47] This is also because, for Benjamin, allegory reconfigures what Baudelaire says of modernity: "to extract from fashion whatever element it may contain of poetry within history, to distill the eternal from the transitory."[48]

Posing the question of the *Trauerspiel* together with French literature means not only shifting a geographical limit, or setting the dramatic genres into play, but also constructing temporal configurations in which histories can appear, even in an entirely hypothetical way. Posing yet another question, a bit surprised, and affirming a figure in the history of truth: *Quoi? Quoi! Oui . . . Oui . . . Il est vrai.*

—Translated by Will Bishop

46. Ibid., 34–35.

47. Charles Baudelaire, "The Swan," translated by Keith Waldrop, *The Flowers of Evil* (Middletown, CT: Wesleyan University Press, 2008), 115–16.

48. Baudelaire, *The Painter of Modern Life and Other Essays*, trans. by Jonathan Mayne (London: Phaidon Press, 1964), 12–13.

CHRISTOPHER BRAIDER

Actor, Act, and Action in Benjamin's French Baroque

In confiding his interest in writing a book about the tragedies of seventeenth-century France, Benjamin mentions the unspecified "addition" he would have had to make to include the French case in the *Trauerspiel* book. I have elsewhere discussed what Benjamin ought to have added—the perspective of comedy his symptomatic preoccupation with tragedy ruled out.[1] I focus here, less polemically, on what he would in fact have added, in hopes of scratching an itch that has tormented scholars of the so-called French "classical age" for a half century and more: the question of the French baroque.

In its character as an addition significant enough to warrant a new book, Benjamin's interpretation of seventeenth-century French tragedy would have disarranged the constellation of ideas that structures the *Origin of German Tragic Drama* as we know it. After all, he managed to incorporate the cases of England and Spain in the *Trauerspiel* book in a way that, far from challenging his interpretation of the German baroque, confirmed it at every point. For example, Benjamin writes tellingly about the "sophistic solutions" that enabled the Spanish Jesuit Calderón to bridge the ontological abyss between creaturely existence and the radiant eternity that awaits in the world to come: a task that defeated the melancholy German Lutherans on whom he concentrated attention.[2] A man of the theater to a degree the earnestly bookish Gryphius, Hallmann, and Lohenstein could never be, Calderón mobilizes the trompe-l'œil machinery of the stage to convert the compelling illusion of earthly life theater purveys into the

1. See my "Talking like a Book: Exception and the State of Nature in Benjamin and Molière," *Comparative Literature* 64/4 (Fall 2012): 382–406.
2. Walter Benjamin, *The Origin of German Tragic Drama*, trans. John Osborne (London: Verso, 1977), 88. Hereafter cited as *OGTD*.

YFS 124, *Walter Benjamin's Hypothetical French "Trauerspiel,"* ed. Bjornstad and Ibbett, © 2013 by Yale University.

still greater illusion of transcendence whose deeply felt impossibility motivates him as much as his German counterparts.[3] And though Shakespeare is sharply distinguished from Benjamin's Germans for creating, in his soliloquies, vivid explorations of the ontology of the primal fall that the leaden-winged, metaphor-clogged set-piece declamations of the German scene failed to achieve, the greatness of the Englishman's *Hamlet* is said to lie in having epitomized the vision of the human condition in which *Trauerspiel* takes root.[4] If something more was needed, it is because French tragedy posed special difficulties that Benjamin could not solve within the extant *Origin*'s framework.

Key to the problematic addition is the "contrast" between French and German versions of *Trauerspiel* to which he alludes. For Benjamin, German tragic drama is quintessentially baroque—a conviction the more salient in that, far from arguing the point, he takes it for granted. Further, as Jane Newman shows, the fact that it is baroque is not just a matter of the peculiar form it takes as an expression of the contingent historical moment to which it belongs. What makes it baroque also makes it *German*, revealing the specifically national experience of post-Westphalian modernity with which German scholars of the Weimar Republic associated the baroque as constituting the uniquely German equivalent of the high Italian Renaissance. The *Origin*'s implicit aim is accordingly to define modern German culture as a whole—a task the more urgent in the wake of Germany's humiliating defeat in the Great War.[5]

The picture drastically changes, however, the moment we cross the Rhine. For French scholars of the 1920s and '30s, and often still today, the French seventeenth century was as incontrovertibly "classical" as the German was baroque. Nor is it simply that, in contrast to what we arguably observe everywhere else in Europe, French poets were guided by classical standards of reason and taste their conceit-drunk contemporaries neglected. The *grand siècle* achieved a self-disciplined

3. Benjamin, *OGTD*, 49, 81–84, 127–28, 132–33.

4. Benjamin, *OGTD*, 135–38; on *Trauerspiel*'s corresponding deficiencies, 123–25, 173, 200.

5. Jane O. Newman, *Benjamin's Library: Modernity, Nation, and the Baroque* (Ithaca, NY: Cornell University Press, 2011). The links between the interpretation of the baroque and German nationalism from 1871 to National Socialism are Newman's presiding theme. See esp. chap. 1 and, on the special relevance of the Great War, the discussion of "Lutheran war theology," 143–69.

urbanity in whose ironic light the baroque emerged as the deformed monstrosity that inspired the term *barocco* in the first place.

True, Benjamin could have found ready examples of the baroque in the French classical age, and in particular in the early seventeenth century of Louis XIII and cardinal Richelieu. Ever since Jean Rousset raised the issue in *La littérature de l'âge baroque en France* in 1954, even diehard defenders of the centrality of French classicism acknowledge the baroqueness of Hardy, Théophile de Viau, Tristan l'Hermite, or Rotrou—dramatists whose tragedies resemble German poets' far more closely than those of the *grands classiques*, Corneille and Racine. Nevertheless, just as Benjamin retains only Shakespeare and Calderón, overlooking the more congenially misshapen productions of Webster, Middleton, and Ford or Lope de Vega, Tirso de Molina, and Alarcón, he would have dwelt above all on the *grands classiques* as such. And a major reason for doing so is that the French scholars he might have consulted did so. If the circumstances of German history from the Reformation to the Great War persuaded German literary historians to identify the national spirit born with the Treaty of Westphalia as baroque, it was integral to French scholars' perception of their own national identity to insist on its classical character.[6]

In stressing the contrast between the cases of seventeenth-century Germany and France, Benjamin's target would, then, have been the myth of French national exceptionalism that classicism sustains. Our question is thus how to read the classicism responsible for French exceptionalism, illuminating in the process the specifically French experience of post-Westphalian modernity. And Benjamin's chief exemplars would have been Corneille and his younger rival and epigone, Racine.

Moreover, since the evidence suggests that this second book would have extended rather than confuted the first, Benjamin's goal would have been to show how the exception proves the rule, ceasing to be

6. See notably Gustave Lanson, *Histoire de la littérature française* (Paris: Hachette, 1894), a book deeply indebted to the theory of French historico-cultural singularity in Hippolyte Taine's *Origines de la France contemporaine* (1876–1894). The strategically central 4th part of Lanson's *Histoire* turns on the creation of the first true French "chefs-d'œuvre" in the seventeenth century. In *Corneille* (Paris: Hachette, 1922), Lanson summarizes the poet's impact on subsequent French literature thus: "Before him, classical tragedy didn't exist. Through him, it existed. He is who wholly detached it from poetic and pathetic Greek tragedy, who turned it into a distinct and opposite species" (187). This same presumption underlies René Bray's still weighty *La formation de la doctrine classique en France* (Lausanne: Payot, 1931).

an exception at all. The theme would accordingly have been a *paradox* in which we discern a Benjaminian version of postwar German revanchism. Though its significance stems from German efforts to define a cultural identity worthy of the political one Bismarck forged, it was the experience of defeat in 1918 that made the baroque the order of the day in Weimar Germany. But, as Benjamin saw it, the experience of defeat defined the unique German insight into the nature of modern experience as such. The point he would have argued about the *grand siècle* would thus have been to show that what made France different also made it the same: a participant in a demoralized modernity shared with the German enemy.

What has always seemed to distinguish French tragedy both from predecessors in the French tradition and from unruly counterparts in the rest of Europe is the perfection of the scenic illusion achieved through the famous unities and mastery of dramatic *vraisemblance.*[7] The prime directive of "classical" drama is to fuse the space-time of performance with that of the world it represents; and this fusion flowed from the principle of immanence informing the Aristotelian demand for the strict internal necessity of the encompassing action. Where diegetic modes of representation in history or romance rely on a mediating narrative to describe the events out of which a plot is formed, theatrical mimesis embodies events themselves. The consequence from the standpoint of theatrical poetics is the need to ensure that the knowledge readers or spectators require in order to understand why the characters act and talk the way they do arises as a spontaneous outgrowth of the situation in which the actors find themselves.

The chief function of French classicism is, then, to produce the kind of sophistic solutions with which Benjamin credits Calderón. Corneille's case proves especially telling here. Like Calderón, he was a committed transcendentalist who shared the Spaniard's Jesuit-inspired faith in the redemptive power of the human will.[8] The Augustinian picture of post-lapsarian corruption that mesmerized all Christian believers from the Reformation on portrays human beings

---

7. To see how deep-seated the traditional French picture of the *grand siècle*'s pan-European authority is, see Jane K. Brown, *The Persistence of Allegory: Drama and Neoclassicism from Shakespeare to Wagner* (Philadelphia: University of Pennsylvania Press, 2007).

8. On Corneille's debts to the Society of Jesus, see Marc Fumaroli, *Héros et orateurs: rhétorique et dramaturgie cornéliennes* (Geneva: Droz, 1990), esp. pt. 2, chap. 6.

as denied direct access to the efficacious grace alone capable of ran-
soming our sins. Even in religious dramas, God's intention is perceived as a rigorously natural function of the human actions theater
represents. In Corneille's *Polyeucte*, the proof of God's providential
presence in the sublunary world is the death the eponymous hero
willingly embraces for his sake, seconded by his wife Pauline's conversion on witnessing his martyrdom. And lest we miss the point, the
imperial deputy Sévère, Polyeucte's initially lucky rival for Pauline's
love, draws the lesson by acknowledging a spiritual power he admires
even if he cannot grasp it. The theoretical result is the *vraisemblance
extraordinaire* Corneille loftily opposes to the more worldly kind he
associates with his competitors, Mairet, Scudéry, or Rotrou.[9] Yet the
fact that the effects he achieves are "extraordinary" in no way dimin-
ishes their underlying verisimilitude. If readers and spectators suspend their disbelief in the way the play means them to, it is because
the action *naturalizes* the triumphant self-overcoming sealed by the
hero's martyrdom.

This is where Benjamin would have set to work. What makes
Corneille "classical" in the eyes of the French commentators of
Benjamin's day is what enables the sophistical Calderón of *La vida
es sueño* to incarnate the baroque dramaturgy his melancholy German contemporaries aspired to. As in *Polyeucte*, vindication of God's
providence takes the form of the hero Segismundo's spontaneous embrace of the theological idea in the play's title. For all the unfolding
story's pressing immediacy, "life is a dream"; and if the audience en-
dorses this sentiment at the final curtain, it is because, a fiction that
has kept us on the edge of our seats throughout, the *play* is a dream
in which we believe as firmly as in the creaturely life it mimics. The
classicism scholars took to distinguish Corneille from his German
counterparts is the fruit of the dramatic sophistry of which Gryphius,
Hallmann, and Lohenstein were incapable.

Benjamin would thus have aimed at the anamorphic reversal by
which what appears to set French tragedy apart from German *Trauerspiel* turns out to be the metaphysical condition it shares with it; and
the entry point for this demonstration would have been French man-

---

9. Pierre Corneille, *Discours de la tragédie*, in *Œuvres complètes*, ed. Georges
Couton, 3 vols. (Paris: Gallimard, 1980–1987), vol. 3, 168–70. References to Corneille's
plays are to this edition.

agement of dramatic action. More specifically, it would have been the relation between the dramatic action and its basic unit of measurement and construction: the individual *act* and its insertion in the self-organizing action it serves. If acts supply the building blocks out of which an action is composed, the action, in turn, *necessitates* these acts as an expression of the overarching logic they articulate. The key to solving the riddle of French exceptionalism is accordingly the self-generating *dialectic* binding act to action, and action to act.

However, the outcome of Benjamin's interpretation of the paradoxical affinity uniting *tragédie classique* and *Trauerspiel* produces a further paradox. Though the apparent French exception turns out to be no exception at all, the playwright who exhibits the strongest contrast with the German baroque is the baroque Corneille. And he is cast in this light by the theology of the act on which his dramatic sophistry depends. The premise that defines the distinctive features of Cornelian action, producing the hyperbolic excess of the *vraisemblance extraordinaire* that makes it baroque, is the power to act—a power, however, the plot sets in tension with the world in which the act takes place. Conversely, the playwright who proves least resistant to the German baroque theology of the fall is the supremely classical Racine. It is not just that, unlike their Cornelian counterparts who not only act but do so as a spontaneous answer to the higher call to love, faith, or duty that defines them, Racinian characters typically *hesitate* in the manner Benjamin prescribes. Once Racine's heroes and heroines do resolve to act, the result is their crushing subjection to the state of affairs they struggle to overcome.

Benjamin's book on seventeenth-century French tragedy would have restated another item found in the critical literature he would have consulted. As the French tradition has argued ever since Jean de La Bruyère first floated the idea, what grants Cornelian heroes and heroines the world-beating self-determination denied their Racinian peers is the fact that, where the latter portray humanity as it *is*, the former represent it as it *should* be:

> Corneille subjugates us to his characters and ideas, Racine conforms to ours; the former paints men as they should be, the latter paints them as they are. There is more in the first of what we admire, and of what we even ought to imitate; there is more in the second of what we recognize in others, and experience in ourselves. The one elevates, astonishes, overmasters, instructs; the other pleases, stirs, touches,

penetrates. What is most handsome, noble, and imperious in reason is handled by the first; and by the other, what is most moving and delicate in our passions.[10]

The key lies in the divergent anthropologies and the related theologies of the will. In this sense, Benjamin's book would have anticipated the work of another conflicted Eastern European materialist of a neo-Kantian stripe, Lucien Goldmann's *Le Dieu caché*.[11] Thanks to the Jesuit doctrine of the will he shares with Calderón, Corneille develops a poetics of the *act*. By contrast, Racine elaborates a poetics of *action* grounded in the crypto-Lutheran sense of the bondage of the will associated with his origins in the Jansenist community of Port-Royal. In line with the principle of immanence that secures the illusion of natural truth, both playwrights represent a world defined by the absence of the God who made it, engendering the evils their characters inherit from the past. But, in Corneille, this absence occasions a version of the "sufficient" grace Jesuits align with the autonomous power of will that enables *Le Cid*'s Rodrigue and Chimène to turn vengeful filial duty into pure self-determined love or that enables *Rodogune*'s Antiochus to distinguish himself from his otherwise indiscernible twin, surmounting the tragic fate to which his melancholy brother succumbs. Conversely, in Racine, the absence of the divine produces *le comble* of tragic irony owing to which each act his characters perform hastens the fate a malign providence reserves.

So what is the act that it should exist in tension with the action it advances? And what is the action if it is greater than the sum of the acts that compose it? It bears witness to the beautiful symmetry the pursuit of this Benjaminian line of inquiry brings to light that the dialectic of act and action is as integral to the poetics of our two French poets as to the metaphysical horizons described by the themes they join.

The status of the act lies at the heart of *La place royale*, last in the string of comedies leading up to Corneille's first tragedy, *Médée*.

---

10. Jean de La Bruyère, *Les Caractères, ou les mœurs de ce siècle*, in *Œuvres complètes*, ed. Julien Benda (Paris: Gallimard, 1951), 84. All translations are mine.

11. Like Benjamin, Goldmann consistently pursues textual analysis projected against the background of a metaphysical absolute relative to which all insights prove inadequate historical approximations—a notion whose Kantian rather than Hegelian (still less Marxist) origins surfaces expressly in his discussion of Pascal's wager. See *Le Dieu caché: Étude sur la vision tragique dans les* Pensées *de Pascal et dans le théâtre de Racine* (Paris: Gallimard, 1959), chap. 15.

The premise is yet a third paradox. The curtain rises on the end of a romantic comedy in which the hero, Alidor, is left in possession of the woman he loves, the beautiful and tough-minded Angélique. Possession of the woman also leaves Alidor in possession of the "place royale" itself, the physical space that forms the communal arena of amorous combat. For Doraste loves Angélique, too, and smarts at the loss his rival's success has caused. The trouble is that Alidor is royally bored. In his capacity as romantic lead, he *always* gets the girl: that is his role, and therefore his fate. So Alidor wants his *freedom* and, as its outcome and condition, he wants *change*. And change is what he gets in that the result of the comic imbroglios the action sets in train is to break the amorous chains that bind hero to heroine.

La place royale is startlingly new—a romantic comedy in which, after mighty struggle, the hero finally rids himself of romantic entanglement, leaving the heroine to storm off to a convent where men will never find her again. This inversion of the romantic norm generates the play's exceptional comic energy. Alidor is so invincibly attractive that persuading Angélique to forsake him turns out to be a Herculean task. Nor do things work out in the end quite as he imagined. Far from setting him free by giving her hand to his rival Doraste, Angélique perjures herself for Alidor's sake, reneging on her promise to marry Doraste only to discover that what she took to be Alidor's arrangements to elope with her are in fact an attempt to kidnap her on Doraste's behalf. The result is not only Angélique's decision to forsake the world but what looks like Alidor's reversion to the role he has desperately tried to shed:

> Since you can accept me without breach of faith,
> My soul, can your rigor persist?
> Am I no longer Alidor? Is your ardor extinct?
> And when my love grows, does it prompt your disdain?[12]

Yet however messy the process, Alidor remains in sole possession of "the place": the heroine's heart, since, when we last see her, she is determined to withdraw from all commerce with men; the stage, in that the play ends with a soliloquy in which he congratulates himself on his narrow escape; and the public, too, inasmuch as his soliloquy

---

12. Corneille, 5.7.1506–09. This apparent revival of love may merely test Angélique's feelings to ensure that she really doesn't love him anymore—assuming it isn't an ironic exercise of the actor's gift of heartless detachment from the emotions he excites in others.

features a metalepsis in which he steps out of the world of the action to address all women fond enough to fantasize about capturing his heart:

> Beauties, think not of awakening my flame,
> Your eyes can never enslave my reason,
> And it would already ask much of my soul
> To make me so much as curious to know your names.[13]

The question *La place royale* poses is thus whether even a hero can truly act; and the form the question takes tells us what an act is: a self-determined product of free will that changes that world in which it happens. This generates a still further paradox. For the act Alidor wants to perform depends on the action as much as the conformity to generic type he rebels against. This is one reason for the hero's striking metalepsis. By breaking the plane of separation between actor and audience, Alidor asserts his autonomy even as he reminds us of its artificiality. But the paradox of the act's dependence on the action also explains why nothing of the kind will happen again. Dating from *Médée*, Corneille will scrupulously obey the firm "classical" proscription of metalepsis as a fatal breach of dramatic verisimilitude.[14] And nowhere is this proscription more pointed than in a tragedy whose testimony to our problem is underscored by the fact that its hero's name is an anagram of the period French for actor, *comédien*.[15]

The avoidance of metalepsis in *Nicomède* in part reflects the title character's dignity as a tragic hero. It is one thing for the idle Alidor to put the ladies of Paris on notice of his immunity to their charms and quite another for a prince to mingle in this way. But Nicomède's heroic dignity also expresses that of the species to which he belongs. Nicomède is a distinctively Cornelian creation: a son whose mission it is to teach his father Prusias how to act, affirming in the process

---

13. Corneille, 5.8.1582–85.

14. Note the loathing expressed for metalepsis in d'Aubignac's *Pratique du théâtre* (Paris: Antoine de Sommaville, 1657), 56–60.

15. See Hélène Merlin-Kajman's discussion of *Nicomède* in *L'absolutisme dans les lettres et les deux corps du roi: passions et politique* (Paris: Champion, 2000), chap. 3. Note, though, that, focused primarily on Corneille's projection of his identity as author, Merlin-Kajman reads the hero's name as an anagram for *comédie* rather than *comédien*. Sacrificing the telltale *n* in order to stress Corneille's status as poet, she is perhaps less attentive to the degree to which the poet grounds his authority in the mediating autonomy he grants his heroes and especially heroines. See my *The Matter of Mind: Reason and Experience in the Age of Descartes* (Toronto: University of Toronto Press, 2012), chap. 3.

a moral autonomy emphasized by the fact that it is he, and not his father, who knows what to do. As a son, he has a predetermined role to play—that of paying the debt of duty he owes the author of his days. The trouble is that the at once moral and political disorder in the play stems from a paternal weakness as exemplary as Nicomède's strength.

For Prusias is incapable of playing the part providence assigns him: that of the sovereign charged with deciding the issue of events.[16] Indeed, compared to his boy, Prusias cuts the very portrait of the hapless Benjaminian tyrant. All but comically impotent in his dealings with his vindictive second wife, who schemes to eliminate his natural successor in favor of her own son, Prusias proves equally powerless in response to the extortions of imperial Rome. Incapable of setting things right in his own house, he is reduced to pitiful wavering in the face of the Roman threat—to borrow Benjamin's wonderful metaphors, he flaps in the wind like a tattered banner, a king of playing cards or a figure out of the paintings of El Greco, distinguished above all by the smallness of his head.[17] The result plunges his kingdom into a Schmittian state of life-and-death exception from which it is rescued only once his legitimate heir in effect usurps the throne by acting like the king his father should be.

The heroic resolve Nicomède displays in the hour of public as well as private need resolves the paradox *La place royale* lays out. What enables Nicomède to act, becoming the sovereign the law of royal primogeniture decrees, is his conscious and deliberate acceptance of the part the occasioning action requires him to play. On the one hand he ceases to be the mere empirical Nicomède, Prusias's son, in order be reborn as the hero who, in assuming the sovereign identity for which his father proves unfit, saves both father and kingdom. However, the very gesture by which he liquidates his private person in order to play his public part shows him to be a true actor in every sense: one whose unwavering conformity to type produces the act that, in preserving his father's realm, changes the political landscape in which the play begins.

The solution of the paradox Corneille confronts is thus as sophistically baroque as anything in Calderón—but the Calderón of the

16. I allude to Carl Schmitt's decisionist theory of political sovereignty, whose relevance to Benjamin's *Origin* is densely documented. For a direct discussion, complete with supporting references, see "Talking like a Book."

17. Benjamin, *OGTD*, 70–72, 123–25.

cloak-and-dagger plays rather than religious allegories like *La vida es sueño* or the *autos sacramentales*. If *La vida*'s Segismundo replaces his father on the throne when, taught by his own bizarre experience that life is a dream, he overcomes the bestial urges to which original sin condemns all human creatures, it is because he takes psychic dictation from the divine stage manager who, like his counterpart in *El gran teatro del mundo*, silently watches over him from the start. By contrast, Nicomède stands alone in that, in the hour of need, his sole resource is his own heroic self. Nicomède becomes a king because the test of events finds him to *be* one—the proof being the resolve with which he acts when the unfolding action wheels round the moment to do so. Where his father behaves like an ordinary mortal in whom we recognize all the hallmarks of the German baroque picture of the fallen human condition, the son not only conforms to the ideal expected of a king but *makes it real*. And he does so because he acts where his father helplessly vacillates.

Which brings us to the problem Benjamin faced in contemplating a book on French tragedy. For *Nicomède* proves most baroque just when it most decisively deviates from Benjamin's model. If the point of the second book is to show how the French exception to the baroque cashes out as a disguised version of the European norm, and if, in Corneille, French tragedy is nowhere less baroque than where it is most so, Benjamin would have had to find his probative example in that dramatist in whom French scholars most unarguably discern the classical ideal that sets their tradition apart, Racine.

Still, Racine's classicism raises more questions than it answers in that it was so multifariously overdetermined. One of the many seminal ideas set out in Roland Barthes's *Sur Racine* is that of the "refus d'hériter" that characterizes the species he calls *homo racinianus*.[18] In the first place, the rejection of an inherited legacy pinpoints the omnipresent weight and authority of a heroic past of which the majority of his heroes and heroines are the self-consciously belated, subheroic legatees. The chief characters of *Andromaque*, for instance, are all burdened by inherited identities that threaten to preempt the ones they attempt to forge for themselves. Pyrrhus is the son of Achilles, Oreste the son of Agamemnon, Hermione the daughter of Helen, and Andromaque the widow of Hector. And if it happens that the one character in the play who does seem genuinely to act lacks a

---

18. Roland Barthes, *Sur Racine* (Paris: Seuil, 1963), 50.

heroic parent to live up to, the title character Andromaque herself, it is because she is prepared for this role by her suicidal readiness to stand in her dead husband's place, giving her life in order to secure a problematic future for a son whose fate it will be to measure up to the example *his* father sets.

But what is true of his heroes and heroines is also true of Racine, a belated poet whose notoriously Œdipal relation to his giant predecessor Corneille accounts for the lamentable violence engendered by the fact that, as mentioned earlier, his characters resemble human beings as they are rather than as Cornelian example shows they ought to be.[19] From this standpoint, even Racine's oft-cited if ill-defined Jansenism turns out to be overdetermined. If Racinian classicism is a thing of quite literally murderous rigor and exactness, shaping plots whose ice-cold regularity ensures that his characters suffer the maximum of pain, it is in large measure because Racine defined himself as the poet who is not the baroque Corneille. If Racine's dramatic personnel are unable to act or, better, if the acts they perform serve only to seal the tragic fate to which the action assigns them, it is because the "place royale" of free creation is already occupied by Racine's elder Cornelian twin. Where, then, Corneille gives us a baroque theater of the act, Racine gives us a stringently classical theater of Aristotelian action. Further, if, as Aristotle's *Poetics* (1449a-1450b) teaches, *ethos* or character is a strict function of the underlying *praxis* or plot to whose immanent logical determinations it is bound, Racine's routine definition of character as ensnared in the toils of identities imposed by the past expresses, at the level of poetics, his own struggle to break free of his inescapable archetype.

But what is this if not exactly the way Benjamin describes the German baroque? It matches the terms of the crucial distinction Benjamin draws between Greek tragedy and German *Trauerspiel*. As Benjamin sees it, the ultimate fruit of Greek tragedy, in direct contrast to *Trauerspiel*, is the dignity human beings achieve in defiance of the fate the gods ordain. Indeed, Greek tragedy is said to usher in a new

---

19. The Œdipal reading of Racine's relationship to Corneille goes way back. The best versions are Terence Cave, *Recognitions: A Study in Poetics* (Oxford: Oxford University Press, 1988), pt. 2, chap. 3, Fumaroli, *Héros et orateurs*, pt. 5, Richard E. Goodkin, *Birth Marks:The Tragedy of Primogeniture in Pierre Corneille, Thomas Corneille, and Jean Racine* (Philadelphia: University of Pennsylvania Press, 2000), and Amy Wygant, "Medea, Poison and the Epistemology of Error in *Phèdre*," *Modern Language Review* 95/1 (January 2000): 62–71.

order of self-determined human law paid for by the proudly sacrificial acts tragic heroes and heroines are shown to make, thereby asserting not only their independence but their superiority to the divinities who kill them.[20] Were we, then, to look for a true counterpart for Greek tragedy in seventeenth-century France, the baroque Corneille is what we would find. The true equivalent to *Trauerspiel* is Racine.

But Racine's competition with Corneille also produces a match for the underlying poetics of *Trauerspiel* in the self-defeating hesitations that bedevil characters' responses to the situations in which they are thrown and the curiously comical form the action takes whenever they try to act. I conclude by drawing attention to a passage in Racine that captures the essence of the case, act two of *Andromaque*.

In conformity with the five-part scheme of classical poetics, act two undertakes the dramatic complication of the initial situation presented in act one. It accordingly develops the plot threads whose "knotting" in act three commits the characters to the tragic end consummated in act five, extinguishing the hope for a happy escape nourished by act four's plot-twisting *péripéties*.

We learn in act one that, despite heading up an embassy on behalf of the Greeks to demand the death of Hector's son Astyanax, an execution for which Pyrrhus is to be rewarded by marriage with Hermione, Oreste is in fact there to pursue his own desire for Helen's daughter, making his performance of an ambassadorial role as ambiguous as he finds it painful.[21] And we also learn that, despite being the son of Hector's killer, Pyrrhus is in love with Andromaque. He is therefore unwilling to give the Greeks what they want since to do so would end all hope of winning her hand.

Act two then begins with the first plot complication in the person of Hermione. Tirelessly stalked by Oreste, whom she loathes, she is passionately in love with Pyrrhus. However, when Oreste presses his suit in 2.2, she promises to marry him if Pyrrhus rejects the Greeks' demand that he surrender Andromaque's boy. Having just heard from Pyrrhus's own lips that he has no intention of surrendering Hector's son, Oreste gloats over the certainty of getting his wish. His behavior in this is unseemly: his soliloquy in 2.3 sounds like the fatuous self-congratulations in which Molière's Arnolphe might indulge—the

20. Benjamin, *OGTD*, 106–110.

21. On Oreste's problematic performance in the role of ambassador, see Timothy Hampton, *Fictions of Embassy: Literature and Diplomacy in Early Modern Europe* (Ithaca, NY: Cornell University Press, 2009), chap. 7.

more so since, having witnessed Andromaque's refusal to submit to Pyrrhus's blackmail in act one, the audience knows that Pyrrhus has changed his mind. Oreste himself only learns the truth in 2.4, when Pyrrhus declares his intention to accept Hermione's hand. The immediate result is the irresistibly comic aside ("Ah dieux!") with which Oreste reels off stage. However, the *comble* of quasi-comical tragic irony comes in 2.5. Having unknowingly gone a long way toward unhinging the powers of reason that will utterly abandon Oreste at the final curtain, Pyrrhus launches into a tirade of vengeful hate for Andromaque whose pathological excessiveness leads his confidant Phœnix rightly to suspect that he is in fact still in love with her.

It suffices to have summarized the action here to make my point. At the same time as Racine orchestrates the plot complications needed to tie the tragic knot, he reveals all of his characters to be Benjaminian puppets, jerked about on the hidden strings of a fate no less malignant for being of divine design. Unlike, say, the Lohenstein of *Sophonisbe*, punning to the point of pedantry on cognates of the word *Spiel* in token of his characters' feckless fatedness, Racine plays his cards artfully close to his chest. Nevertheless, what he produces is nothing if not *Trauerspiel*.

But what is this if not confirmation of the deepest idea shaping Benjamin's hypothetical French *Origin*? What both *Trauerspiel* and Racinian tragedy denounce as fate, a notion that, for all its tragic resonance, continues to reserve a place for the providence the secular turn of post-Westphalian modernity is in the process of effacing, is in reality the determinism of *history* at its most ineffably profane. The Germans of Benjamin's generation knew this, having lost the Great War and endured the hunger and hyperinflation provoked by the draconian war reparations France exacted in the Treaty of Versailles. By contrast, deluded by their victory in 1918, and by their faith in the literary culture that seemed to justify that ephemeral triumph, the French would not come to see it till the Fall of France of May-June 1940. And even then it would take the insights of the dogged French-speaking Switzer, Rousset, to begin to draw the lessons.

KATHERINE IBBETT

Classicism and the Creaturely:
Pierre Corneille's *Polyeucte*

French classicism often seems to shun the creaturely. Let's take even
the most prosaic understanding of that term and think about the status of the human body: when a body is present in classical texts, it
is often merely as a vessel from which a text can be drawn (Racine,
Bajazet) or as a screen on which a propriety-observing blush can be
traced (Lafayette, *La Princesse de Clèves*). Yet while classical theater
famously declaims a yearning for apotheosis and the space beyond,
its stage must rely on the creaturely body of the actor to voice such
desires. Accounts of stagings of classical plays often suggest the awk-
wardness that the body on stage could inadvertently bring about, especially in plays like martyr dramas where some divine access had to
be translated into all too clumsy human terms. In the eighteenth century, Voltaire recalled a staging of Pierre Corneille's *Polyeucte* (first
performed in1642), the most prominent and popular martyr drama of
classical France, stating that "in the past the actor who played Polyeucte, in white gloves and a big hat, took off his gloves and hat to
pray. I don't know if this foolishness still goes on."[1] Since martyr
drama as a genre dwindled swiftly, the answer to Voltaire's question
is that such foolishness didn't go on very long at all.[2] In this essay I
argue that reading French martyr drama's awkward embodiments as

1. *Commentaires sur Polyeucte*, cited in Pierre Corneille, *Œuvres complètes*, ed.
Georges Couton, vol. 1 (Paris: Gallimard, 1980), 1623. My citations from *Polyeucte*
refer to line numbers of this edition, and all translations are mine unless otherwise
noted.
2. I have discussed the genre at further length in *The Style of the State in French
Theater, 1630–1660* (Burlington, VT: Ashgate, 2009), where I argue that the martyr's
contested body figured a wider crisis about bodies on stage and their relation to the
state.

YFS 124, *Walter Benjamin's Hypothetical French "Trauerspiel,"* ed. Bjornstad and Ibbett, © 2013 by Yale University.

Trauerspiel rather than as failed tragic experiments allows us to see that this minor genre touches on some major questions. Where Benjamin's post-Westphalian dramas illustrate a particular political settlement, their French equivalents explore, I suggest, the awkward territory of settlement and compromise in which Catholic France found itself after the Edict of Nantes granted certain rights to Protestants. These plays ask us to consider compromises between ideals of faith and political realities.

The martyr drama's difficulty as a genre is precisely the "tension between immanence and transcendence" that Walter Benjamin places at the center of his elucidation of the *Trauerspiel*'s particularity.[3] Benjamin's exploration of creatureliness draws on the figure of the martyr-king (like Charles I) in the German school dramas of the seventeenth century, tracing the relation between tyrant and martyr. Both are compromised and creaturely figures: as Benjamin puts it, "In the *Trauerspiel* monarch and martyr do not shake off their immanence."[4] Where we expect "transcendental impulse," we find instead that in the dramas Benjamin discusses "the baroque knows no eschatology."[5] In reading French martyr drama through the lens of the *Trauerspiel*, the traditional tragic node of sacrifice appears as a compromised and creaturely affair rather than a reckoning with the transcendent. If the martyr play is concerned with the end story of salvation, the ultimate off-stage space, it nonetheless insists that such an apotheosis can only be told through the creaturely; we, as spectators and worldly creatures, have access to the divine only through the people on stage, and must make do with that.

In the search for a French *Trauerspiel*, *Polyeucte* and the many plays that trailed in its wake make an obvious starting point. As was the case for the German mourning dramas that interested Benjamin, this French outcrop of martyr plays was produced by a generation of writers trained in Jesuit institutions, who knew the long tradition of Jesuit college drama that turned around the representation of saintly deaths.[6] Like most martyr plays of this generation, *Polyeucte*

---

3. Walter Benjamin, *The Origin of German Tragic Drama*, trans. John Osborne (London: Verso, 1998), 66. Hereafter cited as *OGTD*.

4. Ibid., 67.

5. Ibid., 66.

6. On Gryphius's familiarity with Jesuit martyr plays and in particular French Jesuit writing, see Jane O. Newman, *Benjamin's Library: Modernity, Nation, and the Baroque* (Ithaca: Cornell University Press, 2011), 180.

represents the late Empire and early Church to a seventeenth-century audience themselves imagining, in the first decades after the Edict of Nantes, just how divine law and political expediency might be made to work together. The play takes place in Roman Armenia: the local Roman governor, Félix, has just married off his daughter Pauline to a local noble, Polyeucte. Just as Polyeucte is upsetting his father-in-law's political ambitions by converting to the new religion of Christianity, Pauline's old flame Sévère, a Roman military hero thought to have been killed in battle, returns from the dead. Polyeucte continues to insist on his faith and is finally killed for it; following the strictures of *bienséance*, the audience is unable to see his end, unlike in the source text, which details the new Christian's injuries at the hands of his jailers.[7] By the end of the play, Félix and Pauline are nonetheless speedily converted to the new religion by dint of Polyeucte's example, and Sévère is unseverely musing on the importance of religious toleration for the wider society. Despite its lofty eye on the divine, at times the action of the play and in particular the back-chatting between the power-hungry but deeply unintelligent Félix and his resigned but deeply intelligent daughter borders on black comedy, recalling another of Benjamin's key distinctions: "The *Trauerspiel* is conceivable as pantomime; the tragedy is not."[8]

The success of *Polyeucte* and other plays like it came at a somewhat surprising moment in French stage history, given that representations of bodily injury and death, the focus of the standard martyrological narrative, were no longer welcome on the rapidly "regularizing" stage, which disliked such bloody spectacle.[9] In *Polyeucte*, Corneille seemingly works hard to push not just violence but other fleshly traces offstage: Paul Scott has argued that Corneille sublimates the erotic bond between the martyr Polyeucte and his friend Néarque, apparent in the source texts, and describes instead a friendship forged through baptism.[10]

This disappearing of the flesh recalls the argument traced by Eric Santner in his recent book *The Royal Remains: The People's Two*

7. Corneille, *Œuvres complètes*, 977.

8. Benjamin, *OGTD*, 118.

9. For a list of similar plays and an account of this problem, see Ibbett, *Style of the State*, 35.

10. Paul Scott, "Manipulating Martyrdom: Corneille's (hetero) sexualization of Polyeucte," *Modern Language Review* 99 (2004): 328–38.

Bodies and the Endgames of Sovereignty, in which Santner pursues questions raised by his earlier work on the creaturely by entering into conversation with Roberto Esposito's account of the Pauline distinction between flesh and body. Esposito diagnoses Paul's account of the passage from flesh to the corporate unity of the church or body in Christ as a central transition for Western culture:

> More than an expulsion of the flesh, this [passage] concerns its incorporation into an organism that is capable of domesticating flesh's centrifugal and anarchic impulses. Only the spiritualization of the body (or better, the incorporation of a spirit that is capable of redeeming man from the misery of his corruptible flesh) will allow him entrance into the mystical body of the church.[11]

Santner goes on to elucidate this relationship between flesh and its redemption in the *corpus mysticum*, which he calls "the master trope that allowed for the aggregation and sacramentalization of all manner of secular entities."[12]

This flesh/mystical body distinction is a useful starting point for thinking about *Polyeucte*. The Pauline (as in apostolic) passage from flesh to mystical body encapsulates the choices proffered to the play's central character, a new Christian who must choose between a marriage to the aptly named Pauline—with, eventually, the possibility of propagating faith through reproductivity—and the solitary heroism of martyrdom. The play figures the emergent church in two main ways. On the one hand, the church here is a mystical body inspired by the martyr's death; on the other, the church is imagined through a much more prosaic body, that of the potential mother, Pauline, who stands for another kind of birth of the Christian community at a period when the counter-reformation church was loudly proclaiming the importance of motherhood for the propagation of the faith. Critics have frequently commented on the absence of mothers in Corneille's tragedies, but in *Polyeucte* maternity is constantly present as potential. The play explores the New Testament distinction between children of the flesh and children of the spirit even in its opening

11. Roberto Esposito, *Bios: Biopolitics and Philosophy*, trans. Timothy Campbell (Minneapolis: University of Minnesota Press, 2008), 164, cited and discussed in Eric Santner, *The Royal Remains: The People's Two Bodies and the Endgames of Sovereignty* (Chicago: University of Chicago Press, 2011), 29. In response to Santner's *Royal Remains*, see the special issue of the *Journal for Cultural and Religious Theory* 12/1 (spring 2012), edited by Julia Lupton and C.J. Gordon.

12. Santner, *Royal Remains*, 39.

dedication to Anne of Austria, the queen Regent, whom Corneille describes as having "given birth to miracles," a discreet nod not just to her patronage or religious devotion but also to the great relief brought about by the birth of the long-hoped-for future Louis XIV, the year before the play appeared.[13]

The flesh/body distinction, of course, can never be completely straightforward, as Polyeucte's agonizing suggests. For Santner, flesh is a stubborn remainder, something that cannot be wholly transformed or redeemed by the transcendent. As he puts it, for Paul in I Corinthians "flesh is the thorn in the body."[14] Pauline, Polyeucte's wife and Félix's difficult daughter, proves to be the thorn in the body of both the churchly community envisioned by her husband and the imperial dream of her father. It is not only the martyr who is a problematic body in *Polyeucte, martyr*; the wife's troubling physical presence also underlines the play's larger attention to the question of the material world and its compromised objects.

Polyeucte's more material concerns all point to an anxiety about the precise status of the body and the object within Catholic thought of the counter-reformation, and, more particularly in France, within the terms of the post-Nantes settlement. The play's central character proclaims his faith in incarnation and resurrection, but the play also betrays that interest in order to turn around the difficulties of a more human embodiment. Like the *Trauerspiel* described by Benjamin, *Polyeucte* remains mired in the immanent, even as it lurches toward what lies beyond. In this play, religious faith never departs from the terrain of political machination. Here, it is the martyr who figures as Benjamin's famous intriguer; in all Polyeucte's earnest declarations of faith, he remains bound to a very earthly way of imagining salvation as transaction. Polyeucte's desire for death involves a kind of temporal intrigue, Benjamin's "corrupt energy of schemers" in which he wants to die before his newly-baptized grace is eroded by the contingent swings of fortune.[15] He brokers a careful calculation of profit and loss, in which Christian death functions as a kind of insurance policy ("assure" in the original text):

> This greatness fades. I want one which will be
> Immortal, happiness, boundless, assured,

13. Corneille, dedication "À la Reine régente," *Œuvres complètes*, 974.
14. Santner, *Royal Remains*, 39.
15. Benjamin, *OGTD*, 88.

High above envy, above destiny.
Is a poor wretched life too dear a price
Which in a moment can be snatched from me . . .[16]

Charles Taylor's recent reading of religion around "the distinction transcendent/immanent" sets out what he calls the "immanent frame [. . .] a constructed social space, where instrumental rationality is a key value, and time is pervasively secular."[17] Polyeucte operates entirely within that constructed space; his aspirations to the transcendent are rendered only in the basest of instrumental terms.

Like Benjamin, Corneille worries about what happens when we understand something difficult or divine through the prosaic, so that "the profane world is both elevated and devalued."[18] Jane Newman writes of Benjamin's interest in ways that the material can gain a paradoxical power through allegorization, "a power that represents a potentially threatening force capable of blocking—even as it provokes and is necessary to—the Christian allegorist's project to move beyond the realm of facticity."[19] What are we to make of an allegorist who cannot get beyond his material, or a martyr who cannot get beyond his market value?

Benjamin shows how the allegorical world of the *Trauerspiel* leaves its readers floundering: "Any person, any object, any relationship can mean absolutely anything else."[20] But *Polyeucte* gives us a particular French twist on Benjamin's Lutheran crisis of the sign. In representing the interpretive crisis of the late Roman Empire, the play speaks to the anxieties of Catholic France seeking to reestablish one national authority in the decades after the Wars of Religion. So, just as early modern Catholics and Protestants clashed over the proper value of a whole set of religious gestures, in this play the Romans who are confronted with the early church puzzle over how to understand what they see in the world around them; the play even begins with the troubled interpretation of a dream, curtly dismissed as an "extravagance" (line 6) by Polyeucte, who should be better able

16. Pierre Corneille, *Polyeuctus, The Liar, Nicomedes*, trans. John Cairncross (Harmondsworth: Penguin, 1980), 95; original line numbers in *Œuvres complètes*, 1193–96.

17. Charles Taylor, *A Secular Age* (Cambridge: Harvard University Press, 2007), 540.

18. Benjamin, *OGTD*, 175.

19. Newman, *Benjamin's Library*, 181.

20. Benjamin, *OGTD*, 175.

to understand the weight of abstractions in the world. Polyeucte's own gestures are constantly reinterpreted by those around him. Martyrdom, Benjamin tells us, "prepares the body of the living person for emblematic purposes,"[21] and in *Polyeucte* we see the attempts to interpret the body as emblem. The emblem that so intrigues Benjamin, that famously difficult knitting together of word and image, can be unpacked according to one's reading preferences; it mutely offers itself up to various interpretative ends. Likewise the martyr is revealed in this play to be a piece of flesh with a story (or rather multiple stories) attached to it, a flesh made body by the power of the word. If Polyeucte understands the dead body of a Christian to signify salvation, his Roman father-in-law interprets such a sign quite differently. Having imagined that the threat of death would call off the posturing of the new Christians, Félix must be patiently instructed by his daughter Pauline that in fact his very Roman promise of violence only sharpens their resolve. Félix initially plans to persuade Polyeucte to abandon his faith by forcing him to watch the death of his friend Néarque:

> He will be clearer about what he ought to do
> When he sees the slain man who led him on.
> At that grim fate which suggests his own,
> The fear of death and the desire to live
> Will unreservedly win back his soul.
> The sight of death cancels the wish for it.[22]

As we see here, the governor still believes in the corrective power of spectacle. However, Félix's certainty is soon undone by the very different interpretive standards of the Christian community. Pauline assesses the likely results of such a threat very differently, and explains what death means to this strange new body of interpreters:

> For *them*, death's neither shameful nor the end.
> They covet glory, scorn the gods on high;
> Blind to the earth, they set their heart on heav'n;
> Believing death opens the door to it,
> Tormented, rent in twain, no matter what,

21. Ibid., 217.
22. Corneille, trans. Cairncross and modified by the author, 82; original line numbers 879–84.

Tortures to them are what our pleasures are,
And lead to their desires' accomplishment.
The vilest death they christen martyrdom.[23]

Pauline's response underscores the crisis in signification presented by the new Christians: in *Polyeucte*, just as in early modern France more widely, the certainty of the sign has been radically destabilized by a collision of interpretive communities.

In the midst of such confusion Pauline stands as our clear-headed and prosaic guide; even before her conversion in the final scene she figures a certain model of wifehood, able to acknowledge and navigate the shoals of signification without losing a sense of the quotidian business of (proto-)Christian womanhood. *Polyeucte* explores Benjamin's creatureliness through the notion of marriage and its fleshly commitments; where his tension is between the martyr and the tyrant, here Corneille sets up a stand-off between the martyr and his wife. The play's centerpiece, set apart through the use of stanzas, is a monologue by Polyeucte in jail. Alone, he weighs up whether to move toward martyrdom or to privilege instead his earthly marriage with Pauline. In the opening lines, Polyeucte addresses the temptations that draw him to Pauline:

Source of delight, fertile in misery,
What do you want of me, deceiving joys?
Shameful attachments of the flesh and world,
Why not leave me, when I have left you?[24]

Here, flesh is invoked only in order for it to be rejected; this "flesh" is the only occurrence of the word in Corneille's considerable dramaturgical *corpus*. Polyeucte's rejection of the world is contrasted with his embrace of the "saintly sweetnesses of Heaven, adorable ideas": the abstractions of religion are to be preferred to a fleshly fecundity that represents only misery.[25] Though in his 1660 "Examen" of the play Corneille argued that "its representation satisfies both the pious and society people [*les Dévots et les gens du Monde*]," in 1642 those representatives of the *monde* in the audience might have felt themselves rebuked by Polyeucte's pious prison utterances (although

---

23. Corneille, trans. Cairncross, 86; lines 946–53.
24. Corneille, trans. Cairncross (modified), 93; lines 1105–8.
25. Corneille, line 1145, my translation.

they may, anticipating Voltaire, have been sniggering at his hat and gloves).[26]

If *Polyeucte* is written in the context of a post-settlement France, it is also very distinctly a play concerned with what happens after a more domestically familiar settlement: marriage. Mitchell Greenberg has noted that *Polyeucte* shows us a rare "already-there of marriage, the already-there of sexual union, whose realization in [Corneille's] other plays had only been a distant, flickering mirage."[27] And the play represents a range of ways to respond to the reality of marriage: if Polyeucte seeks to flee it, his eyes on a mystic and Churchly corporation, Pauline in contrast pragmatically faces up to her very peculiar husband, even after her beloved Sévère has reappeared, telling her confidante Stratonice, "This is what is left to us, and the ordinary effect of the love we are given, and the vows made to us."[28] Here marriage, after the event of the ceremony, is in itself a kind of leftover; it represents the quotidian grappling with the stuff of life, dealing in "ordinary effects" rather than waiting for the miraculous. Telling her story to Stratonice she falters and says "You know about the rest": the "rest" is the stuff of women's knowledge in the world.[29] For Polyeucte, in bitter contrast, these remainders are to be left behind: "Let us make God triumphant: he'll look after the rest."[30] The women's attention to the "reste," to worldly matters, points to the end of the play, when Pauline goes, along with her newly, meekly Christian father and the remarkably tolerant Sévère, to bury the bodies left behind.[31] *Polyeucte* is not unusual in consigning women to the sphere of immanence, but Corneille seems to make a particular virtue out of that location, granting a particular moral significance to those who are left behind to grapple with the world. Just as his tragedy *Horace* tells us the fallout effect of martial heroism by affording us the insights of those too feeble or too female to embody the nation, so *Polyeucte* draws us to imagine what forms of virtue are lived by those

26. Corneille, "Examen de *Polyeucte*," *Œuvres complètes*, 980.

27. Mitchell Greenberg, *Canonical States, Canonical Stages: Oedipus, Othering, and Seventeenth-Century Drama* (Minneapolis: University of Minnesota Press, 1994), 128.

28. Corneille, lines 131–2.

29. Corneille, line 207.

30. Corneille, line 717.

31. For a broader reading of Corneille's language of the *reste*, see my "Heroes and History's Remainders: The *Restes* of Pierre Corneille," *Modern Language Quarterly* 69/3 (September 2008): 353–66.

who are left behind.[32] What happens *after* the ending of things—of treaties, marriages, deaths—is central to the new political settlement imagined at the close of the play.

In *Polyeucte* as elsewhere in classical theater, women are persistently described using a language of the object: "O, too beloved object that has so charmed me" says Sévère of Pauline.[33] But if a woman is a thing in this play, the objectification of Pauline and her rejection by Polyeucte also recalls the other leftover objects repeatedly and more violently rejected by Christianity, the pagan idols. Yet it is precisely from these things left behind—women, objects—that we must build up the meaning of the play, just as in the *Trauerspiel* we shore up "That which lies here in ruins, the highly significant fragment, the remnant [. . .], in fact, the finest material in baroque creation."[34]

The ruined fragments of the idols whose destruction animates the action of *Polyeucte* have a very particular status in the play. The audience never sees the scene of iconoclasm, instead hearing it through the account of Pauline's confidant Stratonice. But the first readers of the play, in the edition of 1643, did see the scene, which featured as its frontispiece: a behatted Polyeucte, quite the seventeenth-century noble, smashes a statue in what looks very much like a church, reminding the reader of the scenes of Protestant iconoclasm in France's not-so-distant Wars of Religion. Where theater must fail at absolute representation, the "play for readers" that Benjamin imagines the *Trauerspiel* to be is, then, able to supplement representation with one last fragment. The breaking of the idols must be imagined as an echo of France's own recent violent history, now supposedly redeemed by the 1598 Edict of Nantes.

Later in the play, Polyeucte himself voices his dismissal of the idol as object, describing the idol to Pauline as "Insensible and deaf, impotent, injured, of wood, of marble, or gold, as you prefer."[35] The object is briefly reanimated only in order to be cast aside; it is

32. On the relation between heroism and what it leaves behind in *Horace*, see especially Susan Maslan, "The Dream of the Feeling Citizen: Law and Emotion in Corneille and Montesquieu," *SubStance* 35/1 (2006): 69–84; Hélène Merlin-Kajman, *L'absolutisme dans les lettres et la théorie des deux corps: Passions et politique* (Paris: Champion, 2000), 190–206, and in a slightly different vein, "Réécriture cornélienne du crime: le cas d'Horace," *Littératures classiques* 67 (2009): 101–114.

33. Corneille, line 495.

34. Benjamin, *OGTD*, 178.

35. Corneille, lines 1217–18.

personalized only to be described as useless. The idol then figures a personhood drained of agency, what Benjamin calls the "dead object," which nonetheless wields real power: "once human life has sunk into the merely creaturely, even the life of apparently dead objects secures power over it."[36] In *Polyeucte*'s world, which is strictly speaking pre-Westphalian but (as Catholic representation) post-Tridentine and (as a French play) post-Nantes, the anxiety over the immanence or otherwise of the idol inflects all forms of relation and existence. Even in the midst of Christianity's early and exemplary heroism, we are already consigned to the creaturely world of compromise.

This remorseless reiteration of the idol's thingness, which seems to infect even human striving, can be contrasted with the human-object relation glimpsed in the strange genre of almost-contemporary texts known as the *histoires tragiques*. These turbulent and often didactic tales appeared just before the great flourishing of French classical theater, and provided the source for the German school plays of which Benjamin writes in at least one instance. Gryphius's *Catharine of Georgia*, for example, draws on the "Histoire De Catherine Royne de Georgie" found in Claude Malingre's collection of *Histoires tragiques de nostre temps* (1635). In this gruesome tale, Queen Catherine's martyrdom is described in particular and painful detail:

> Having stripped her naked, and tied her hands behind her back, they pulled from the fire large iron pincers, burning red, and pulled at her breasts with them, and burnt her cruelly, so that one breast was cut and ripped away from her. [. . .] The other breast was cut and torn away so that one saw all the ribs underneath, and her guts laid bare; her blood, streaming all down her torn-up breast, served to cover the nakedness of her body.[37]

The unpiecing of Catherine's body is described at some length; she is eventually so undone that finally she comes to resemble "a wooden statue, or a log chopped at from all sides, as deformed to the eyes of men as it was pleasing to the eyes of God and the Angels."[38] The body of the queen is first approximated to the objectness of the idol, a thing

---

36. Benjamin, *OGTD*, 132.

37. Claude Malingre, *Histoires tragiques de nostre temps dans lesquelles se voyent plusieurs belles maximes d'Estat et quantité d'exemples fort memorables, de constance, de courage, de generosité* (Rouen: D. Ferrand et T. Daré, 1641), 528–29 (my translation).

38. Ibid., 530.

of wood, but that status as object is very swiftly recuperated. The human becomes object so that she can be redeemed as fully human through Christ:

> When the flesh [*chair*] of this precious victim of Jesus Christ was all consumed by the fire, some Christians who were present gathered and reassembled all her bones [*tous ses os*], without losing one of them.[39]

This formulation recalls the set phrase "en chair et en os," meaning "alive" in seventeenth-century French; Furetière's dictionary notes that "One says that a man is still *en chair et en os*, to mean, that he is still full of life. Jesus Christ appeared to his disciples *en chair et en os*, that is to say, really and in corporeal nature."[40] And the aliveness of the redeemed body of Catherine comes about precisely in its passage from flesh to body: the bones of the material body are gathered up by and into a Christian assembly. As a genre, the *histoire tragique* is committed to showing us the flesh in all its horror, but it manages to move beyond that and to redeem the objectness of the body through a clear affirmation of the injured body's redemption and incorporation in the body of the Church. Not one single bone remains: in Santner's terms, the flesh becomes body. *Polyeucte*, in contrast, is stuck on the flesh, and in that stuckness bodies forth the French *Trauerspiel*.

Fittingly, a play that has tussled with immanence and transcendence ends with two versions of faith. Firstly and most obviously, we must pass through Polyeucte's martyrdom offstage in an apotheosis that we can never see. But the play closes with another form of leadership, gesturing toward a strange and melancholy form of religious toleration. The former Roman hero Sévère, who once figured absolute martial transcendence, now points to a new political path for the Empire. While distinguishing himself from the Christians, Sévère allows us to understand his intellectual sympathies with them, and points to a moment at which he could, possibly, become one himself:

> I always liked them, be they so reviled.
> I see none die that does not make me grieve;
> Perhaps one day I'll know them better. I
> Meanwhile approve that each should have his gods,
> Worshipping freely, with impunity.[41]

39. Ibid., 531.
40. Antoine Furetière, *Dictionaire universel* (La Haye: Leers, 1690), s.v. "chair." My translation.
41. Corneille, trans. Cairncross, 119; lines 1795–99.

Sévère's unsevere sighs over the deaths of the Christians constitute a new political melancholy, far from Polyeucte's burning certainties of faith; his gentle prevarications point to a new and creaturely sovereignty that must find its path not in religious absolutism but in secular solutions of toleration. In Sévère, France finds the tentative voice of a post-Nantes compromise. Even these people who cause such trouble by smashing idols might, perhaps, meanwhile, as Sévère puts it, be worth getting to know; even in what looks like a religious play, the melancholy place of the secular begins to be established.

The heyday of the martyr play was a brief one, and the genre has largely been regarded as something of a failed venture, unable to transcend its historical moment. Martyr plays are the leftovers of a literary history that has been too eager to praise classicism as apotheosis; in recent years, as classicism's smooth surfaces have been ruffled by readings against the grain, they have come to attract more critical attention precisely because of their strangeness.[42] Since the appearance of martyr plays on the French stage, critics have wrestled with the question of how to understand the place of *Christian* tragedy, in which the promise of what Benjamin calls "a guaranteed economics of salvation" seems to radically displace the tragic form.[43] But reading this genre as *Trauerspiel* allows its strangeness to remain intact, neither absorbed into classical triumph nor dismissed as a dusty failure. If Benjamin's *Trauerspiel* teaches us about the significance of the fragmentary, then the martyr play's importance is that it performs the difficulty of France's fragmented post-Nantes position even at the heart of the bold newness of the classical.[44]

42. See, in addition to the work of Paul Scott whose *Polyeucte* article is cited above, the recent dissertation of Christopher Semk, "Performing Martyrdom: The Poetics of Suffering on the French Stage 1600–1633" (Indiana University, 2010).

43. Benjamin, *OGTD*, 216.

44. This work was supported by the Radcliffe Institute for Advanced Study at Harvard University.

CLAUDE HAAS

The Dramaturgy of Sovereignty and the Performance of Mourning: The Case of Corneille's *Horace*

Walter Benjamin's comments on the *tragédie classique* are not only sparse; they also seem contradictory at first glance.[1] In the notes to a planned, but never realized project on French drama he speaks of the "contrastive nature"[2] of the *tragédie classique* in comparison to the German *Trauerspiel* ("mourning play"); and yet he claims to have hit upon the "first thought" for the *Trauerspiel* book while seeing the "crooked crown" of the king in a Geneva production of the *Cid*.[3] These two frequently quoted remarks, however, correspond much more strictly to each other than one might assume.

In fact, it would be quite right to assert that the crowns in both the baroque *Trauerspiel* and the *tragédie classique* are always and princi- pally crooked. In this sense, the Geneva production of the *Cid* staged something—albeit inadvertently—that is deeply rooted in German as well as French seventeenth-century drama. The symbolic dimension of the politics of these plays and their emblems of power cannot in- vest the monarchs appearing in them as political entities appointed by God.[4] The crooked crown would thus illustrate rather bluntly the

1. This essay was written in the context of a project on *Trauerspiel* and tragedy running at the Center for Literary and Cultural Research Berlin until December 2013 which will result in a book coauthored by Daniel Weidner and myself. I would like to thank Daniel Weidner very much for long conversations on Walter Benjamin and the *tragédie classique* without which I would not have been able to write the essay in this form. This is especially true for the passages on the performative aspects of mourning.
2. Walter Benjamin, *The Correspondence of Walter Benjamin 1910–1940*, ed. Gershom Sholem and Theodor W. Adorno, trans. Manfred R. Jacobson and Evelyn M. Jacobson (Chicago: Chicago University Press, 1994), 315.
3. Benjamin, *Gesammelte Schriften*, ed. Rolf Tiedemann and Hermann Schwep- penhäuser (Frankfurt a.M.: Suhrkamp, 1985), vol. 6, 534.
4. In a recent and impressive study drawing on Benjamin, Romain Jobez has shown this for the *German Trauerspiel* and French drama prior to the *tragédie classique*. See

YFS 124, *Walter Benjamin's Hypothetical French "Trauerspiel,"* ed. Bjornstad and Ib- bett, © 2013 by Yale University.

precariousness of the power that these monarchs wield. However, *Trauerspiel* and *tragédie classique* tend to draw very different conclusions from this precarious status of power. Without wanting to overstrain the image, one is tempted to say that the baroque *Trauerspiel* lets its quiet critique of power unfold in the allegorical contemplation of crooked crowns, while the *tragédie classique* of Corneilian provenance—at least according to its own dramaturgic intentions — musters the modern politics of absolutist sovereignty in order to, as it were, "straighten" the crown. In this respect, it is indeed correct to point out a "contrastive nature" of the two dramatic models that, nevertheless, emerge from shared religious and political interests. Acknowledging this tension also means that a reading of the *tragédie classique* against the backdrop of the *Trauerspiel* book is interesting precisely because Benjamin's observations are not easily transferable to French drama. We can bring up new questions with the help of Benjaminian insights, but we cannot rely on Benjamin's answers.

In what follows, I will engage in such a reading of Pierre Corneille's *Horace*, pointing out both the striking thematic and structural affinities the play evinces to Benjamin's conception of the German *Trauerspiel* and the significantly different stance it takes in view of its politics. Three issues are of particular interest to me: the potentially non-tragic character of heroic figures' sacrificial deaths in the framework of a sovereign dramaturgy; the sovereign's political self-legitimization in the state of exception; and the performative dimension of mourning for the dead as a genuinely theatrical objection to the politics of sovereignty.

*   *   *

That Corneille's plays do not belong to the form of tragedy is a thesis scholarship has not tired of reformulating.[5] Therefore, it has almost become a commonplace to address the early *tragédie classique* as a quintessentially non-tragic "tragedy." As different as the arguments

---

Romain Jobez, *Le théâtre baroque allemand et français. Le droit dans la littérature* (Paris: Garnier, 2010).

5. See Jacques Maurens' programmatic title: *La tragédie sans tragique. Le néo-stoïcisme dans l'œuvre de Pierre Corneille* (Paris: Armand Colin, 1966). For the probably most prominent exception, which lets tragedy begin with the "death of God" already present in Corneille, see Serge Doubrovsky, *Corneille et la dialectique du héros* (Paris: Gallimard, 1963), 497.

offered in favor of this thesis may look in particular, at least with respect to Benjamin's distinction between tragedy and *Trauerspiel*, one
is likely to assert that Corneille's early plays subscribe to the absolutist state model inasmuch as they insistently rule out all potential
ambivalence and dialectics from the figure of tragic sacrifice, rather
than trying to integrate it entirely into *raison d'état*.[6]

Nevertheless, the genuinely *temporal* ambivalence that Benjamin
grants to tragic sacrifice—and which, moreover, he holds responsible
for the end of tragedy already in antiquity—still proves instructive for
the non-tragic deaths of Corneille's figures. For Benjamin, the tragic
sacrifice is always "at once a first and a final sacrifice. A final sacrifice in the sense of the atoning sacrifice to gods who are upholding an
ancient right; a first sacrifice in the sense of the representative action,
in which new aspects of the life of the nation become manifest."[7]
Instead of subjecting his figures' deaths to such an ambivalent constellation, Corneille aligns them to a linear dramaturgic development
enacting a politics of sovereignty. Although his figures die violent
deaths because they abide by an "old law," this law is coded less in
terms of a "divine" than of a feudal and pre-sovereign order. The dramaturgy of Corneille's early plays in particular shows a violent death
to be justified and legitimate when it consolidates the absolutist state
model.

And yet Corneille must go to great lengths to stage the genuine
meaningfulness sovereign politics give to death. This is most evident
in the way his drama is persistently confronted with a phenomenon
necessarily at odds with such a meaningfulness, namely mourning,
and especially familial mourning. Consequently, sovereignty's claim
to justifying death depends most of all on the exclusion of mourning and thereby simultaneously marks this exclusion as the hidden
center of Corneilean drama. These plays cannot be tragedies because
the *Trauerspiel* undermines them by displaying, and surreptitiously
criticizing, their *lack* of tragedy.

It is not coincidental that this configuration culminates in a play
that undertakes the *coup* of proving necessary a total of six deaths
for the consolidation of sovereign power. This play is, moreover,

---

6. For the genealogy of this discourse and its function in Corneille, see the defini-
tive study by Katherine Ibbett, *The Style of the State in French Theater, 1630–1660:
Neoclassicism and Government* (Burlington: Ashgate, 2009).

7. Benjamin, *The Origin of German Tragic Drama*, trans. John Osborne (London:
Verso, 1998), 106–7. Hereafter cited as *OGTD*.

generally deemed the first *tragédie classique* because of its exemplary adherence to the normative poetics of French classicism: *Horace*, premiered in 1640 in Paris. Corneille takes his plot from a well known episode of Roman history recorded by Livy: in order to avoid further carnage Rome and Alba Longa, two cities battling for supremacy, each chose three warriors to decide the outcome of the war in a man-to-man fight. The family (as well as the emotional) ties between the three Horatians and the three Curiatians—the warriors chosen by the two cities—are extremely close: Horace and Curiace are not only good friends, they are almost double brothers-in-law. Horace's wife Sabine is Curiace's sister, Curiace in turn is the paramour of Horace's sister Camille. Although Horace emerges as the winner and the sole survivor of the battle, the only one to honorably receive him at home is his father. In contrast, both his wife and his sister insist on their right to mourn their slain brothers—and in Camille's case also the dead lover—and to criticize categorically the killing that was so eminently meaningful for the state's consolidation. When the situation escalates and Camille begins to insult her brother, Horace does not hesitate to kill her too. When the sovereign appearing in the final act acquits Horace of this crime, he brings to a close a play that, from the beginning, has been fighting a losing battle against grief and tears. Understood as the expression of a family affiliation threatening to undermine sovereign law, tears and grief not only mark but also negotiate the borderline between family rights and state law. The central significance this issue of mourning takes on in the play is made clear when the war between Rome and Alba Longa—in spite of occasional references to two states (l. 1742)[8]—is characterized as a war of *one* people living in two cities (l. 291) and, thus, as a "civil war" (l. 292). This is why the family ties between Horatians and Curiatians do not remain exterior to but rather stand at the center of the political conflict.

Historically speaking, Corneille is most certainly reacting to the domestic strife that had been ravaging France since the late sixteenth century. The dedication to Richelieu makes the intentions of his play unmistakably clear: the "civil wars" are to be ended by centralized absolutism. The old feudal structures relying on the principle of hereditary nobility must be destroyed *by* and *for* the emerging monar-

8. Pierre Corneille, *Horace. Tragédie* in *Œuvres complètes*, ed. Georges Couton (Paris: Gallimard, 1989), vol.1, 831–901.

chy: family rights, represented in the play by mourning and tears, must be transformed into state law, represented by a heroic readiness to make sacrifices that seeks to leave tears behind once and for all.

Horace's confrontation with Curiace at the beginning of the second act illustrates this opposition. From the start, Horace anticipates his own death, and the glory it will bring imbues him with pride:

> But though this combat means my death, the glory
> Of being chosen swells my heart with pride.[9]

Incapable of understanding this form of heroic determination, Curiace foresees the sorrow that the fight will entail for both the Horatians and the Curiatians: "In any case I shall have tears to shed."[10] Horace, in contrast, deems tears a completely mistaken response to heroic self-sacrifice.

> What! Thou couldst weep for me if I should die
> Serving my country? For a noble heart,
> That is the fairest of all deaths. The glory
> Which follows it, permits no tears; and I
> Would welcome it, blessing my happy fate,
> Should this in some wise benefit the State.[11]

Even when asserting that he could (only) "bless" his "destiny" if Rome and the state lost less through his death, Horace is by no means implying that self-sacrifice is inassimilable to the state. On the contrary: while Rome would certainly lose an important warrior in him, the ever-living glory he would bestow on the state in dying would provide a symbolic surplus that is even higher for the dead hero and his family than for the state itself.

Despite Curiace's inability to understand Horace's position, the play does not present their dialogue as the exchange of equally valid antagonistic positions. Instead, the teleological focus of the sovereign dramaturgy manifests itself by stylizing Curiace as a fundamentally *backward* figure.[12] As much as he might feel Horace to be a "barbarian," the orientation of the drama with its political (i.e. sovereign)

---

9. *The Chief Plays of Corneille*, trans. Lacy Lockert (Princeton: Princeton University Press, 1957), 121. Original line numbers in the French, 377–78.

10. Corneille trans. Lockert, 121 (French, line 394).

11. Corneille trans. Lockert, 122 (French, lines 398–402).

12. John D. Lyons, to whom I am indebted here, has made this point in *The Tragedy of Origins. Pierre Corneille and Historical Perspective* (Stanford: Stanford University Press, 1996), 49–50.

implications claims the opposite. Horace is importantly ahead of Curiace in terms of "sovereign" civilization because he has understood that the glory offered by the state must put an end to mourning. Hence, the play characterizes emotions, tears, and grief as pre-heroic and pre-sovereign states of consciousness, driving this position home in the adverbs of time used in the dialogue. Because of his "humane attitude," Curiace sees himself as a kind of evolutionary late-comer that "still" grieves and feels:

> I thank the gods that I am not a Roman
> So as to keep some human feelings still.[13]

In contrast, Horace's self-understanding presents him as the protagonist of a "no more." When Curiace is officially named combatant by Alba Longa, Horace severs all family ties to him: "Alba names thee, and I no longer know thee."[14]

Against this "no more" Curiace is only able to muster yet another "still": "I know thee still; that is what breaks my heart,"[15] probably without knowing how right he is. For the play will indeed suggest that the figures placing family ties (and, thus, also mourning) above the state's offers of heroism will infallibly perish. More importantly still—and this is the real dramaturgic coup of the play—the destruction of these renegades is fully incorporated into the sovereign logic of sacrifice. The most prominent example next to Curiace is Horace's sister Camille, whose death is explicitly effected and justified by tears and mourning. Instead of giving her brother the recognition he thinks is due him as the victor returning home, she merely offers him the tears she believes she owes most of all to Curiace: "Take, then, my tears. They are his due from me."[16] In the ensuing dialogue she then repeatedly insists that neither Horace nor Rome have the right to proscribe her tears, which is also why she finally insults the entire state.[17] No one articulates this more clearly than Horace himself, right after he kills her:

> Thus whoever dares lament
> An enemy of Rome should find swift payment.[18]

---

13. Corneille trans. Lockert, 124 (lines 481–82).
14. Corneille trans. Lockert, 124 (line 502)
15. Corneille trans. Lockert, 124 (line 503).
16. Corneille trans. Lockert, 146 (line 1257) (translation modified).
17. Corneille trans. Lockert, 147 (lines 1283–87).
18. Corneille trans. Lockert 148 (lines 1321–22).

Camille's offense, according to Horace, is that she does not let *raison d'état* curb her emotions. In her backward recalcitrance she is just like her paramour Curiace: "still" seeing, and mourning, a "human being" in the citizen proclaimed an "enemy" by the state.[19]

Although the play—and the sovereign appearing at the end of it—make it plain that Horace should not have killed his sister, it is equally clear that they consider Camille's mourning to be a crime. Even her own father calls her a criminal and stresses that, because of this, she herself does not deserve to be mourned either: "Je ne plains point Camille, elle était criminelle."[20]

However, the fact that the sovereign simply dismisses old Horace's objection that, as his son acted in the heat of the moment, he did not commit a crime when he killed his sister shows that the sovereign fully realizes that his most important subject and henchman is also "criminal." But it would be amiss to interpret the sovereign's words as an explicit critique of sacrifice that would posthumously justify Camille's tears. In fact, the ending of the play takes the opposite stance when it fully and exemplarily integrates Horace—precisely because of his criminal act—not only into *raison d'état*, but also into the genuinely absolutist structure of sovereign law. The king will even go so far as to address the criminal Horace as the (co-) founder of this law. Thus Camille's death, instead of following a logic of sacrifice that cannot be assimilated by sovereignty, becomes the most important "sovereign" sacrifice of the entire play.

In order to grasp the consequences of this process it is indispensable to consider briefly the functioning of absolutist legislation. Carl Schmitt's attempt to define the principle of sovereignty and sovereign law with a famous recourse to the infamous "state of exception" dates its historical emergence back to modern absolutism. It is no coincidence that Schmitt invokes Jean Bodin's late sixteenth-century theory of sovereignty, which conceives of the sovereign *making* a law as someone *breaking* the law and then systematically derives all legal acts from this paradoxical figure: "All the other attributes and rights of sovereignty are included in this power of making and unmaking law, so that strictly speaking this is the unique attribute of

19. See, in this context, Susan Maslan's fascinating suggestion of reading the Camille figure as a transgression of the antagonism of citizen and human being already latent in the seventeenth century, in Maslan, "The Dream of the Feeling Citizen: Law and Emotion in Corneille and Montesquieu," *SubStance* 35/1 (2006): 69–84.

20. Line 1411: "I pity not Camille; she was wicked." Corneille trans. Lockert, 150.

sovereign power."[21] Schmitt focuses sovereignty on precisely this paradox: "The exception reveals most clearly the essence of the state's authority. The decision parts here from legal norm, and (to formulate it paradoxically) authority proves that to produce law it need not be based on law."[22]

The king in *Horace* explicitly calls upon such a paradox when he puts Horace's killing of Camille to trial in the final scene of the play. He insists that Horace's victory over the Curiatians does not make him the ruler over two states. Rather, Horace allows him to make his appearance as an eminently law-making figure: "But for him I would obey instead of making the law."[23] In as much as the king himself, however, repeatedly considers the killing of Camille as a "crime,"[24] he must, at one and the same time, break an established law when he pardons Horace. The act that makes a law is an act that breaks the law; and the king, in his function as king, lets the criminal both partake of, and precede, his own law-making breach of law.

> 'Tis in such subjects that a king's strength lies;
> And such as they are hence above all laws.[25]

Moreover, Horace's crime allows the sovereign to establish a foundation myth that guarantees and perpetuates the (re-)foundation of sovereign law as a breach of law. In his speech, the king recasts Horace as a second Romulus and urges Rome to treat the murder of Camille just as it treated the killing of Remus:

> She well can overlook in her deliverer
> That which she overlooked in her first founder.[26]

Romulus and Horace become mythical murderers who retroactively certify the (renewed) foundation of sovereign law in the form of an authorized crime. In as much as he declares both of them as "founders" of Rome, the king also endows his own (breach of) law with mythical authority. For his sovereign re-enactment legitimizes their crime by committing a crime that legitimizes itself. Just like Remus,

21. Jean Bodin, *Six Books of the Commonwealth*, trans.T. M. Tooley (Oxford: Basil Blackwell, 1955), 83.

22. Carl Schmitt, *Political Theology. Four Chapters on the Concept of Sovereignty*, trans. George Schwab (Chicago: University of Chicago Press 2005), 13.

23. My translation, line 1745.

24. Lines 1735, 1740.

25. Corneille trans. Lockert, 160; lines 1751–54.

26. Corneille trans. Lockert, 160; lines 1757–58.

Camille is (re-)inaugurated as the necessary sacrifice on which sovereign power will not only found itself from now on, but, as it were, will have "always already" founded itself in a mythical time.[27] This recourse to myth tends to obfuscate the temporality of the sovereign act of foundation and political self-legitimation: the king pretends to be sanctioning a political order allegedly in place for some time already, although he is actually legitimizing himself politically in the present state of exception.

Significantly, Romulus was already mentioned in the play's first scene when Sabine (while leaving out the fratricide) stressed that he originally hailed from Alba Longa. This origin allows the sovereign to sound the symbolic political death knell of the conquered city in the final act. By asserting that Alba Longa has also always already participated in the foundation (as well as the re-foundation) of Rome, Tulle, the king, does not only put an end to the civil war, he also manages, on an imaginary level, to fully incorporate the enemy city into the new sovereign Rome. These image politics culminate in a decree to bury the corpses of Camille and Curiace in a common grave. This posthumous wedding monumentalizes—that is, both exposes and preserves—the entire civil war as a sacrifice that was necessary for the establishment of sovereignty. Hence their monument is not intended as a site of familial mourning, but one of sovereign triumph.

The conception as well as the figuration of sovereign self-legitimation in *Horace* thus stand in an extremely complex tension to Benjamin's comments on the state of exception in the baroque *Trauerspiel*. In a critical appraisal of Carl Schmitt, Benjamin argues that the sovereign's self-empowerment in the state of exception is thwarted by his affectivity, exposing his "indecisiveness."[28] Hence, the state of exception reveals to the audience the sovereign's "state of creation"[29] and thus also the groundlessness of his reign. From this point of view, Corneille's play simply seems incomparable to the German mourning play. But at second glance it becomes evident that the insight into the groundlessness of a modern sovereignty enacted solely by the sovereign himself also founds *Horace*'s dramaturgy of the state of exception. Unlike in the *Trauerspiel*, however, *Horace*

27. On a principal legal level, Maslan is thus correct to observe, with reference to Agamben, that the king sketches an image of Rome that "has been since its very origin a state of exception." Maslan, "The Dream of the Feeling Citizen," 73.

28. Benjamin, *OGTD*, 71.

29. Ibid., 85.

is not interested in sorrowfully exposing this groundlessness. On the contrary, the play attempts to conceal the political arbitrariness of worldly power by means of a decisionistic act—or better, enactment—introducing a mythically founded crime as the eternal source of both the sovereign's and its own legitimation. This is reflected in the monumentalized proscription of mourning in a memorial of sacrifice that is not to be mourned.

On the level of dramaturgy, it is no coincidence that the play closes with words spoken by the sovereign. The audience's acclamation is the only thing that can possibly follow upon the law breaking/making act, the absolutist re-foundation of the state, and the mythical transfiguration of the criminals as well as the victims. But it is an entirely different question whether the king also *has the final say* in the play. In order to address this question it is necessary to consider the performance and the meta-theatricality of the play, which are in deep conflict with its dramaturgy and with its official politics of sovereignty.

This conflict is decisive because it allows the play to introduce a critical corrective to the conception of sovereignty it itself unfolds. For the performance, the meta-theatricality, and the scenic potential of mourning persistently disrupt, and thereby successfully thwart, the teleological orientation of the "sovereign" dramaturgy. In remaining precarious throughout the play, all prohibitions of mourning formulated in the text then ultimately threaten to affect the audience as well.

This problem is already manifest in the unity of place to which the play strictly and prototypically adheres. Underneath the register of the "Persons of the Play" Corneille specifies: *"The scene represents a hall in the home of the Horatii, in Rome."*[30] The meaning of the unity of place, so frequently analyzed in the scholarship, is not restricted to the classicist *bienséance* rule formulated later, in order to ban the onstage representation of bloodshed,[31] although Corneille is certainly also promoting this rule by moving all war operations off stage and representing them on stage in messenger's reports. But in *Horace* this

30. Corneille trans. Lockert, 110.
31. For the unity of place in *Horace*, and the precarious distinction of private and public sphere based on it, see the astute poetologically oriented reading of Hélène Merlin-Kajman, *L'absolutisme dans les lettres et la théorie des deux corps. Passions et politique* (Paris: Champion, 2000), 90–101.

has a remarkable consequence: the heroic feats and the overcoming of family ties to which the play programmatically subscribes are banned *from* the stage, while the tears and the grief the play is trying so hard to ban are almost the only things shown *on* stage. Although excluded on the political level, mourning remains omnipresent on the performative level. This is not to say that mourning becomes a nonpolitical phenomenon. On the contrary, it will prove eminently political because it pleads for non-sovereign politics and thus initiates, on a formal level, a reflection on tragedy immanent to the "classical" model of drama Corneille inaugurates.

The reasons in favor of banning grief given in, and by, the play take on a poetological and meta-theatrical dimension because they are articulated throughout in terms of spectatorship. Seeing sorrow and tears harbors the fundamental threat of affecting and consequently also of demoralizing the spectators. At the sight of a weeping Camille, Curiace fears he will lose his courage and he therefore threatens her with shame and misery.

> Curiace: Allez, ne m'aimez plus, ne versez plus de larmes,
> Ou j'oppose l'offense à de si fortes armes.

> Go, go! love me no more and weep no more,
> Or I shall strike back to defend myself
> Against such potent weapons.[32]

As the rhyme of "larmes" and "armes" indicates with remarkable clarity, tears prove a weapon that can overpower all weapons of war—and thus also sovereignty. If Curiace can be demoralized by merely watching Camille cry, then tears most certainly also pose a threat to the play's audience, which is, after all, again and again confronted with such a "sad sight."[33] The meta-theatrical level becomes even more obvious when Horace, of all people, tells his father to remove all weeping women from the battle field:

> Father, restrain these women; they are frantic;
> And above all, I beg thee, do not let them
> Go forth. Their love would bring them, with great noise
> Of cries and tears, to hinder our encounter;
> And what they are to us would make it natural

32. Corneille, lines 577–88; Corneille trans. Lockert, 127.
33. Corneille trans. Lockert, 127; line 579.

That folk should think their coming thus a vile
Artifice we contrived.[34]

These words complicate the dialogue between Curiace and Camille
at a decisive point. If Curiace remained a purely immanent mirroring
of the audience, Horace's verses now introduce the weeping women
themselves as *spectators that are to be excluded*. Unlike Curiace, he
is less afraid of being demoralized by the women's cries (although his
monologue does not categorically rule out this possibility). What he
fears most, though, is that the women will disrupt the entire battle.
For then the Curiatians could accuse the Horatians of having secretly
employed the female spectators to precisely this end; that is: of having used a "vile artifice" to hide their cowardice.

However, under close scrutiny the play exposes itself as such a
"vile artifice" inasmuch as it does not follow, but rather reverses, the
clear-cut spatial arrangement of combatants and mourners—or better yet: mourning spectators—thus also inverting the distinction of
public and private space. The play bans the heroes fighting in public
from the stage while opening a space for the women crying in private
on the stage; a space that ceaselessly threatens to affect the (public)
auditorium.

Far from overcoming this problem, the constant talk of necessary distinctions between family and state, private and public space
makes it all the more visible. The old Horace tries to keep Camille
from crying after the battle has ended by pointing out to her that
it is wrong to mourn "domestic losses" if they have given rise to
"public victories."[35] The play however, despite a dramatic development at first glance entirely in support of them, removes these "public victories" from the public space of the theater, while giving the
"domestic losses" center stage in it. This potential reversal of public
and private spheres also haunts the compromise Sabine offers Horace
after he kills Camille. She too differentiates between private and public space in order to establish the private realm as a legitimate place
for crying:

Let us participate in the public triumph
In public. In our own home let us mourn
Our private woes and think not of the blessings

34. Corneille trans. Lockert, 130; lines 695–700.
35. Corneille, lines 1175–76.

Common to all, but heed alone the heartache
Belonging to ourselves.[36]

On a meta-theatrical level, her hope of restricting tears to the private house proves futile because this private house is all the public theater audience ever sees. Thus, Sabine's proposition takes on an almost ironical note in the final line: the domestic "we" to whom she wants to confine seeing and grieving the "ills" that concern only "us" ("belonging to ourselves"), can have always already included the play's collective audience.

Because this possibility that the familial exclusivity "turns inside out" is always lurking on a performative level, the first representative *tragédie classique* threatens to transform its audience into "sad spectators." And this threat is strictly tied to the play's attempt to fully incorporate death into a sovereignly warranted logic of sacrifice. Mourning and tears, dramaturgically and thematically excluded for political reasons, reassert themselves performatively with full force, and the play exposes this tension again and again. In this sense, tears continue to be shed beyond the final act. That the sovereign re-founds his state in the house could be understood as a subjective effort to counteract this tendency and yet his transgression of public and private space will hardly suffice (the play is suggesting) to dry the tears that can so easily pass from stage to auditorium. For, if the play's performance thwarts the attempt to characterize grief and mourning as pre-sovereign phenomena, it also shows that the audience might be crying because of the sovereign act of foundation itself. The grave of Camille and Curiace, instead of banning mourning, would then become the place where the audience mourns nothing but the sovereign's dramaturgic triumph.

The way in which a baroque *Trauerspiel* (at least in Benjamin's view) and a *tragédie classique* conceive of and engage grief might differ fundamentally. In *Horace* at least, there is no trace of the empty heaven and the eternally mournful discrepancy between representation and meaning that Benjamin sees epitomized in the allegory. The fact that mourning in *Horace*, however, is also situated on a hardly controllable threshold between private and public space intimates a common *political commitment to mourning* shared by the *Trauerspiel* and the *tragédie classique*. For both models tie mourning to the

---

36. Corneille trans. Lockert, 149; lines 1371–74.

unfoundedness of sovereign power, illustrated in their kings' crooked crowns. Where the baroque *Trauerspiel* mourns, and by mourning also exposes, the crookedness of the crown, *Horace*, in contrast, mourns the sovereign act of trying to straighten the crown.

This momentous difference determines how the two dramatic models immanently reflect on their form and their genre, simultaneously distinguishing them from, and aligning them to, one another. The baroque *Trauerspiel* on the one hand, by mourning the historical loss of tragedy, grieves at the absence of an ambivalent tragic sacrifice capable of inaugurating a different kind of politics. The *tragédie classique* on the other hand, by opposing the ambivalence of sacrifice to a sovereign positing a non-ambiguous meaning of death, mourns his usurpation of potentially ambivalent, and hence also non-sovereign, politics. What joins the two models is thus a desire for tragedy that, despite the different perspectives determined by their "contrastive nature," characterizes both of them as *Trauerspiele*.

—Translated by Michael E. Auer

TIMOTHY HAMPTON

La foi des traités: Baroque History, International Law, and the Politics of Reading in Corneille's *Rodogune*

> Ruins of cities and castles were piled up
> in a jumble, next to great treasures.
> When he asked he was told that these represented
> treaties and badly hidden plots.
>
> —Ariosto, *Orlando furioso*, 34.79[1]

I. POLITICAL READING

In April of 1547, the Holy Roman Emperor Charles V invaded Germany. Charles had been working for several years, both diplomatically and militarily, to limit the spread of Protestantism in Central Europe, all the while hoping to impose and strengthen Imperial control over the stubbornly independent German states. At the Battle of Muhlberg on April 24, he defeated a coalition of German princes headed by Landgraf Philip of Hesse. Following the battle a treaty was hammered out between Charles and Philip, with help from Philip's nephew, the ambitious Maurice of Saxony. After initial hesitation, caused by the fear that the Emperor was adding new clauses to the agreement as they went along (such as the requirement that all of Philip's subjects abjure Protestantism), Philip consented to sign. The treaty stipulated that Philip would raze all of his fortresses, give up his artillery, abandon all earlier treaties, turn over all prisoners, promise to support the Emperor against the Turks, and pay 150,000 écus in gold. Upon signing he would be free to return home.

Or so it seemed. Philip signed a draft of the treaty and fell to his knees before the Emperor. Upon rising he was taken into custody. Charles's deputies met his protests with the claim that his captivity

---

1. All translations in this essay, unless otherwise indicated, are by the author.

YFS 124, *Walter Benjamin's Hypothetical French "Trauerspiel,"* ed. Bjornstad and Ibbett, © 2013 by Yale University.

was sanctioned by the very treaty he had just signed. The Emperor insisted that the clause in the treaty stipulating that Philip should not be held a prisoner for a single day—in sixteenth-century German, "nicht in enich tag"—in fact read that he should not be held prisoner eternally—"nicht in evich tag." The dispute spun around the difference, in sixteenth-century script, between the letter N and the letter V, between *enich* (once, only) and *evich* (permanent, eternal), a graphic uncertainty which, in this case, marks the difference between immediate freedom and indefinite imprisonment. "When will my imprisonment end?" cried the incensed Landgraf in the account provided by Jacques-Auguste de Thou, the great chronicler of the period. "When it pleases His Majesty," answered Charles's minion, the unctuous Duke of Alba, adding that this might not come for fourteen years. "His Majesty would never do anything against his sworn word," he added—a remark which, according to de Thou, plunged Philip into despair.[2] As it turned out Charles kept Philip in custody for close to four years, claiming that he had legal right to do so because of the treaty that Philip himself had signed.

De Thou notes that Charles's perverse demonstration of "subtlety" in reading the treaty had the effect of harming his credibility in the eyes of many of his followers. The Duke of Eblebe, who had brokered the initial terms of the agreement, was so affected by the "sad end" of the negotiation that he died of melancholy soon after. Philip's nephew Maurice begged Charles to release his uncle, regardless of whether there had been an error in spelling or a mistake in pronunciation, noting that many men of honor had given their word in support of the treaty. Charles refused, believing that he could keep Maurice under control by holding onto his uncle. For his part, Maurice concealed his resentment of the Emperor, waiting until a propitious time to avenge what he called "the intolerable, brutal and continual degradation coming from Spain."[3] The settling of accounts came in 1552, when Maurice and his allies won the support of the new (Catholic) king Henry II of France, through the Peace of Chambord. Whereas Henry's father Francis I had only given money to the restive German princes against the hated Hapsburg Emperor, Henry was willing to commit

2. Jacques-Auguste de Thou, *Histoire universelle depuis 1543 jusqu'en 1607* (London, 1734), 1:267. De Thou's history, originally written in Latin, first appeared in 1604 and was republished many times in both Latin and French over the next two centuries.

3. I quote from Wim Blockmans's *Emperor Charles V: 1500–1558*, trans. Isola van den Hoven-Vardon (New York: Arnold Publishing, 2002), 98.

troops, and they helped drive Charles into a humiliating retreat. This in turn led to the withdrawal of support for the Empire by Maximilian of Hungary and forced Charles to make major concessions on the legitimacy of the (Protestant) German princes. The German princes themselves took the dramatic step of withdrawing from further participation in the meetings of Christian leaders that were just getting underway in Italy—those meetings would later come to be called the Council of Trent and would decide the future shape of Christendom.

Much as I might like to, I don't presume to claim that Charles V's deliberate misconstrual of a single letter in a peace treaty led to the eventual breakup of Christianity. However this strange episode in the history of reading (which subsequently became a commonplace among political theorists) helps set the context for my argument in this essay.[4] For one thing, it engages the tensions during the period between structures of international, ecclesiastically based, political order (in this case, the Holy Roman Empire) and emerging national states—a topic that is important for a consideration of the French dimensions of Walter Benjamin's work on tragedy. Second, it introduces the important political tool of the peace treaty, which, I will argue, functions as a synecdoche, in early modern literature, of new developments in international political culture. I will argue that a consideration of the treaty can help us grasp some of the issues that Benjamin links to the rise of historically based tragic drama.

The moment of political reading just evoked places us at the heart of the great shift that Benjamin links to the origin of the German baroque *Trauerspiel*. Benjamin describes the form of the *Trauerspiel* as involving the grafting of traditional Christian literary forms onto the "pragmatic events" associated with classical politics. He notes that the medieval genres of the mystery play and medieval chronicle come down to the baroque only in fragmentary form, as vestiges of an earlier order of Christian transcendence that now no longer exists. Whereas Christian forms present all of world history as a story of redemption, "the *Haupt- und Staatsaktion* deals with only a part of

---

4. See my discussion of Bodin, below. Also, several decades later the French political theorist Gabriel Naudé would evoke Maurice's strategic counter-attack as one of the first instances of what he would call the "coup d'état," the "modern" political gesture deployed by rulers to save their sovereignty at the cost of their moral ideals. See Gabriel Naudé, *Considérations politiques sur les coups d'état*, ed. Louis Marin (Paris: Éditions de Paris, 1988): 102. Naudé's notorious "secret" treatise on political violence dates from 1639.

pragmatic events." By the time of the German baroque, says Benjamin, "Christendom or Europe is divided into a number of European Christian provinces whose historical actions no longer claim to be integrated in the process of redemption." To respond to this rupture between political disunion and spiritual longing, the "formal world" of the *Trauerspiel* "is revealed."[5]

It might be useful to think about Benjamin's contrast between Christian eschatology and "pragmatic events" in more explicitly formal terms than he does. As he hints, the "part of pragmatic events" that the tragedy attempts to engage implies a set of very specific actions, a moment of crisis that he calls the *Haupt- und Staatsaktion*, but that students of French tragedy would recognize as the limited scope of events surrounding tragic action. By contrast, as he notes, the great martyr dramas of the Germans and of Calderón bring human contingency to expression through dialogue with larger theological themes and more extensive narrative forms.

These formal differences are also ethical differences. The Christian thematics of redemption mean that early modern tragedy—in all of its guises—bears, in varying degrees of intensity, the traces of Christian and classical moral philosophy (themes of charity, friendship, fidelity), even as they seem to point to an emerging world order in which these themes perdure as mere quaint echoes of an earlier dispensation. Tragic form struggles to mediate these two sets of values.

These tensions are imprinted on Benjamin's own discourse. He asserts that the *Trauerspiel* emerges when "Christendom or Europe" has become fragmented. Yet "Christendom" and "Europe" are not the same, as Benjamin's account of the emergence of modern political culture indicates. It is the role of the baroque to mediate the transition from a Christian imperial model of history to a modern world of competing states from which the possibility of transcendence has receded.[6] But Benjamin's own formulation suggests that the baroque must also mediate between local, or "national" political cultures and

---

5. Walter Benjamin, *The Origin of German Tragic Drama*, trans. John Osborne (London: New Left Books, 1985), 78. Hereafter cited as *OGTD*.

6. The distinction between theological order and political order goes, in fact, to the heart of Charles V's invasion of the German states. For the invasion itself was an ambiguous sign. Like the treaty, its meaning depends on how we read it. Officially, it was undertaken to heal the wounds of the Christian community and thereby to guarantee the redemption of those who had fallen out with the Church—that traditional function of the Christian community the eclipse of which underpins the emergence of the *Trauerspiel*. Yet secretly Charles acknowledged that his actions were designed

the changing dynamics of "international" relations. The key figure in Benjamin's account of baroque culture is the sovereign who is, Benjamin notes, "the representative of history." The sovereign must be so deeply versed in political history as to become himself the ideal author of tragedy. Baroque culture places him in a situation of instability or "emergency," caught between a theocratic order and a modern stable political system. His response to this instability is to claim his power as dictator: "The ruler is designated from the outset as the holder of dictatorial power if war, revolt, or other catastrophes should lead to a state of emergency."[7]

It is worth considering Benjamin's list of threats to the sovereign—"war, revolt, or other catastrophes." "War" and "revolt" are themselves forms of catastrophe that unfold on very different stages, and the difference between them was a matter of debate among theorists of the age. The notion of "revolt" points to the entire current of thought—beginning with Luther's comments on the peasant wars—on the question of dealing with local insurrection. The problem of "war" is the problem of what we now call "foreign policy." Thus within Benjamin's own discussion of the breakup of Christianity into diverse "European Christian provinces" there is also inscribed the problem of how baroque culture can engage with new forms of international relations and the accompanying development of international law. Benjamin argues that the *Trauerspiel* takes on the burden of resolving two visions of history, of offering "a secular solution" to the theological and moral problem of the individual soul in search of transcendence. I will suggest that baroque culture also takes on the task of mediating the relationship between the contingent space of discrete "court cultures" and the emergence of the broader space of a new international order.[8]

The break-up of the Holy Roman Empire and the decline of a unified Christendom are mediated by a number of new political tools. Among these was a newly important genre of political writing—the

---

to "punish those who disobey[ed]" his political authority. I quote from a letter from Charles to his son Philip II cited in Blockmans, 94.

7. Benjamin, *OGTD*, 65.

8. On the problem of the national and the international in conceptualizations of the baroque, see Jane O. Newman, *Benjamin's Library: Modernity, Nation, and the Baroque* (Ithaca: Cornell University Press, 2011), especially chap. 1. For a strongly "nationally" oriented modern baroque, see Marc Fumaroli's preface to Victor Tapié's *Baroque et classicisme* (Paris: Livre de Poche, 1980), 7–42.

peace treaty. During the years around the Peace of Westphalia (1648), leading to the development of the so-called "states system" of European foreign relations (replacing the early fictions of Empire and *respublica christiana* whose demise Benjamin alludes to), the production, authorization, and interpretation of peace treaties was an important theme in political theory, history writing, and literature. I will argue in what follows that the dynamics of treaty-making and treaty-reading raise a particular set of problems that shape certain aspects of the new forms of historical drama that come to prominence in seventeenth-century France. To be sure, these problems help shape the emergence of new dramatic forms across Europe. However the French response to the great problems that preoccupy Benjamin is distinct, and I will point to some of the features of French historical drama that both intersect with Benjamin's account of the *Trauerspiel* and lend the French tradition its specificity.[9]

The emergence of what we might call a "baroque" historical vision—a newly international focus that replaces the dynastic and national histories of the Renaissance—intersects with the new political tool of the negotiated treaty in ways that have both thematic and formal implications for literature. Not only does literary culture in the early seventeenth century begin to confront the dynamics of an international space defined increasingly by discrete national states—in contrast to the imperial and Christian fictions of earlier centuries—but political disorder is often depicted as a problem of linguistic disorder. Thus Montaigne, writing in the 1570s, laments that political unrest and linguistic misprision are intrinsically linked.

> Most of the occasions for the troubles of the world are Grammatical. Our legal conflicts are born from debates over the interpretation of laws; most of our wars are born of the failure to express clearly the agreements and treaties between princes.[10]

9. For background on the history of the treaty-making during the period, see the opening chapters of Mario Toscano's *The History of Treaties and International Politics* (Baltimore: The Johns Hopkins Press, 1966). On the period that interests me specifically in this essay, the mid-seventeenth century, see Peter Sahlins, *Boundaries: The Making of France and Spain in the Pyrenees* (Berkeley: University of California Press, 1989), chapter 1, and Jesús María Usunáriz, *España y sus tratados internacionales: 1516–1700* (Pamplona: EUNSA, 2006), chapters 3–4.

10. Michel de Montaigne, "Apologie de Raymond Sebond," in *Œuvres complètes,* ed. Albert Thibaudet and Maurice Rat (Paris: Gallimard, 1962), 508.

This connection between the circulation of texts and the eruption of violence raises the question of how cultural discourses—the writings of philosophers, theorists, poets, historians, and so on—work to mitigate the political dangers of such moments of fragility. What kinds of hermeneutic strategies are worked out to help frame or corral moments at which the reading of a single text can have disastrous consequences for the lives of peoples?

The relationship between political organization and literary interpretation had been raised as early as 1516. Erasmus of Rotterdam, the great humanist, had argued in his manual of political advice, the *Education of the Christian Prince* (dedicated to the future Charles V, whose hermeneutic wizardry we have just seen at work), that all treaties should be read allegorically. If your neighbor seems to have violated the letter of the treaty, suggests Erasmus, that doesn't mean he has violated its spirit. One should ignore specific violations to preserve the sense of charity and "public utility" that governs the relationships between princes. Erasmus may be the last major European writer to claim that the narrative of Christian redemption mentioned by Benjamin can operate in equilibrium with more secular forms of political power.[11]

Modern accounts of the treaty as a text appear in the decades after Erasmus, with the two great Continental founders of modern international statecraft, Jean Bodin and Hugo Grotius. In the fifth book of his 1576 treatise *De la république*, Bodin locates the dynamics of what would later come to be called "foreign policy" in the changing nature of the "faith" that peoples place in each other. For it is faith, he notes, that is the single "foundation" for the justice on which all republics, alliances, and societies are "founded."[12] Yet the problem with international politics, says Bodin, is that faith is undermined by the process of treaty-making itself. For treaty-making is inherently "unjust," that is, unbalanced. Since most treaties take place between unequal partners it is no wonder that they are generally broken. The key to making a good treaty is thus to make certain that both sides

11. Erasmus of Rotterdam, *The Education of the Christian Prince*, ed. Lisa Jardine, trans. Neil M. Cheshire and Michael J. Heath (Cambridge: Cambridge University Press, 1997), 93–95.

12. Jean Bodin, *Les six livres de la république*, ed. Christiane Frémont (Paris: Fayard, 1986), 5:189. The entire sixth chapter of Book V, "La foy des alliez," is relevant to the discussion of treaties.

have entered into it free of duress and that all ambiguity has been scrubbed from the language of the agreement. For example, Bodin notes that treaties often stipulate that signatories must not engage in activities that are iniquitous; and that both sides are required only to engage in activities that are "just." However, he points out that these phrases, intended to be general in nature, are then taken in specific as a way of justifying political advantage: "he who is bound will take the general term 'just' and apply it to a specific instance."[13] Misreading the language of the treaty authorizes political advantage, as in the egregious demonstration of "subtlety" we saw in the example with which I began, where Charles V, in Bodin's account (the episode had now become a commonplace) "performed his subtlety on a single letter" in order to keep control of Philip of Hesse.[14] For this reason, says Bodin, one must "clarify and make specific all cases that one thinks iniquitous."[15] The key to making treaties is to account for all specific possibilities. Otherwise, the general categories of moral obligation—those very aspects of the treaty that link it to the large moral and ethical concerns of Christian princes—become escape hatches.

For Bodin the language of the peace treaty bears the burden of offering the "secular solution," to recall again Benjamin's phrase, to the disintegration of Christian harmony. The treaty is a text that must mediate the pressures brought to bear by the two conflicting models of history evoked by Benjamin: the morally inflected narrative of Christian redemption history and the amoral demands of the current "emergency."[16] For Bodin, treaty-making is a question of justice and fairness, of the "faith" between princes. Yet treaties are no sooner signed than they are pushed to the breaking point by the "subtleties" of their readers.

Bodin's concern with the nuances of political language is picked up and developed in legal terms in Hugo Grotius's famous book *On the Laws of War and Peace* (1625), which inaugurates the discourse of modern International Law. Grotius devotes Chapter 16 of Book 2 of that work, titled "On Interpretation," to the language of treaties.

13. Ibid., 190.
14. Ibid., 210.
15. Ibid., 190. On the variety of factors shaping oath-taking generally during this period, see Paolo Prodi, *Il Sacramento del potere* (Bologna: Il Mulino, 1992), especially chapter 8.
16. See Benjamin, *OGTD*, 77–85.

His focus is on developing techniques of reading and writing that can bring the "internal acts" [*interni actus*] that shape treaty-making into phase with the language that is enjoined to express them. To do this he studies the "inference of intent" that may be drawn from the language of the treaty. "The measure of correct interpretation is the inference of intent from the most probable indications."[17] Put differently, the interpretation of the treaty must account for and choose among all possible implications that might have been intended in its language, or that might emerge from it. A serious reading of a treaty must forestall from the outset the kind of misreading we saw Charles V undertake in the scene depicted earlier. Like Bodin, Grotius worries about the tension between what he calls "broad meanings" and "narrow meanings" of words. He stresses that the "common advantage" must always be given consideration, and when several meanings are possible, "that which is broadest should be chosen, just as the masculine gender is taken for the common gender, and an indefinite expression for a universal."[18]

It should be clear, even from this brief survey, that as we move from Erasmus, to Bodin, to Grotius, we can see an increasing shift away from the moral underpinnings that shape interpretation in the Christian commonwealth toward a concern with fixing writing and reading in such a way as to forestall the possibilities for "subtleties" of the kind practiced by Charles V. For Erasmus, the interpretation of treaties is rooted in a concern for the integrity of the Christian community. For Bodin, what is at issue is fixing the language of the treaty. For Grotius, what matters is developing a hermeneutic approach that can respond to the variety of meanings extracted from that language. Yet in all of these instances the treaty is acknowledged to be at once binding and imperfect. It is never sufficient in itself to shape human action. It is a document designed to impose structure on human desire across time. However it can never stand alone. Theorists of the political agreements seek constantly to ground political action in the letter of the treaty, all the while hinting at allegorical or moral reading strategies that might supplement a literal reading and guard against interpretive distortion.

17. Hugo Grotius, *De Jure Belli ac Pacis Libri Tres*, trans. Francis W. Kelsey (Oxford: Clarendon Press, 1925). This work is in two volumes, volume 1 contains the translation. I have just cited 1:411 and, for the Latin, 2:274.
18. Grotius, 1:414; 2:278.

II. DRAMATIC READING

The link between linguistic text and political action set forth by theorists such as Grotius and Bodin takes on interesting resonances when it is placed in dialogue with that literary form that most directly engages issues of action, historical contingency, and individual will. This is the historical drama that comes to the forefront in Europe at the end of the sixteenth century, with Marlowe and Shakespeare, then Lope de Vega, then Pierre Corneille. It is Corneille whom we might take as the French counterpart to the tradition of German *Trauerspiel* evoked by Benjamin.

After his early dabbling in comedy and the first great political cycle of plays that made his reputation (*Le Cid, Cinna, Polyeucte, Horace*), Corneille turned his hand to a number of different dramatic projects. These included a trilogy of plays that seems to reflect the political struggles of the Fronde (*Nicomède, Don Sanche d'Aragon, Pertharite*), followed by an immensely long reworking of the story of Jason and the Argonauts, *La toison d'or*. Yet whereas most of the great early tragedies had focused on the establishment or foundation of a state, beginning as early as the 1640s thematic material increasingly involved the management of empire, the relationships between large and small states, between colonies and central imperial authority—that is, questions of international relations and treaty-making. Corneille first engaged the question of the treaty in a central way in 1644, in *Rodogune, Princesse des Parthes*, a play to which I would now like to turn.[19]

Corneille took the material for *Rodogune* principally from the Hellenistic historiographer Arrian. It is the one play he wrote, said Corneille later in his "Examen," for which he had the greatest tenderness.[20] Here is a bare-bones résumé of the backdrop to the play: When Nicanor, the king of the Syrians, betrays his wife Cléopatre to take up with Rodogune, a princess from the enemy kingdom of Parthia, Cléopatre has him killed. Through a series of political reversals she then takes Rodogune as her prisoner. However, she is soon threatened

---

19. For an account of Corneille's engagement with problems of diplomatic recognition and tragic form see Timothy Hampton, *Fictions of Embassy: Literature and Diplomacy in Early Modern Europe* (Ithaca: Cornell University Press, 2010), chapter 5.

20. Pierre Corneille, *Théatre Choisi*, ed. Maurice Rat (Paris: Garnier, 1961), 353. All references to *Rodogune* will be line numbers of this edition (translations mine).

militarily by the Parthians, and to appease them she agrees to a treaty according to which she will give her oldest son's hand in marriage to Rodogune. The new couple, one a Syrian and one a Parthian, will then usher in an age of peace and harmony. As the play opens, Cléopatre is about to set in motion the realization of the treaty through the betrothal.

Thus Corneille sets up from the outset a treaty that hangs over the entire action that follows. The background to the play projects a scenario of peacemaking in the marriage of the Syrian prince and the Parthian princess. There are, however, as we might expect, complications, and much embellishment on the basic historical material. First off, in Corneille's version Cléopatre turns out to have two sons, Antiochus and Seleucus, whom she has had raised in a neighboring province and only brought back to Syria just before the action of the play begins, in preparation for the betrothal that will seal the treaty. The treaty has established peace, but it exists only in a virtual form, awaiting final implementation. Moreover, not only are there two sons, but those sons are twins. So Rodogune has two potential mates. And the hitch is that nobody, except Cléopatre, knows which is older. She has kept the order of their birth a secret in order to maintain her hold on power. Now, as the play begins, Cléopatre is about to reveal who the oldest son is and therefore who will marry Rodogune and take over the throne according to the dictates of the treaty.

At one level, Cléopatre has solved the great political problem that haunts many of Corneille's early plays—the problem of royal succession and the threat posed by ambitious sons to their parents. Here, because the sons are potential rivals, there's no point in killing the parent, since one would only be helping one's rival. Yet the sons, it turns out, are not rivals. We learn very early on, in Act 1, scene 2, that Cléopatre's sons have no interest in murdering Rodogune. *Au contraire*, they are both in love with her. They agree that whoever was born first should rule and marry Rodogune, not because either of them wants political power, but because the woman they love deserves to be a queen. As Cléopatre's confidant Laonice puts it in the set-up to the action: "La paix finit la haine, et, pour comble aujourd'hui,/ Dois-je dire de bonne ou mauvaise fortune?/ Nos deux princes tous deux adorent Rodogune" ["Peace has put an end to hatred and, as the climax today,/ Should I say the good news or the bad?/ Both of our princes adore Rodogune"] (286–88).

So far so good for treaty-making, we might assume. However, no sooner does the action get underway than Cléopatre calls in both sons and reveals that since she is the only one who knows which son is older, she will designate as oldest that son who is most willing to do her bidding. Whoever wants to rule must kill Rodogune, thereby exacting vengeance for her having stolen the heart of Cléopatre's dead husband: "If you want to reign, here is the price of the throne: /Between two sons whom I love equally/ The only right of primogeniture is adherence to my cause/ The eldest will be named by the death of Rodogune."[21] Against the reconciliation of the "happy day" that, in Laonice's opening words will "stifle vengeance," Cléopatre proposes what Naudé called the "coup d'état," a violent political action designed to keep herself in power.[22]

For her part, Rodogune soon learns of Cléopatre's plan and considers escape. However her informant, the Phraatian ambassador Oronte, points out that in the eyes of the world—and especially her own father—she will be seen to have violated the terms of the treaty: "And the king, more irritated against you than Cleopatra/ Seeing you bring on a new war,/ Will blame your fears and our wavering,/ For having dared to doubt the faith of the treaties."[23] The treaty binds Rodogune and keeps her in Syria. The only option, says Oronte, is to stay put and find a way to turn the plot around, to follow what Rodogune calls a moment later "the order of treaties," while escaping alive.

Thus the play is built on the opposition between, on the one hand, a legal document that structures the possibilities for action on the part of the characters, and, on the other, the capacity of political agents to generate plots—both political and literary. Corneille uses the motif of the peace treaty to posit a baseline of literalness, a set of constraints against which the actions of the characters must unfold—the very kind of thing envisioned by Bodin as he tried to imagine a treaty that would not be prey to "subtlety." Yet all of the actors are

---

21. (642–45).

22. On the strangeness of this political succession see Michel Prigent, *Le héros et l'État dans la tragédie de Pierre Corneille* (Paris: Presses Universitaires de France, 1988), 225–30. The dynamics of the relationship between the brothers has been explored with insight by Richard Goodkin in *Birth Marks: The Tragedy of Primogeniture in Pierre Corneille, Thomas Corneille, and Jean Racine* (Philadelphia: University of Pennsylvania Press, 2000), Chapter 6.

23. *Rodogune*, lines 811–14.

engaged in what we might call creative acts of reading. The two boys are willing to submit themselves to both the letter and the spirit of the treaty, giving up love to the terms of inheritance it stipulates. By contrast, Cléopatre has elected for a reading of the treaty that is based in deferral. She has kept her boys away in order to prepare her own actions. By pretending to embrace the terms of what she later calls the "shameful peace," she buys time to overturn it.[24] "Time is a greater treasure than most people think," as she says sententiously, early on.[25] Rodogune, by contrast, must remain in Syria to satisfy the letter of the treaty, even as she seeks to undermine its spirit.[26]

Clearly Corneille is asking us to think about the possibilities and limitations of an emerging political culture based upon international laws and agreements. The social stakes of this questioning of the treaty are made clear in Act 4, when Antiochus confronts Rodogune. Just like Cléopatre, Rodogune has been playing her cards close to her vest and no one knows what her heart holds. Antiochus asks her to reveal whether she could love one of the two brothers. He says that he would gladly sacrifice himself if peace could be established and she could be made queen; but he and his brother need to know if she could take one of them as a mate. She reveals that she does indeed love one of them, and that it is he. But she cannot simply marry him and accede to the throne. For the very fact that he has come and asked her to make a choice between him and his brother has suddenly brought back to her memory Cléopatre's assassination of her former lover, Nicanor, Antiochus's father and Cléopatre's husband. Before she can love anybody, says Rodogune, Nicanor's death must be avenged by the murder of Cléopatre:

> A strict duty opposes this love:
> Don't blame me, you are the reason;

---

24. Ibid., line 647.

25. Ibid., line 515.

26. On the theme of dissimulation and plot making, see Hélène Merlin-Kajman, *L'absolutisme dans les lettres et la théorie des deux corps* (Paris: Champion, 2000), Chapters 5–6, as well as Katherine Ibbett, *The Style of the State in French Theater, 1630–1660* (London: Ashgate, 2009), 97–108. The psychological dimensions of Cléopatre's mad obsession with power are explored in Mitchell Greenberg's *Subjectivity and Subjugation in Seventeenth-Century Drama and Prose: The Family Romance of French Classicism* (Cambridge: Cambridge University Press, 1992), 87–112.

> You brought it back to life by forcing on me a choice
> This breaks the favorable laws of your treaties.
> Witness the strange destiny, for me, of a dead father,
> If you leave me free, I must avenge him.[27]

The beautiful irony here is that the dead father whom she must avenge is Antiochus's father, not hers. Yet even more striking is the sense that so long as the treaty was in place as a kind of virtual structuring document ("the favorable laws"), without having been fully realized, she could forget the past. Now, since Cléopatre has brought things to a crisis, the treaty can be only be fulfilled through a gesture of matricide. As Rodogune continues a moment later, "Let us return to the strictures imposed on me by the peace, / Since freeing myself would mean losing you forever."[28] Only under the shadow of the treaty, in the limbo that has preceded the play, can Rodogune love Antiochus and not demand that he commit matricide. Indeed, the very attempt to force her to choose and act on her choice has brought back to life a sleeping desire for revenge. Whereas Cléopatre first confronted her sons by instructing them to act according to her precepts, what she called "the faith of a mother,"[29] Rodogune now echoes that phrase when she herself is unable to remain within the precepts of peacemaking: "a memory brings back a remembered task/ Which the faith of the treaties can no longer control."[30] The tension between the "faith" of the mother and the "faith" of treaties is what the play must resolve.

Thus it would seem that we can have modern political culture, based on agreements and treaties, but only if we also engage in matricide. This sense of a barely repressed desire for vengeance reminds us of the historical context for the play. It comes at a key moment in French foreign and domestic policy, before the Fronde years, directly after the death of Louis XIII and in the wake of recently uncovered secret alliances between Gaston d'Orléans, Cinq-Mars, and Spain. Here it is precisely the deployment of the treaty that is presumed to erase the ancestral and nobiliary rivalries that characterized much of the early decades of the century. As Antiochus says to Cléopatre a moment later "Should we have been able to predict this hidden hatred/

---

27. *Rodogune*, lines 1211–16.
28. Ibid., lines 1225–26.
29. Ibid., line 183.
30. Ibid., lines 1016–18.

Which the faith of the treaties had not succeeded in extirpating?"[31] The good faith of treaty-making is supposed to scrub away hidden hatred, to cleanse the world of the dynamics of revenge culture. But it can only do so as long as it is not fully implemented. Now, however, says Rodogune to Antiochus, his own dead father is speaking to his son through her very voice. "He borrows my voice in order the better to be heard."[32] In lieu of the modern representatives who speak with the voices of their princes to negotiate peace, here we get a voice from the dead. Shades of Hamlet![33]

The action of the play thus involves a series of readings of, to use Grotius's phrase, the "implications" of the treaty. For the two boys, the treaty imposes a duty that they are willing to accept only because they have agreed to respect their "perfect friendship," a notion of concord that goes back to Renaissance and classical theories of friendship. Indeed, for the brothers the treaty can work precisely because concord already subtends it (and in this regard they seem very close to someone like Erasmus, for whom treaties reside on ideals of community).[34] Put differently, they can fulfill the treaty because they have no need of a treaty to begin with. By contrast, for Rodogune the treaty can be fulfilled through matrimony, but only if it is also violated through a matricide that seems to rekindle the ancestral revenge culture that it would appear to be designed to dispel. For Cléopatre the treaty must be used as a delaying document, as she prepares her own coup. Here, no less than in Charles V's strange reading of his accord with Philip of Hesse, the vehicle of the treaty itself, as a political tool, seems to be on trial. In Corneille's world peace treaties emerge as documents that place constraints on political action, yet by so doing they unleash powers of the very type that they were designed to neutralize.

The resolution of the plot seems to underscore the instability of moments of negotiated concord. Unable to break apart the bond of

31. Ibid., 1307–8.

32. Ibid., 1172.

33. The curious obsession with past events that permeates the play has been noted by John Lyons in *The Tragedy of Origins: Pierre Corneille and Historical Perspective* (Stanford: Stanford University Press, 1996), 76. It is explored with insight by Christopher Braider in Chapter 2 of *Indiscernable Counterparts: The Invention of the Text in French Classical Drama* (Chapel Hill: University of North Carolina Press, 2002).

34. For a nuanced and learned account that traces the friendship of the two brothers back to the "parfaite amitié" of Renaissance and classical moral philosophy, see Ullrich Langer, *Perfect Friendship: Studies in Literature and Moral Philosophy from Boccaccio to Corneille* (Geneva: Droz, 1994), Chapter 7.

friendship between her two sons, or to derail their love for Rodogune, Cléopatre proceeds to give primogeniture to Antiochus and betroth him to Rodogune. In this way, she says, she can stay true to the letter of the treaty—"follow point for point the peace treaties."[35] So at last she seems to have embraced the world of international concord. The treaty is about to be fulfilled by marriage—yet only at the instant that it will be destroyed. For, mistrustful of her "oldest" son, Cléopatre has poisoned the wine that Antiochus and Rodogune will drink to seal their union. As they raise the poisoned chalice the action is interrupted by a messenger, who reveals that Cléopatre has murdered her other son, Séleucus. Unmasked, Cléopatre drinks the poison herself, leaving vengeance, as she puts it, to the gods. So the treaty is fulfilled as a dramatic plot device. Rodogune and Antiochus remain to celebrate marriage and the melding of their two peoples. Yet it is not fulfilled as as a document designed to forge peace out of the political situation at the play's outset. For it is now no longer needed. One of the signatories has committed suicide. It remains as a mere ruin of its own intentions, brought to actualization by the unfolding of tragic form.

III. REDEMPTIVE WRITING AND TRAGIC FORM

The death of Cléopatre brings us back to the problem that preoccupied Walter Benjamin, the question of how a symbolic form like the *Trauerspiel* might mediate the eschatological impulse of Christian history with the particularities of everyday struggles for political domination. For Benjamin the mediating structure that brings those two areas of experience together is the allegorical "play within the play," the characteristic literary trope of the baroque which offers a vision of eternal beauty that nevertheless knows itself to be contingent and fabricated.

By contrast, says Benjamin, the "new drama throughout Europe" to which Corneille belongs is marked by "the rejection of the eschatology of the religious dramas."[36] Yet narrative redemption from time takes its own, secular form in Corneille. In the tradition of classical French drama that Corneille both authorizes and defines, the struggle for transcendence is a struggle not for Christian salvation, but for domination through time and of time. This domination is emblema-

35. *Rodogune*, line 1586.
36. Benjamin, *OGTD*, 81.

tized by the peace treaty, which aims to structure the future through a kind of speech act. However, that text is in tension, in the world of *Rodogune*, with the impulses of the characters, who want to write their own future.

This will to persevere takes its most powerful form in the figure of Cléopatre, who, when she declares her willingness to base the birth order of her sons on her will to power, becomes a maker of fictions. The tyrant is indeed, as Benjamin says, "the representative of history." Yet here that domination of history is rendered problematic by the presence of the peace treaty. Cléopatre emerges as the figure for the historian or writer who shapes the narrative of royal domination through succession. Yet she must struggle to define the relationship between, on the one hand, the textual artefact that is the peace treaty, with its insistence, following Bodin, on the letter of the law, and, on the other hand, the capacity of those in power to write their own plots through fiction-making, dissimulation, trickery. Indeed, what is remarkable about *Rodogune* is that it deploys the peace treaty as a kind of ideal instance of political writing aimed toward the future, and against which all of the characters must somehow struggle. The treaty is the ideal text that nonetheless must be supplemented by tragedy. In this regard, the treaty stands as the document that structures the play and toward which, through the unfolding of tragic form, it aims. For a writer like Corneille, whose career is co-extensive with the rise of International Law and the birth of a new, post-Imperial European order, the peace treaty functions as a kind of ghostly text. It recalls the ideals of community evoked by Benjamin's account of the breakup of Christendom, even as it becomes a central structuring element in the emergence of a new cultural and political order. Whereas Cléopatre seeks to work against the peace treaty to write her own narrative, Corneille absorbs it into his text, as both endpoint and origin.[37]

---

37 This gesture of fiction making or "plotting" has been read in diverse ways. For Ibbett, *The Style of the State*, 120–122, it helps us understand the author's relationship to political power. For Braider, *Indiscernible Counterparts*, 153–55, it is linked to a new sense of textual culture. For Merlin-Kajman, *L'absolutisme*, chapter 5, it defines a break in the history of royal authority. In a slightly less dialectical mode, Serge Doubrovsky's *Corneille et la dialectique du héros* (Paris: Gallimard, 1963), 295ff, takes Cléopatre's fictionalizing of history as evidence of an existential struggle over the nature of the self. I see it as a response to the genre of the treaty.

JANE O. NEWMAN

Afterword: Re-Animating the *Gegenstück*, or the Survival of the French *Trauerspiel* in the German Baroque

> I sometimes think about writing a book on French tragedy as a coun-
> terpart [*Gegenstück*] to my *Trauerspiel* book. My plan for the latter
> had originally been to elucidate both the German and the French
> *Trauerspiel* in terms of their contrastive nature . . .
>
> —Walter Benjamin to Hugo von Hofmannsthal (June 5, 1927)

> gegenstück, n. 1) in der kunst, "zwei figuren von einer grösze, welche
> so gestellet sind, als ob sie sich einander betrachteten", franz. *com-
> pagnon, pendant* Adelung; vergl. *gegenpart*. Bei Campe auch für pa-
> rodie. 2) daher übertragen: man sieht, dasz die aesthetische idee das
> gegenstück (*pendant*) einer vernunftidee sei. Kant 7, 175 (1790) . . . 3)
> aber auch mit hervortreten des gegensatzes (wie *gegenpart* ursprün-
> glick): das sanguinische temperament und sein gegenstück das melan-
> cholische. Kant 10, 319 . . .

> [gegenstück, n. 1) in art, "two figures of the same size that are posi-
> tioned such that they appear to face one another," French, *compagnon,
> pendant* (Adelung, cf. also *gegenpart*). Campe also uses it for parody. 2)
> Thus, in a figurative sense: "we see that the aesthetic idea is the *ge-
> genstück* (*pendant*) of the rational idea" (Kant, 7, 175 – 1790) . . . 3) But
> also with an emphasis on opposition (as originally in the term *ge-
> genpart*): "the sanguine temperament and its *gegenstück*, the melan-
> choly temperament" (Kant, 10, 319) . . .]
>
> —*Grimm Wörterbuch* (1854 ff.)[1]

RE-ANIMATIONS

In their Introduction to the present volume, Hall Bjornstad and Katherine Ibbett quote a letter that Walter Benjamin wrote to Gretel Adorno

---

1. *Deutsches Wörterbuch von Jacob und Wilhelm Grimm*. 16 volumes. Leipzig
1854–1961. Quellenverzeichnis Leipzig 1971. http://dwb.uni-trier.de/de/ – Accessed
January 30, 2013.

YFS 124, *Walter Benjamin's Hypothetical French "Trauerspiel,"* ed. Bjornstad and Ibbett, © 2013 by Yale University.

in July of 1940 as he made his way south toward the Spanish border, trying to stay ahead of the Gestapo. Citing Benjamin, they write that, "alone in [his] room," he "call[ed] on" the French "Grand Siècle" of Cardinal de Retz.[2] But why did Benjamin call on Retz (1613–79)? For solace in a moment of despair? Perhaps. Given the nature of Retz's account in his memoirs of the day-to-day dissimulations required to survive the deadly chaos of the Fronde years, however, when, during the precarious days of August, 1648, for example, everyone at the Parisian court is said to have been acting "the several parts of a *comédie*,"[3] it seems more likely that Benjamin turned to French early modernity for lessons *not* about the classical unities and *bienséance*—which, had he found them there, would have made the "Grand Siècle" the *Gegenstück*-opposite of his own desperate times. Rather, what he might have sought in Retz was a vivid reminder of the similarities of past hazards to the ones he was confronting—which would have then made early modern France another kind of *Gegenstück* for him. For, in the famous Grimm *Wörterbuch* quoted above (the standard reference work for the historical meaning of German words today, just as it was in Benjamin's time), the primary definition of *Gegenstück* is not "contrasting opposite" (a secondary meaning), but, rather, *compagnon*, or *pendant*. In this construction, the absolutist state of Retz's France (regardless of its wobbly condition in the years he describes) might well have served for Benjamin as something like a companion-piece to the more modern authoritarian state whose lethal reach he sought to elude. We might even want to imagine him pausing as he read what he claims here was the only book he had with him to ponder whether any of the tragicomedic strategies depicted by Retz might also be of use to him as a way of safely navigating the distressingly similar political waters upon which his melancholy ship was so desperately foundering at the time. Or at least this is how I think we might understand another reference to Retz in a letter Benjamin

2. Walter Benjamin, *Gesammelte Briefe*, vol. 6, ed. Christophe Gödde and Henri Lonitz (Frankfurt am Main: Suhrkamp, 1995), 470.

3. Of the scene in Paris on August 24, 1648, for example, Retz writes: "The truth is, the Cabinet seemed to consist of persons acting the several parts of a comedy." The Project Gutenberg ebook of *The Memoirs of Jean François Paul de Gondi, Cardinal de Retz*, Book II. http://www.gutenberg.org/files/3846/3846-h/3846-h.htm – Accessed February 2, 2013. On this passage, see also Hélène Merlin-Kajman, "L'exemplarité romaine, entre la tragédie et la farce," in *Le rire ou le modèle? Le dilemme du moraliste*, ed. Jean Dagen and Anne-Sophie Barrovecchio (Paris: Honoré Champion, 2010), 89–107.

wrote to Hannah Arendt at around the same time, when, deeply depressed ("dans un cafard . . . noir") about the parlous state of affairs he faced, Benjamin quotes La Rochefoucauld on Retz to the effect that it was his (Retz's) "lethargy" ("paresse") that "sustained" him "with glory" "in obscurity" for many years.[4] I comment here on Benjamin's second reference to Retz as a way of recalling that just two months after writing this letter, Benjamin actually did succeed in breaking out of his depression, but only just long enough to perform the single act that his "cafard . . . noir" allowed, when he took his own life "in obscurity" in a hotel in Port-Bou. Just how "glorious" that death was is a matter of debate.

Five years on and after the war, another non-French scholar of French early modernity likewise summoned up the past as a way of dealing with modern catastrophe in a brief essay entitled "Les poètes de la vie fugitive." The piece appeared in the Swiss journal *Lettres* in 1945, where it served as the Foreword to a series of translations into French of *German* early modern poems by Paul Fleming, Andreas Gryphius, Angelus Silesius, and Georg Weckherlin.[5] Like Benjamin, the translator seems at first glance to have sought to understand the dreadful calamities of the present through the lens of their "earlier appearance" "in historical dress."[6] The five years between these two appeals to the seventeenth century—and the differential situations of the two men (one not a Jew who had survived the war, the other, a Jew who did not)—nevertheless made all the difference, and the contrast between their competing glosses of early modernity is stark. The purpose of the translation project, our author writes, is to provoke a debate about what a postwar Francophone audience should think of Germany and its traditions in the face of the atrocities signified by Benjamin's choice of suicide, described here as the kind of evil "of which we have seen too much these last twelve years." Rather than inscribing the history of German culture into a narrative

4. Benjamin to Hannah Arendt, July 8, 1940, in Benjamin, *Gesammelte Briefe*, vol. 6, 468.
5. Jean Rousset, "Les poètes de la vie fugitive," in Rousset, *L'aventure baroque*, ed. Michel Jeanneret (Geneva: Éditions Zoé, 2006), 27–31.
6. The quote is from the same letter from Benjamin to Hofmannsthal in which the hypothetical book on the French *Trauerspiel* is mentioned, and refers to Benjamin's interest just as much in "the French spirit . . . in its contemporary appearance" as in that "spirit" [*Geist*] in "its earlier, or older, appearance . . . in historical dress." See Benjamin, *Gesammelte Briefe*, vol. 3, 259.

of horrible inexorability, however, with all roads leading straight to National Socialism, we are told that the charge to the present is to undertake (without pardoning Nazism's crimes) the urgent mission of "re-animating" an "other" moment of German history when "there was a Germany capable of humanism." The author goes on to point out that it was precisely this earlier "Germany"—as represented by the four poets, who are present-day Germany's humane "betters"— that had already been "re-animated" in the acts of the modern "authentic German Resistance," whose fighters had faced off against the Nazis in often invisible and sometimes fatal ways. Set in the scales of memory as a true *Gegenstück*-counter-weight to Nazism's barbarism, it is these men's and women's bravery to which the translations pay homage.[7] Modern scholars of Fleming, Gryphius, Angelus Silesius, and Weckherlin may find the association of explicit acts of opposition to tyranny with these poets' work perplexing. Such incongruities do not seem to have been our author's point. Rather, it appears to have been largely the fact that Gryphius et al lived and wrote poetry amid the conflagrations of the earlier and equally devastating conflict of the Thirty Years' War that allowed them to be reborn into the role of *contrastive* "counterparts" to the modern evils of both Nazism and (and for my purposes, perhaps more importantly) Benjamin's "lethargy."

The mystifying doubleness of "le mal" and "le bien" in National Socialist Germany, and the choice between inertia and resistant action as two possible responses to it, reappear in the gloss that the German poems receive in the second part of the *Lettres* essay. "La vie fugitive"—in German, the human condition of *Vergänglichkeit*, or transitoriness—takes "two forms" in these texts. One version is somber, melancholy, and "desolate" in the face of humanity's entanglement in a dark world of both natural mortality and tragedies of its own making; the other version is "drunk" with immersion in the "small nothings" of now-time, whose immediacies resist decay and transcend death when they become the stuff of verse. Given that our author "re-animates" the "antitheses" of *German* poetry—which

---

7. This may in fact have been another origin of the term; the *Gegenstück* was the "opposing piece," the weight put in the other side of a scale to see how much an object to be measured weighed. In this case, acts of resistance might "even out" history's judgment of the German soul. I am grateful to Professor Kai Evers (UC Irvine) for noting this etymology.

Benjamin in his "Barockbuch" calls the "dizzying," "spiritual contra-dictions" of the era from which texts like the poems derive[8]—in order to point the way forward for the *French*, it should come as no surprise to discover that the translator, whose name I have deliberately not mentioned up to this point, was none other than Jean Rousset, who, just shy of a decade later, invented an equally doubled vision of the French seventeenth century in his *La littérature de l'âge baroque en France: Circé et le paon* (1953). The Swiss Rousset had spent some of the darkest days of World War II (1938–43) teaching French in Halle and Munich; Michel Jeanneret suggests that he had contact with the German Resistance through his students during these years.[9] If this is true, then understanding the Baroque as a time when courageous defiance was possible in the face of a proto-totalitarian state makes a certain amount of sense. Moreover, as I show below, Rousset was not the only one to have found the hope of a better past and a pro-totype of resistance in the "classical" literature produced during the supremely unruly Westphalian period, when the sovereign territo-rial state-*pendant* of Hitler's Germany was allegedly on the rise. My point here, however, is that it was originally in *Germany* that Rousset found his "other" version of *French* classicism, the period that later in life he called "mon Baroque."[10] From the very beginning, then, the literary-historical possibility of finding, or inventing (from *invenio*, to find) a *Gegenstück* of the French "Grand Siècle" was based on "re-animating" things found on the other side of the Rhine.[11] The authors of the essays collected in the present volume are thus in good com-

8. See Benjamin, *The Origin of German Tragic Drama*, trans. John Osborne (Lon-don/New York: Verso, 1977), 56. Hereafter cited as *OGTD*.

9. See Jeanneret, "Au coeur de l'œuvre, le Baroque," in Rousset, *L'aventure ba-roque*, 7.

10. See Rousset, *L'aventure baroque*, 49–62.

11. Rousset was of course not the only foot soldier in what Marc Fumaroli, citing Pierre Charpentrat in the latter's *Baroque et Classicisme* of 1957, calls "la guerre de reconquête" waged by the Baroque on French classicism in the postwar years. Others, including the Spaniard Eugenio d'Ors and Victor Tapié, also participated. But these ef-forts are different, I think, from Rousset's in the 1945 Foreword, which was in turn also not the same as the ideologically motivated "discovery" by French Occupation Forces-sponsored initiatives during these same years of another kind of "other" Germany in an anti-Prussian Baroque not in France, but in southern Germany. On these initiatives, and for an account of the French invention of the Baroque in the 1950s and 1960s, see Marc Fumaroli, "Préface," in Victor L. Tapié, *Baroque et Classicisme*. Second edition (Paris: Pluriel / Librarie Générale Française, 1980), 9–42.

pany when they turn to the "crude theater" of Benjamin's German seventeenth century for help in locating a French *Trauerspiel*.[12]

As for Rousset, so too in the essays collected here, Benjamin's German Baroque plays midwife to an (if not "better" then at least) alternative version of "classical" *grandeur*. For some of the authors (Ibbett, Lyons, Méchoulan, Merlin-Kajman), a baroque classicism defeats, or at least puts in question, the characteristics and values often associated with "les grands auteurs." For others (Braider, Haas, Hampton, and Maslan), it appears to co-exist (if uneasily) in dialectical fashion with neo-classicism as it is conventionally understood. I remain agnostic as to whether a baroque "Grand Siècle" would be "better" than a classical one; both terms and versions of the period are in any case anachronisms, as Merlin-Kajman points out and, as John Lyons wrote already in 2001, the invention of "post-seventeenth-century history of literary and cultural study."[13] I *am* convinced, however, that the French seventeenth century, recast in these essays as something entirely other than a "regularized" era in harmony with a consolidating national state, will, when thrown in the balance, make it difficult for future scholars to invest in oversimplified cartoons of a "classical" French literary tradition.

Yet, the question remains: Why "call on" a baroque "Grand Siècle" triangulated through things German, and why do so now? Why is it so urgent, in other words, to renew French (neo)classicism one more time by creating an updated version of the period through the lens of something so dated and apparently foreign to it as Benjamin's account of the bizarre plays of the "Second Silesian School"? Is this project anything more than an instrumental gesture that shores up the study of an earlier canon (yet again) under attack (perhaps for ideological or perhaps, this time, for merely budgetary reasons) by associating it with the name and the myth of Benjamin as—like the Baroque—a permanent outsider?[14] I would say yes. There is something greater

12. Benjamin refers to the "crude theater" of the German baroque *Trauerspiel* in *OGTD*, 158.

13. John D. Lyons, "What Do We Mean When We Say 'Classique'?" in *Racine et/ou le classicisme*, ed. Ronald W. Tobin, Biblio 17, 129 (Tübingen: Gunter Narr, 2001), 505.

14. On the tradition of considering the Baroque as "a site inhabited by freaks," see Timothy Hampton, "Introduction: Baroques," in *Yale French Studies* 80 (1991): 1. Lyons ("What Do We Mean," 503) refers to Hélène Merlin-Kajman's argument in her *Public et littérature en France au XVIIème siècle* (1994) about the ideological rejection of classicism by Roland Barthes's generation.

at stake in the way these essays use Benjamin to contest the tired nationalist disciplinary geographies to which even a relentlessly globalizing postmodern academy all too often succumbs. The essays also offer a welcome alternative to the hierarchies of value and relevance endorsed by this same academy's endlessly presentist investment in implicitly progressivist periodization schemes. The two problems are related. That is, when classicism is understood in presentist fashion as coincident with nationalism, as it so often has been (eighteenth-century Weimar "classicism," the "deutsche Klassik" of Goethe and Schiller, as it was celebrated by a National Socialist academy, is a case in point), it functions as a "mirror" that "reflects back histories" of the nation only as it has allegedly become.[15] (As it was understood in Benjamin's time—and sometimes even by Benjamin himself—and since, the Baroque did not escape being interpellated into a narrative of this kind.)[16] When earlier periods are understood in this way only as the beginning of a present-day end, the result is the elision of the possibility of an anti-progressivist engagement with a past that understands that both "classical" literary canons and literal nation-states were "baroque" in a different way from the very start, both internally riven and always embedded in international networks. Re-animating a doubled version of early modernity's political profile in particular by means of a Deleuzian historiography that reads the past and the present—and the nation and its others (both on the outside and within)—as always already implicated in one another might be wise in the present context, when, as any number of International Relations theorists argue, we have moved into a "post-Westphalian" era.[17] We are, in other words, now beyond the forms of consolidated

15. On this version of presentism, see Kathleen Biddick, "Bede's Blush: Postcards from Bali, Bombay, and Palo Alto," in Biddick, *The Shock of Medievalism* (Durham, NC: Duke University Press, 1998), 83–84. It might be useful to note here that when Benjamin refers in the *Trauerspiel* book to the stand-off between "Baroque" and "Classicism," he may in fact not have been referring to French classicism at all, as Merlin-Kajman notes in passing in her essay, but, rather, precisely to Weimer Classicism, which was traditionally claimed to have been what "overcame" the Baroque in Germany. On this quite traditional stand-off between (German) Classicism and the German Baroque, see Newman, *Benjamin's Library: Modernity, Nation, and the Baroque* (Ithaca: Cornell University Press, 2011), 35–38.

16. See Newman, *Benjamin's Library* 6–9, and Fumaroli ("Préface," 13–15) on the "nationalist" versions of the Baroque that sprang up in central and eastern Europe during the Cold War.

17. See, for example, Richard Falk, "Revisiting Westphalia, Discovering Post-Westphalia," in *The Journal of Ethics* 6 (2002): 311–52; Seyla Benhabib, *The Rights*

statehood said to have taken their beginnings around the time of the Treaty of Westphalia (1648)—which was of course also the time of both French classicism and its *pendant*, the German Baroque.

In what follows, I turn to an earlier generation of students of the Romance languages and literatures who explicitly understood the "Grand Siècle" as a *Gegenstück*—in both senses—to their own times. Emerging out of the collective scholarly din of a nationalist discipline that saw modern (e.g. post-Franco-Prussian War and post-Versailles) Germany's relation to modern France figured in its relation to classicism writ large and to Corneille in particular are two dissenting voices of particular relevance here. They are the great German-Jewish Romanist and Comparatist Erich Auerbach (1892–1957), and Werner Krauss (1900–1976), Auerbach's junior colleague in Romance Languages at Marburg, who, because he was not Jewish, was able (with Auerbach's permission) to take over Auerbach's courses and responsibilities when Hitler's race laws forced the latter to flee to Istanbul. Both Auerbach and Krauss wrote books and essays that look quite a bit like the study of the seventeenth-century French *Trauerspiel* that Benjamin failed to produce, and did so at approximately the same time. For them, as for Benjamin, early modern drama never ran the risk of being either disdained or forgotten. Rather, it was full of difficult "analogies" to the present day.[18] Understanding the issues at the heart of their not-at-all hypothetical versions of the French mourning play may suggest further ways in which "re-animating" the *Trauerspiele* of both French and German early modernity may be useful for us.

THE NOT-SO-HYPOTHETICAL FRENCH *TRAUERSPIEL*: THE "GRAND SIÈCLE" BEYOND THE RHINE

That Benjamin's hypothetical *Trauerspiel*-book remained, well, hypothetical, may have been because he seems in fact not to have been able to decide exactly what he thought about French classical drama.

---

of Others: Aliens, Residents, and Citizens (Cambridge: Cambridge University Press, 2004); and Wendy Brown, *Walled States, Waning Sovereignty* (New York and Boston: Zone Books / The MIT Press, 2010).

18. Benjamin writes at length in the *Trauerspiel* book about the difficult "analogies" many of his contemporaries both justifiably and unjustifiably see between early modern Germany and the early twentieth century in Germany. See *OGTD*, 53–56.

In the famous letter to Hofmannsthal of June 5, 1927, for example, he refers to the plays about which he already intended to write as both "die französische Tragödie" and "das französische Trauerspiel," thus apparently forgetting the distinction he had taken such pains to make between tragedy and the mourning play in the chapter entitled "*Trauerspiel* and Tragedy" of the text meant to serve as his *Habilitation*, the post-doctoral thesis that would have enabled him to lecture at a German university.[19] That Benjamin remained uncertain about what kind of *Gegenstück* French "classical" tragedy might have been to the German Baroque *Trauerspiel* might have been because he in fact does not seem to have read very many French classical tragedies. Unlike the works of Calderón, for example, which appear at numerous points in the list of books Benjamin claims to have read between c. 1917 and 1939 (a list that is available in volume VII of the Frankfurt Benjamin edition), not a single text by Corneille or Racine is named. Indeed, although he famously recalls having *seen* Corneille's *Le Cid* performed in Geneva when he was a young man, Benjamin seems to have *read* only one dramatic text from the French seventeenth century. Interestingly, it was the play that Chris Braider calls both the "greatest comedy" and the "greatest tragedy" of the French classical era: Molière's *Dom Juan*.[20]

There were, however, other German scholars who seem to have known exactly what they meant when they referred to the texts of French classical drama and to the plays of Corneille in particular at the time. As Michael Nerlich has shown, early twentieth-century Ro-

19. The rejection of the thesis by the faculty at Frankfurt is thus often said to be a *Trauerspiel* of its own, the "tragic" beginning of the end of an academic career for its author, the final act of which unfolded in 1940, as we have seen. See Burkhart Lindner, "Habilitationsakte Benjamin. Über ein 'akademisches Trauerspiel' und über ein Vorkapitel der 'Frankfurter Schule' (Horkheimer, Adorno)," in *Zeitschrift für Literaturwissenschaft und Linguistik* 53–54 (1984), 147–65.

20. Christopher Braider, "Talking like a Book: Exception and the State of Nature in Benjamin and Molière," *Comparative Literature* 64/4 (2012): 391–92. Adriana Bontea ("A Project in its Context: Walter Benjamin on Comedy," *MLN* 121 (2006): 1041–71) discusses Benjamin's hypothetical comedy based on an undated, unpublished fragment he wrote entitled "Molière: Der eingebildete Kranke (The Imaginary Invalid)." In that fragment (*Gesammelte Schriften* II-2, ed. Rolf Tiedemann and Hermann Schweppenhäuser et al [Frankfurt: Suhrkamp, 1977], 612–13), the context appears to have been a production of the play that he saw. For Molière as he appears on Benjamin's list, see Benjamin, *Gesammelte Schriften* VII-1, "Nachträge," ed. Tiedemann and Schweppenhäuser et al (Frankfurt: Suhrkamp, 1991), 450.

mance Studies in Germany were generally a nationalist affair.[21] The chauvinism of the discipline had of course already been shaped by the Franco-Prussian War (1870–71); it then took an exceedingly bad turn both during World War I and after Versailles, and deteriorated even more drastically in the interwar years and through the occupation of France. Several generations of wars were thus waged "by other means" in school classrooms and university seminars and in the pages of countless journals and books. Darko Suvin notes that during the interwar and World War II years in particular, those Romanists who studied Iberian and Italian literature and culture were on somewhat safer ground than the so-called "Gallo-Romanists," whose object of study had already belonged to the *Kulturgut* of the enemy nation of choice for quite some time before Hitler again declared France to be "the implacable, mortal enemy of the German *Volk*" in *Mein Kampf*.[22] To belong to the micro-community of German scholars who studied things French during this period thus constituted something of an a priori risk. Indeed, as Leo Spitzer writes in his 1946 "Das Eigene und das Fremde. Über Philologie und Nationalismus" (The Self and the Foreign: On Philology and Nationalism), even those scholars who were not Jewish or otherwise politically undesirable and thus could continue to teach mostly kept their heads down; the worst joined up with disciplinary initiatives in support of what was called the *Kriegseinsatz*, the academic "war effort" of the intellectuals that began around 1940 and continued to contribute articles to such Party-sponsored volumes as *Die Romanistik im Kriege* (Romance Studies in the War) as late as 1944.[23]

As a result, most early to mid-twentieth-century German scholarship on the French classical tradition in particular disdained the

21. Michael Nerlich, "Aufklärung und Republik. Zum deutsch-französischen Verhältnis, zur Frankreichforschung und zu Werner Krauss," in *Lendemains* 69–70 (1993): 8–87.

22. *Mein Kampf* cited in Nerlich, "Aufklärung und Republik," 38. On the differential components of Romance Studies in early twentieth-century Germany, see Darko Suvin's interesting review of Peter Jehle's book on Werner Krauss in *New Left Review* 15 (2002): 157–64.

23. Leo Spitzer, "Das Eigene und das Fremde. Über Philologie und Nationalismus," in *Die Wandlung* I (1945/46), vol. 7, 576–94, and Nerlich, 45–50. On the academic "war effort," see Frank-Rutger Hausmann, "Werner Krauss und der 'Kriegseinsatz' der Deutschen Romanisten 1940–1941," in *Werner Krauss: Wege-Werke-Wirkungen*, ed. Ottmar Ette, Martin Fontius, Gerda Hassler, and Peter Jehle (Berlin: Verlag Arno Spitz, 1999), 11–39.

period precisely because it represented "La France." Corneille had been a problem since Lessing's dismissal of his work in favor of the German "bourgeois mourning play" (*bürgerliches Trauerspiel*) (which was not the same *Trauerspiel* as the Baroque "mourning play") in the eighteenth century. This meant that later generations were able to see him (Corneille) as worthy of attention only through the lens of a Crocean celebration of the disinterested aesthetic unity of his work, or as the author whose heroes provided a model for the selfless rejection of the personal realm in the interest of the (German) state's greater good. Any of Corneille's texts that did not fit this model were dismissed.[24] Examples of this kind of early twentieth-century German work on Corneille can be seen in two articles published by the Basel scholar Ernst Merian-Genast, in 1937 and 1938 respectively, "Corneille als Dichter des Stolzes" (Corneille as the Poet of Pride) and "Corneille-Renaissance" (Corneille Renaissance), in which the great playwright is celebrated as a "classical" "poetic personality" and Stefan George-like poet genius outside of time and place.[25] Auerbach's and Krauss's work was contemporaneous with this scholarship, but proposed some pretty clear alternatives to it.

That Erich Auerbach, the author of the famous *Mimesis: The Representation of Reality in Western Literature* (orig. 1946), was originally a scholar of the Romance traditions in particular is not well known today. He wrote his dissertation on the novella of the early French and Italian Renaissance and his first book on Dante in 1929. He then went on to publish *Das französische Publikum des 17. Jahrhunderts* (The French Audience of the Seventeenth Century) in 1933.[26] With this book, a revolutionary method for studying the plays of the French seventeenth century in their historical sociopolitical

24. See Peter Jehle, *Werner Krauss und die Romanistik im NS-Staat* (Hamburg: Argument Verlag, 1996), 84.

25. See *Romanische Forschungen* 51 (1937): 83–109, here 83, and 279–304, and *Romanische Forschungen* 52 (1938): 41–54. French Romance Studies—and students of Corneille in particular—were of course themselves not innocent of such celebrations at the time. See Jehle, "Zur literaturwissenschaftlichen Corneille-Rezeption im deutschen Faschismus," in *Romanistische Zeitschrift für Literaturgeschichte* 18 (1994): 126–49.

26. See Erich Auerbach, *Das französische Publikum des 17. Jahrhunderts* (Munich: Max Hueber Verlag, 1933). Parts of the argument of the book, which has not been translated into English, appear in the later essay, "La cour et la ville" (orig. 1951), available to English readers in the translation by Ralph Mannheim in *Scenes from the Drama of European Literature* (New York: Meridian Books, 1959). On Auerbach's argument, see Hélène Merlin-Kajman, "Le public au XVIIe siècle et au-delà selon Auer-

context was launched. It would be difficult to overstate the innovation that Auerbach's study represented. We are now used to studying early modern theater in terms of the sociopolitical developments contemporary to it, as Katherine Ibbett's *The Style of the State in French Theater, 1630–1660: Neoclassicism and Government* (2009) and Claude Haas's and Tim Hampton's essays in the present volume show.[27] In 1933, however, Auerbach's way of reading the French seventeenth century as a complex historical period of dangerously shifting social and political relations, in which tragedy—and its authors—had lost both its moral and political compass, was a novelty. In 1934, Krauss wrote one of the only reviews of the Jewish Auerbach's book that appeared; in a fascinating essay entitled "Über die Träger der klassischen Gesinnung im 17. Jahrhundert" (On the Proponents of the Classical Mind in the Seventeenth Century), Krauss previews the thoughts that he then went on to develop at greater length in his own book on Corneille, *Corneille als politischer Dichter* (Corneille as a Political Poet), published in 1936, after his mentor, Auerbach, and more than a fifth of all university Romanists, had been dismissed from their posts.[28]

Krauss's 1936 book is even less well known today than Auerbach's 1933 study. At the time, however, it was widely reviewed and seen as revolutionary in Corneille criticism in both French and exile German publications.[29] More recently, his method has been aligned with that of Antonio Gramsci, Raymond Williams, and Lucien Goldmann.[30] Krauss's analyses of Corneille's plays are even more daring than Auerbach's. They ultimately turn not only on the importance of looking

---

bach," in *Erich Auerbach. La littérature en perspective*, ed. Paolo Tortonese (Paris: Presses Sorbonne nouvelle, 2009), 91–115.

27. Katherine Ibbett, *The Style of the State in French Theater, 1630–1660: Neoclassicism and Government* (Burlington, VT: Ashgate, 2009).

28. Krauss's review, "Über die Träger der klassischen Gesinnung im 17. Jahrhundert," appeared in the *Zeitschrift für französischen und englischen Unterricht* 33/1 (1934): 27–38. His *Corneille als Politischer Dichter* was published in 1936 by the Verlag von Adolf Ebel in Marburg, where he taught.

29. For an account of the reception of Krauss's Corneille book, see the "Editorische Anmerkungen" in the collected works of Krauss, *Das wissenschaftliche Werk*, vol. 3: *Spanische, italienische und französische Literatur im Zeitalter des Absolutismus*, ed. Peter Jehle (Berlin/New York: de Gruyter, 1997), 612–17.

30. See Suvin, *New Left Review* 15, and Sabine Kebir, "Historisches Denken und Aufklärung bei Werner Krauss, Antonio Gramsci und Bertolt Brecht," in *Werner Krauss. Literatur, Geschichte, Schreiben*, ed. Hermann Hofer, Thilo Karger, and Christa Riehn (Tübingen and Basel: A. Francke, 2003), 167–78.

for possible avenues of resistance to the burgeoning apparatus of an absolutist nation-state, but also of analyzing why such resistance ultimately fails, particularly when it is undertaken by characters who are, in his reading, figures for an educated bourgeoisie that had sold out to the court out of venal self interest. The question was clearly more than academic for Krauss, who was himself condemned to death by the Nazis in 1942 because of his work with the Resistance after he—and more than 100 others associated with a group called the "Rote Kappelle" ("Red Orchestra")—was arrested for posting satirical pamphlets about the "paradise offered by National Socialism" around a number of neighborhoods in Berlin.[31] Krauss awaited execution for two years in various prisons in Berlin, daily hearing his fellow prisoners, many of them his young friends from the Resistance, being led off to be hanged.[32] It was only his more or less "Aryan" background, combined with the efforts of a host of colleagues, including such famous Romanists as Karl Vossler and Ernst Robert Curtius, as well as, perhaps surprisingly, Hans Georg Gadamer (who wrote a series of letters to the Nazi judicial authorities testifying that Krauss was "mentally unbalanced"), that seems to have gotten his sentence commuted to a five-year prison term in 1944, which, with the end of the war, he did not have to serve out. Offered a position at his old institution, Krauss was disgusted with the reinstallation in Marburg of scholars and administrators who had been sympathetic to the Nazi regime; he left West Germany for the east, where he took up a position as the Chair of Romance Studies at the University at Leipzig and taught a more or less undogmatic form of Marxist criticism for many years.[33]

31. On Krauss's work with the Resistance, his trial, and imprisonment, see Karlheinz Barck, "Werner Krauss im Widerstand und vor dem Reichskriegsgericht," in *Lendemains* 69/70 (1993): 137–50.
32. Incredibly, during these years, he took the opportunity of his enforced "leave" from his work with the translators' "company" of the Nazi military (into which he had been drafted precisely as a philologist with excellent language abilities) to write and have smuggled out of prison a scholarly study of the Spanish Baroque philosopher and political theorist, Balthasar Gracian (*Gracians Lebenslehre*, Gracian's Lessons for Life), composed, as Krauss notes in the first edition, "under special circumstances" in 1943. See Krauss, *Gracians Lebenslehre* (Frankfurt: Vittorio Klostermann, 1947), "Vorbemerkung," 7.
33. For an account of Krauss's later life, see Hans Ulrich Gumbrecht. *Vom Leben und Sterben der großen Romanisten. Carl Vossler, Ernst Robert Curtius, Leo Spitzer, Erich Auerbach, Werner Krauss* (Munich: Carl Hanser Verlag, 2002).

As noted above, Auerbach's book on the French seventeenth century appeared in the fateful year of 1933.[34] The entirely heterogeneous seventeenth-century world he describes was one in which playwrights and their plays belonged to a social order caught in the midst of profound economic and political change. According to Auerbach, the aristocracy was well on its way to losing its influence and power and the bourgeoisie on its way to gaining prestige as the *noblesse de robe*; shedding their former loyalties as well as their old functions, the two classes met in the middle to form a new social unity that Auerbach calls the "parasitical" class, the worth of whose members rested solely on their ability to mime a homogenizing "bienséance" and "honnêteté," *and* to be recognized as good (and quiescent) apparatchiks by the minister and the king. Auerbach's book and its footnotes are as cluttered as the streets of Paris and the ranks of the parterre in the theater he describes, with information about ticket prices jostling for visibility with descriptions of both the owners of the shops on the rue Saint-Denis and of those shops' wares. Long lists of the social background and religious affiliation of the leading intellectuals of the period compete with analyses of the visibility of these complex social and economic relations in the characters of countless plays. The book culminates in a series of sweeping claims about the "de-Christianizing" secularization of the period, which led to the development of an autonomous moral sphere above, beyond, and disengaged from the political world, a world that was in any case out of the reach of the mere mortals of the parterre who, because they could not intervene in it, complied instead. This was, according to Auerbach, the stuff of Corneille's plays as well as of Racine's; here, he cites his own earlier essay on "Racine und die Leidenschaften" (Racine and the Passions, 1926). The argument provides the nucleus of his discussion of French classicism in chapter fifteen of *Mimesis*, where he claims—contra several of the essays collected here—that it was actually the *loss* of, and not the persistence of, "creatureliness" that made French tragedy "classical."[35] Had the plays been more "creaturely," more involved with the world, they might have been as baroque as

34. In what follows I refer to Auerbach's analysis in *Das französische Publikum*, 12–53.

35. Auerbach, *Mimesis. Dargestellte Wirklichkeit in der abendländischen Literatur* (Tübingen and Basel: Francke Verlag, 1946), chapter XV: "Der Scheinheilige" ("The Faux Dévot"), 356, for example. It should be noted that in *Mimesis*, Auerbach makes

Auerbach's friend Walter Benjamin, five years earlier, had claimed that the plays of their German counterparts were.

In his *Corneille als politischer Dichter*, published in 1936, it would seem that Krauss would have had to be considerably more circumspect than Auerbach three years before. Yet, his interrogation of Corneille's plays through the lens of contemporary theories of the State, and most prominently those of Jean Bodin, reads like nothing other than an assessment of how the National Socialist *Machtstaat* had prevailed using exactly the same techniques as early modern French absolutism, destroying any authentic notion of civil society by investing the sovereign with absolute rights as long as he kept his part of the bargain or contract, especially with the bourgeoisie, to respect his subjects' property, freedom, and rights.[36] Maybe Krauss thought the Nazi censors would get lost in the footnotes. But these fascinatingly dense seven pages of social and political history make it fairly clear that the close reading that follows of the entirety of Corneille's œuvre is meant as a political allegory of contemporary times. In this section, Krauss goes into excruciatingly well-documented detail about the cover provided to the hegemonic state by Bodin's theory of the limits on monarchical power. At the same time, he gives a thorough account, (aptly) based on the resistance pamphlet literature of the time, of the arguments those pamphlets contained for limiting the sovereign's absolute authority—arguments based precisely on a recognition of the infringements of these legal rights by Richelieu. As one reads through these pages, it is difficult to overlook the fact that what Krauss is really talking about is an example of the absolute state that was, for him, much closer to home.[37] Richelieu slides almost imperceptibly from being referred to as "der Kardinal" to being designated as a "Diktator," whose political aim was the erection of a "Führerstaat"; his (Richelieu's) reactions to even less than overt political opposition are cast in the language of arrests undertaken to short circuit "Zellenbildung," the development of oppositional cells.[38] The

---

something of an exception for Corneille, who, he writes, was "conflicted" about the un- "creaturely" style demanded of him by the court (362).

36. In the following, I cite *Corneille als politischer Dichter* after Werner Krauss, *Das wissenschaftliche Werk*, 344–95. The pages discussed here are on 355–62. All translations are my own.

37. University records show that Krauss had been lecturing on French absolutism at Marburg since the winter semester of 1932–33 and continued to do so up through the publication of his book. See "Editorische Anmerkungen," 612–13.

38. Krauss, *Corneille als politischer Dichter*, 358–60.

ruthless crushing of any lingering possibility of "Volkssouveranität" is seen as another characteristically absolutizing move, which explains how Louis XIV can be labeled a "Despot."[39] Readers are thus primed to read for the parallels between Corneille's plays and their own times when Krauss turns to the dramatic texts—and they apparently did, if the review of the book by exile scholar Ulrich Leo, writing in the Italian publication *Archivum Romanicum* in 1937, is any indication. Leo points out how Richelieu's machine—and its harsh response to any "oppositional efforts"—is vividly rendered by Krauss for readers "of our days," who are familiar with such struggles "from their own experiences."[40]

When Krauss turns to the plays, his initial interest does not appear to be in any clear acts of resistance to the "triumph of the idea of the State" as it was consolidating around Corneille and visible in the controversy about the *Cid*. Rather, what the scholar seems to deliver are "only" readings of the plays. But in the analyses of *Horace* as it dialogues with *Cinna* in particular, Krauss shows how Corneille's dramas clearly display the compromising of Bodin's contractual theory of sovereignty by the sovereign when, in *Horace*, for example, the "defense" of the state allows, indeed, demands the harm of the family. Krauss also dwells on the incredible poverty of motivation that drives even those who would appear to resist hegemony in *Cinna*. It may well be that Krauss's anger at what he sees expressed in *Horace* in particular is only audible in the German: "Der Aufschrei der verletzten Menschlichkeit bricht sich ungehört an den Mauern des Staats" ("the cry of an injured/trespassed-upon humanity breaks upon the walls of the state, unheard"), referring of course to the death of Camille. It is an anger that Krauss then goes on to recast as a stimulus to action (here, the future resistance fighter may be heard): "these very walls constitute at one and the same time also the limits of the state, the end of which Camille—Antigone's sister—announces." By showing its absolute disdain of the family and the individual and (in this case) her rights, the point of Corneille's *Horace* is thus to reveal the ugly side of absolutism—and its successor, the totalitarian (nation) state—and thereby to call for resistance to it. In light of his own actions some five to six years later—and the brush with death that they precipitated—it is uncanny to listen to Krauss when he writes in his commentaries on

---

39. Ibid., 345, 386.
40. Leo's review, cited in "Editorische Anmerkungen," 61.

Rodogune and *Polyeucte* that the only viable mode of resistance to a corrupt, but really existing *Machtstaat* such as the one that looms over Corneille's plays is one that follows an absolute moral principle and inexorable "necessity" of character and belief and, more importantly, whose agents are prepared for and indeed reckon with personal "self destruction." In his description of the character of Antiochus as a "kaum gereiften Menschen," a young man barely grown up, who is prepared for just this possibility, the profiles of the future young martyrs of the Berlin pamphleting action can be seen.[41]

There is much more to be said about Krauss's book on Corneille and how he reads the playwright not at all as a classical writer (*pace* Braider, Maslan, and Méchoulan in this volume, this would be Racine for both Krauss and Auerbach), but, rather, as an explicitly "baroque" author who draws the tensions of a life being lived at the time of the consolidating *Machtstaat* into the very fabric of his plays. Krauss's readings of Corneille thus do a good job of approximating what Benjamin's readings of the "mourning plays" of a French Baroque might have been.

But that was not all. In 1948, Krauss held his inaugural address in Leipzig on the topic of the Christian martyr in French classical drama. A newspaper report and private letters indicate that he had already given a version of the lecture at the University of Freiburg in the fall of 1940.[42] This earlier lecture, held, ironically, just a month after Benjamin killed himself, appears to bring Krauss very close to channeling Benjamin's thoughts on the French *Trauerspiel*; it is thus no surprise to find a reference to Benjamin's "intellectually rich study" of the *Trauerspiel* in the notes to an undated typescript of various fragments found among Krauss's papers, which carries the heading, "The Aesthetic Problem of the Martyr Play (The Saint as Hero)." Another undated outline, perhaps of the lecture, contains the (for 1940) astonishingly bold title for one section, "Martyr dramas as the resistance literature of the era of Absolutism." Krauss himself eventually published all of this earlier work in an essay entitled "The End of Christian Martyrdom in French Classical Tragedy" in 1951.

In the 1951 essay, Krauss "re-animates" not only Auerbach's rich description of the unstable sociopolitical world of the "Grand Siècle," but also the rootedness in that century's unruly class conflict and

---

41. Krauss, *Corneille als politischer Dichter*, 362–71.
42. The texts discussed in what follows are available in Krauss, *Das wissenschaftliche Werk*, 397–409, with "Editorische Anmerkungen" on 617–42.

brew of religious factions of the brief and "anachronistic" "episode" of an outpouring between 1610 and 1650 of what Ibbett in this volume calls the "minor genre" of the martyr play.[43] First, Krauss analyzes what he calls here the "the secularization of religion" in the service of class-specific needs of the nobility by the Christian humanist Francis de Sales (1567–1622), which he argues was designed to give the nobles' Fronde-affiliated political efforts greater energy by allowing the issue of faith to emerge into what Krauss calls the clear "light of a classical day." He then turns to the "bourgeois" authors, Jean-Pierre Camus, Desfontaines, Rotrou, and of course Corneille, who were also aware of the dwindling power of their class under Richelieu (the argument is inherited almost word for word from Auerbach) and wrote plays that foregrounded the fact that "only divine and natural law can protect [us] from the omnipotence of the state"; "the free state is to be secured only by means of the sword of faith and the exemplary act of sacrifice." The center of the essay is (inevitably) occupied with a detailed reading of *Polyeucte* that somewhat counter-intuitively, but in moving fashion, pitches the conversion of the "ambitious" "provincial bureaucrat" Felix against the "classically" humane and "pure" Sévère, whom Krauss more or less pillories for not being able to find the "strength" in himself to take the "final step" to convert. There is almost a sense of loss, or regret, in Krauss's claim that it is Sévère's "enlightened" "skepticism" that places him, "Pilate"-like, on the side of a disabling law (*Gesetz*) rather than of enabling "grace" (*Gnade*). While not exactly the same as Auerbach's lament about the "de-Christianization" of the period at the end of his 1933 *Publikum* book, what Krauss seems to be saying here is that in order to act, one has to be able to call upon some deeper resources in a counter-classical—because still sacrally informed—political-theological economy, the Gallican *Gegenstück* perhaps, as Ibbett suggests in her essay, of Benjamin's de-eschatologicalized Lutheran world. The curtain falls on the efflorescence of the French "martyr play," Krauss writes, after the "defeat of the Fronde," when a "political poetry of resistance" becomes irrelevant.

43. Krauss, "Das Ende des christlichen Märtyrers in der klassischen Tragödie der Franzosen," in *Das wissenschaftliche Werk*, 397–409. In a work in progress, Christopher Semk (Yale) dates the period of the martyr play in France slightly differently. I am grateful to Semk for sharing with me his canny reading of the challenge to doctrinal belief represented by the staging of martyrological tragedy even after the defeat of the Fronde.

It is worth noting, in Krauss's reading of the French martyr-drama here, that whereas he argues that it was the French world's "religious incompetence" that allowed the secular arm of the state to declare victory first under Richelieu and then definitively under Louis XIV, the resistant "martyr" continued to "play his role" with gusto elsewhere and with a special longevity "in German Baroque tragedy" in the years that followed. By implication, then, for Krauss, it was the particular tradition of the "classical" French martyr play that was the "origin" of the Baroque *Trauerspiel* that flourished after 1650 on the other side of the Rhine. There, he continues, it issued the "first battle cry" against the "sacrilegious institution of despotism" in the very plays about which Benjamin wrote.[44] It is difficult to imagine what Krauss is proposing here if not a cunning reading of the way Benjamin's German *Trauerspiele* were in fact precisely *not* melancholic. Rather they were meditations on the dangers, but also on the rewards, of fighting back against the system of states that the Treaty of Westphalia had called into existence, the very same system of sovereign polities whose autonomy had opened the door to the possibility of atrocities like those of the Holocaust in the first place. When a French classical "poetry of resistance" wanders in 1940 across the border to Germany as a model for a baroque fight against despotism in plays that become evidence of something like an earlier "Germany capable of humanism," we find ourselves back where we started, namely in Rousset's version of the German seventeenth century as an age that, if properly "re-animated," could provide the model of an "authentique Résistance." Perhaps this is the other history that the authors in this volume of *Yale French Studies* have begun to tell, a history of the modeling forth in early modernity of what Hall Bjornstad in his essay calls "baroque hope," the possibility, that is, of imagining the *Nachleben* of the Baroque in a "post-modernity beyond nationalism" that could be the *Gegenstück* to the tragedy of modernity that began around 1648.[45]

44. Krauss, "Das Ende", 408–409.
45. I am grateful to Colin Devane (UC Irvine) for sharing his Masters' Thesis, "'Faire germer là une maison spirituelle': Sacrificial Conceptions in Sixteenth-Century Huguenot Martyrology" (October, 2012), with me, as well as for many conversations with him about Krauss's work on French martyr drama. The description of the urgent task of the post-Westphalian imagination as a search for a "post-modernity beyond nationalism" is Devane's.

Contributors

Michael E. Auer is an assistant professor of German at the Ludwig-Maximilians-Universität München, Germany. He is the author of *Wege zu einer planetarischen Linientreue? Meridiane zwischen Jünger, Schmitt, Heidegger und Celan* (Fink, 2013) and is currently working on a book project concerning the political ode and the rise of literary criticism in the eighteenth century.

Will Bishop received his doctorate from the University of California, Berkeley. He lives in Paris where he teaches and translates. His most recent translation is Peter Szendy's *Kant in the Land of Extraterrestrials* (Fordham, 2013).

Hall Bjornstad is assistant professor of French at Indiana University, Bloomington and the author of *Créature sans créateur: Pour une anthropologie baroque dans les "Pensées" de Pascal* (Laval, 2010; reissued by Hermann, 2013); the editor of *Borrowed Feathers: Plagiarism and the Limits of Imitation in Early Modern Europe* (Oslo, 2008) and the translator of Pascal's *Pensées* into Norwegian (2007). He is currently working on the changing expressions of royal exemplarity in early modern France.

Christopher Braider is Professor of French and Comparative Literature at the University of Colorado, Boulder, and author of *The Matter of Mind: Reason and Experience in the Age of Descartes* (Toronto, 2012); *Baroque Self-Invention and Historical Truth: Hercules at the Crossroads* (Ashgate, 2004); *Indiscernible Counterparts: The Invention of the Text in French Classical Drama* (North Carolina, 2002); and *Refiguring the Real: Picture and Modernity in Word and Image, 1400–1700* (Princeton, 1993). He is currently working on two new book projects, *Giving*

YFS 124, *Walter Benjamin's Hypothetical French "Trauerspiel,"* ed. Bjornstad and Ibbett, © 2013 by Yale University.

Up the Ghost: The Experimental Method in the Humanities and *Persons and Portraits: Experimental Selves in Early Modern Europe.*

EMMA GILBY is a University Senior Lecturer in the Faculty of Medieval and Modern Languages at Cambridge University and Fellow of Sidney Sussex College. She is the author of *Sublime Worlds* (Legenda, 2006), the editor of *Pseudo-Longin: De la sublimité du discours* (L'Act Mem, 2007), and the co-editor of *Method and Variation: Narrative in Early Modern French Thought* (Legenda, 2013). She is working on a book called *Descartes's Fictions.*

CLAUDE HAAS is Senior Researcher at the Center for Literary and Cultural Research Berlin with the project "Tragedy and *Trauerspiel.*" He is the author of *Arbeit am Abscheu. Zu Thomas Bernhards Prosa* (Fink, 2007) and the co-editor of *Der Einsatz des Dramas. Dramenanfänge, Wissenschaftspoetik und Gattungspolitik* (Rombach, 2012). He is currently working on the representation of heroism and sovereignty in the French and German classical drama.

TIMOTHY HAMPTON is Professor of French and Comparative Literature at the University of California, Berkeley, where he chairs the French Department. He is the author of *Fictions of Embassy: Literature and Diplomacy in Early Modern Europe* (Cornell, 2009); *Literature and Nation in the Sixteenth Century: Inventing Renaissance France* (Cornell, 2000; winner of the MLA's Scaglione Prize); and *Writing from History: The Rhetoric of Exemplarity in Renaissance Literature* (Cornell, 1990; winner of the Bainton Book Prize). He is currently working on a book about Rabelais and a book on the history of cheerfulness.

KATHERINE IBBETT is Reader in Early Modern Studies in the Department of French, University College, London; in 2012–2013 she was a Fellow of the Radcliffe Institute for Advanced Study. She is the author of *The Style of the State in French Theater 1630–1660: Neoclassicism and Government* (Ashgate, 2009). She is working on a book called *Compassion's Edge*, about compassion and its limits in early modern France.

JOHN D. LYONS is Commonwealth Professor of French at the University of Virginia. He was formerly the chair of the Comparative Literature Program at Dartmouth College. His books include *Before Imagination* (Stanford, 2005) and *The Phantom of Chance* (Edinburgh, 2012). He is currently editing *The Cambridge Companion to French Literature.*

Susan Maslan is associate professor of French at the University of California, Berkeley, and the author of *Revolutionary Acts: Theater, Democracy, and the French Revolution* (Johns Hopkins University Press, 2005). She is working on a book about literature and human rights in early modern France.

Eric Méchoulan is professor of French at the Université de Montréal and most recently the author of *La crise (du discours) économique : travail immatériel et émancipation* (Québec, 2011); *D'où nous viennent nos idées? Métaphysique et intermédialité* (Montréal, 2010). He is a co-editor of the journal *Sub-Stance* and was from 2004–2010 directeur du programme at the Collège international de Philosophie (Paris). He is working on a book on the natural history of political sentiments in early modern France.

Hélène Merlin-Kajman is Professor of French at the Université de la Sorbonne Nouvelle-Paris III. She has published many books, including *Public et littérature en France au XVIIe siècle* (Belles Lettres, 1994), *L'absolutisme dans les lettres et la théorie des deux corps: Passions et politique* (Champion, 2000), *La langue est-elle fasciste? Langue, pouvoir, enseignement* (Seuil, 2003), as well as several novels (among others, *La désobéissance de Pyrame*, Belin, 2009). She is currently finishing a book entitled "Espèce humaine, espèce littéraire? Essai d'anthropologie culturelle." She is also theDirector of the literary movement *Transitions* <http://www .mouvement-transitions.fr>.

Jane O. Newman is Professor of Comparative Literature at UC Irvine. She is the author of *Benjamin's Library: Modernity, Nation, and the Baroque* (Cornell, 2011); *The Intervention of Philology: Gender, Learning, and Power in Lohenstein's Roman Plays* (North Carolina, 2000); and *Pastoral Conventions: Poetry, Language and Thought in Seventeenth-Century Nuremberg* (Johns Hopkins, 1990). She is working on two books, one on the legacy of Erich Auerbach and the other provisionally entitled *Pre-Modern Lessons for the Post-Westphalian Age*. She has recently translated a selection of Auerbach's essays, *Time, History, and Literature: Selected Essays of Erich Auerbach*, ed. James I. Porter (Princeton, 2014).

Yale French Studies is the oldest English-language journal in the United States devoted to French and Francophone literature and culture. Each volume is conceived and organized by a guest editor or editors around a particular theme or author. Interdisciplinary approaches are particularly welcome, as are contributions from scholars and writers from around the world. Recent volumes have been devoted to a wide variety of subjects, among them: Levinas; Perec; Paulhan; Haiti; Belgium; Crime Fiction; Surrealism; Material Culture in Medieval and Renaissance France; and French Education.

Yale French Studies is published twice yearly by Yale University Press (yalebooks.com) and may be accessed on JSTOR (jstor.org).

For information on how to submit a proposal for a volume of *Yale French Studies*, visit yale.edu/french and click "Yale French Studies."